Our Sense of Gratitude

Our Sense of Gratitude

For Christopher Ricks

Edited by Michael Autrey

SENEX
PRESS

Senex Press
Boston, Massachusetts
www.senexpress.org
"We publish the best books."

"Gratitude is among those human accomplishments that literature lives to realize. Art enjoys the power not only to voice gratitude but to prompt it, even to restore us to a state in which *grateful* might come again to mean at once *feeling gratitude* and *feeling pleasure*—as though it once was, and ought always to be, impossible to be granted something gratifying and not be grateful for it."

~ Christopher Ricks,
"The Best Words in the Best Order," *Along Heroic Lines*

Contents

List of Abbreviations

Allusion to the Poets – ATTP

Along Heroic Lines – AHL

Beckett's Dying Words – BDW

Dylan's Visions of Sin – DVOS

Essays in Appreciation – EIA

Keats and Embarrassment – KE

Milton's Grand Style – MGS

Reviewery – R

Tennyson (2nd Edition) – T

The Force of Poetry – TFOP

True Friendship: Geoffrey Hill, Anthony Hecht, and Robert Lowell Under the Sign of Eliot and Pound – TF

T.S. Eliot and Prejudice – TSEP

Acknowledgements

This book is made possible by the Association of Literary Scholars, Critics and Writers (ALSCW), an organization that Christopher Ricks, honoree of this volume, helped found. Four current long-time members who have all served or are currently serving the organization deserve special mention and thanks for realizing this volume: David Mikics, Lee Oser, Rosanna Warren and Ernest "Ernie" Suarez. The volume would not exist without them, or without the generosity of the contributors. A few of them deserve special mention as well. Seamus Perry gave sound, face-saving advice early in the process. Jeffrey Gutierrez, Jim McCue and Susan Wolfson helped me find contributors here and in the United Kingdom. Last but not least, thanks to Anthony Rudolf for moral support.

Grateful acknowledgment is made to Faber and Faber Limited to reproduce "The Late Wasp" by Edwin Muir from *Edwin Muir: Selected Poems*, edited by Mick Imlah (2008).

Grateful acknowledgment is made to Faber and Faber Limited to reproduce "Be sure that Possums can't refuse" from *The Poems of T.S. Eliot: The Annotated Text*, Vol. II, *Practical Cats and Further Verses*, edited Christopher Ricks and Jim McCue.

Grateful acknowledgment is made to Faber and Faber Limited to reproduce "Counting," and "Talking in Bed" by Philip Larkin from *The Complete Poems of Philip Larkin*.

Grateful acknowledgment is made to reproduce Ruth Stone, "In an Iridescent Time" from *What Love Comes To: New and Selected Poems*. Copyright © 1959, 2008 by Ruth Stone. Reprinted with the permission of The Permissions Company, LLC on behalf of Copper Canyon Press, coppercanyonpress.org.

Grateful acknowledgment is made to Saskia Hamilton to excerpt from "All Souls" from *All Souls: Poems*. Copyright © 2023 by Saskia Hamilton. Reprinted with the permission of The Permissions Company, LLC on behalf of Graywolf Press, graywolfpress.org.

Grateful acknowledgment is made to the *Times Literary Supplement* where Tim Parks's piece appeared earlier, in shorter form, under the title "Sublimating Envy."

Grateful acknowledgment to Faber and Faber Limited for the rights to reproduce "Jamesian" by Thom Gunn from *The Man With Night Sweats*.

Grateful acknowledgement is made to Farrar, Straus and Giroux for permission to reprint "Jamesian" from *Collected Poems* by Thom Gunn. Copyright © 1994 by Thom Gunn. Reprinted by permission of Farrar, Straus and Giroux. All Rights Reserved.

Grateful Acknowledgement is made to Farrar, Straus and Giroux for permission to reprint "Counting" and "Talking in Bed" from *The Complete Poems of Philip Larkin* by Philip Larkin, edited by Archie Burnett. Copyright © 2012 by The Estate of Philip Larkin. Reprinted by permission of Farrar, Straus and Giroux, New York, and Faber and Faber Ltd., London. All Rights Reserved.

Thanks to Monica Tranströmer for allowing us to publish Bill Coyle's translation of "Östersjöar" by her late husband Tomas. And thanks to Megan Murton and Lilla Kopar for providing prompt help with Coyle's query regarding the accuracy of his translation of Tranströmer's Old Swedish into Middle English.

Preface

"Since a preface," according to Christopher Ricks, "is the place for saying what one has not done," this is the place for saying what could not have been done.[1] This volume is incomplete, and could not pretend to be complete or representative of the generations of literary scholars, critics and writers Christopher Ricks has taught, supervised, corrected, edited, inspired, surprised, encouraged, excoriated, educated and appreciated. Many of those who were fortunate enough to be his students, friends and colleagues, are no longer with us. And many more, who picked up his books and discovered they couldn't and didn't attend to words on the page or in the world the same way after having read him, who might have had something worthwhile to say on and about the extraordinary transformation they underwent while reading him, could not be located, did not respond to an invitation, or are no more. To provide a true accounting of all those he has touched and influenced, a volume as capacious as an encyclopedia would have been required.

This volume is no more than a sliver, a cross section of the generations of students, colleagues and friends from his major phases: Oxford, Cambridge, Boston University and the Editorial Institute. Ricks was one of the founders of the Association of Literary Scholars, Critics and Writers (ALSCW), and many of those contributing here know him from his work for the Association, and were introduced to the Association by him. He is still encouraging his students to join the organization, and is, on at least one occasion cited in this volume, paying their dues.

Christopher Ricks is a dear friend to many, and an example to many more, even to those who have never met him except on the page or listened to him from the back of a dark stuffy lecture hall, or found him directing his piercing stare off-camera, towards his almost inaudible, overmatched interlocutor, on Youtube. The world

---

1   *T*, 2nd ed., vii.

works in mysterious ways. Gratitude is one of the imperishable forms of demystification.

U.N. Autre

Our Sense of Gratitude

In *A New English Dictionary* (the Oxford before the Oxford) there are three definitions of "gratitude" and thirty definitions of "sense."[1] The editors of the NED divide those thirty definitions into four categories: "I. Faculty of perception or sensation. II. Actual perception or feeling. III. Meaning, signification. IV. *attrib.* and *Comb.*, as *sense-consciousness, -impression* . . .." Gratitude belongs to two of the four: gratitude is sensory, and is a source of meaning and signification.

All of those contributing to this volume owe Christopher Ricks a debt of gratitude, all have a sense of gratitude. To owe a debt of gratitude is a debt paradox, not a debt trap. For the debt of gratitude need not be repaid, interest and dividends to be collected by us debtors forever. Gratitude, a currency never depreciating, cannot be devalued. As our honoree has claimed: "To give gratitude is to be the richer, not the poorer, for the giving."[2]

"A sense of gratitude" is a feeling, a sensational feeling, and yet if we shift the emphasis, then gratitude *is* a sense, belonging explicitly to the first of the four categories of "sense" in the NED. If after the big five—sight, hearing, smell, taste, touch—comes proprioception, essential but taken for granted; as the liver is called the silent organ, proprioception might be understood as the silent sense; and if, as is attested in the unforgettable opening of Wilma Stockenström's 1981 novel *The Expedition to the Baobob Tree*, in J.M. Coetzee's translation, "the seventh sense is sleep," then gratitude, I suggest, is our eighth. Yet if gratitude *is* a sense, it is among the higher or "first order" senses, since it can reach its objects while remaining at a distance. Thankfully, gratitude has not been subject to any principle of prohibition, as there has been—or used to be—about the need to first distinguish and then separate, permanently, in our minds and hands, sight from touch

---

1   *A New English Dictionary on Historical Principles* (13 vols.; The Clarendon Press, 1888-1933).
2   *DVOS,* 52.

("Look with your eyes and not with your hands," as my grandmothers used to chide).

Significantly, Ricks ends what he has said will be the final volume of essays with a flourish of gratitude, Samuel Beckett's one-sentence contribution to a book published to celebrate the Joyce centenary: "I welcome this occasion to bow once again, before I go, deep down, before his heroic work, heroic being."[3] A gracious way to bow out, that, letting a writer of fewer and fewer words have the last word. We hear so much about the last word, too much about last words, which is one of the reasons why I want to take off from the beginning of Ricks's "The Best Words in the Best Order," the first essay in *Along Heroic Lines*. The title taken from Coleridge, the first and last words of Ricks's final book are quotations (and for those of you thinking I have missed the Prefatory Note, it begins not with a quote but with a nod to Samuel Johnson). It should come as no surprise that the first word of the first essay of this last volume is "Gratitude"; and the first words, adapted from his inaugural lecture as Professor of Poetry at Oxford, make a welcome claim for the work of literature: "Gratitude is among those human accomplishments that literature lives to realize." A whole theory of human evolution lingers in the interpretative, oxygen-rich air around this principle. Literature isn't alive, only writers and readers are, and yet the force of "lives" in this sentence is vigorous and uncontained; in "lives to" it is hard not to hear the American English sense of the verb active in the phrase "I live *for*": as in "I *live* for Penelope Fitzgerald." There is a theory of history too, at least of art history, waiting on pointe in the wings of this short opening paragraph that concludes: "Art enjoys the power not only to voice gratitude but to prompt it, even to restore us to a state in which *grateful* might come again to mean at once *feeling gratitude* and *feeling pleasure*—as though it once was, and ought always to be, impossible to be granted something gratifying and not be grateful for it" (the emphases are Ricks's). In these sentences Ricks imagines a prelapsarian world, from which a fall need not permanently disable gratitude's preternatural sense. Art can restore our sense of gratitude, and not only for what is lost. Gratitude is both found, made, and lasting; after all it is a sense. "As though it once was, and ought always to be" is a form of words reaching back and offering a promising look ahead. We should be grateful not to the promise, which may never be fulfilled, but to the promissory form of the words available to us now. A sense of gratitude

---

3   *AHL*, 326.

for the vows, and not only or necessarily for their fulfillment. And a sense of gratitude for Ricks's willingness to prepare the audience of his inaugural speech for demonstrations of literature alive to its own responsibilities to gratify the gratifying senses.

Gratitude promises much, and like the other first-order senses it can and does reach back into the past and into the far future. Just as sight can become vision, gratitude—and not just our sense *of* it—can be sharpened, enlarged. Our sense of gratitude is transitive. It calls up, for and out to examples, instances, persons, places and things; gratitude is bound up with all of these roles of nouns and binds us to them. Gratitude compounds, unifies and unites. The feeling, however, does not belong to its object, singular, or to its objects, plural. Our sense of gratitude, like our sense of sight, predisposes us: predisposes us *to*. Like all the other senses, even when it does not or cannot name what draws it, gratitude grounds us, earths us in nouns.

Gratitude takes us out of ourselves towards an other, so the sense of gratitude is the very opposite of othering. In this instance, on this occasion, we are gratified that our honoree exists, grateful for what he has done and allows and encourages, invites and dares, us to do; and his example is not permissive but principled. Gratitude is principled, and might be a principle if that didn't risk sounding like a command. An order to be grateful is at minimum grating, and like many a sensation that is called up only because it is called for, considered 'appropriate,' it is to be at minimum questioned and possibly disobeyed.

Ricks does not take pleasure in what displeases him, in what he considers wrong, but as this anecdote offered by his colleague Meg Tyler demonstrates, there is pleasure to be taken in observing his efforts to right wrongs:

> I recall a time at Harvard, a day-long event on William Empson hosted by the English Department. When Helen Vendler (another recently lost star!) began to speak, Christopher rose in indignation, his face as red as a valentine, and critiqued her misguidedness about Empson. I am not even sure why it pleased us so much that he became so irate. Because he is both perspicacious and feels things strongly? He is certainly willing to express his dissent.

"As red as a valentine!" I take pleasure in and am grateful for that phrase, for Ricks's willingness to express dissent that in this case is not simply loyalty to Empson, one of his heroes, but is evidence that our sense of gratitude engenders loyalty without sycophancy. Note that in her parenthesis Tyler is gracious, generous and faultless, seeing

Vendler, a star, lost to the living but belonging in the constellations of critics that will fall and rise.

Lucian Freud said that his ambition was to paint a picture such that it was impossible to imagine that it had not existed before. He lived to realize this ambition. This cannot be understood as a philosophical claim, for it could be said, I think, of electric light in a time of gaslight, and—since a pad of them is ready to hand—of post-its. With the arrival of new forms—of art, illumination and note-taking—it became increasingly hard to imagine life before they existed. Yet Freud's statement is of the kind that means something more exacting than what it says. I believe he means something very like what T.S. Eliot claims in "The Function of Criticism" when he defines literature "not as a collection of the writings of individuals but as 'organic wholes,' as systems in relation to which, and only in relation to which, individual works of literary art, and the works of individual artists, have their significance. There is accordingly something outside the artist to which he owes allegiance, a devotion to which he must surrender and sacrifice himself in order to earn and to obtain his unique position."[4] Eliot's phrase "'organic wholes'" suggests organisms, these writers that "live to realize." Lucian Freud was devoted, some would say excessively devoted, to a certain strain of the figurative tradition. His ambition was to compete with those who had secured their "unique position." (While "unique position" is another possibly meaningless phrase, in this context the sense is not in doubt.) What Eliot, Freud and Ricks share is a conviction that lasting works enlarge our sense of gratitude, and that the making of lasting works is impossible without gratitude—or envy, its leering twin.

To pick two big targets: I recall Philip Roth, who was said to greet his reflection every morning in the mirror above the sink with: "Attack! Attack!"[5] Roth's imperatives conjure for me the words of Robert Lowell, another writer demoted to art monster, from "Florence": "Pity the monsters! / Pity the Monsters!" Pitiless? Self-pitying? The (art) monsters know only too well what they do. We know from their biographies that both writers behaved badly. In a note to a review of three Roth biographies in *The New York Review of Books*, in reference to a scene from Roth's scatological *Sabbath's Theatre*, Michael Gorra

---

4   "The Function of Criticism" in *Selected Essays: New Edition* (Harcourt, Brace and Company, 1950), 12-13.
5   "Roth Agonistes," Nathaniel Rich, LXV:4, *The New York Review of Books*, (March 8, 2018).

passed summary judgement: "Roth took the incident from [his first wife's] behavior at her own mother's death. Unforgivable, and on the page unforgettable."[6] The unforgivable and the unforgettable are incommensurate, and yet this note is not the cunning of an apologist. This is, perhaps, the binocular sense of gratitude at its sharpest. Our sense of gratitude intact, we can take searching looks at the worst without turning stony; our literatures grant us glimpses of the unfeeling world feelingly. For gratitude is not the only human accomplishment literature lives to realize. It is too easy to forget that the monster in *Frankenstein* remains nameless, and that that book's title brings us back again and again to all-too-human hubris. It is the monster who earns our pity, and his example inoculates us against self-pity.

Given their bodies of work, Roth and Lowell lived for literature, for literature to realize. Their works are more generous than their lives, and we are not in a position to judge their lives or their livings: literary criticism has never been a question of work/life balance. As Ricks reminds us about Geoffrey Hill's complicated relationship with T.S. Eliot: "There are aspects of this that are not of Hill's making, for poets are characteristically more generous than critics, and poems will often prove more generous than their poets."[7] That poems could prove more generous than their composers is more evidence of the literal sense of Ricks's claim that "*literature* lives to realize." Ricks's "this" refers to what he quotes immediately before, P.N. Furbank's "perplexity" at the severity of Hill's critical writing, the forensic attitude of Hill's critical judgment, the thorny hedges in the prose existing in remarkable contrast to a spacious openness in the poetry. Ricks, acute, goes on: "*But then gratitude itself is a form of generosity. There is a revealing (but not betraying) turn in* The Orchards of Syon *XLV: 'The topos / of the whole is gratitude.'*"[8] We betray gratitude if we reserve it only for those works that appear grateful.

If—even if—one believes the museums and the libraries are fit for burning, and is convinced that now the time has come to burn out the eyes of the male gaze; to make art when one is so confident in the knowledge of the past's oppressive failures is to be, whether one

---

6   "Philip's Theater," Michael Gorra, LXVIII:6, *The New York Review of Books*, (April 8, 2021).

7   In 2003, Ricks phrases this same ideal in terms of magnanimity: "But just as creators are more magnanimous than critics, so creations—works of art—have a way of being more magnanimous than their creators." *DVOS*, 187.

8   *TF*, 18. My italics.

admits it or not, grateful for all that which has been so provoking. What the dead have realized will not die. To hate Lucian Freud, as many are proud to say they do, is to grant his work enormous power.[9] *Ing*ratitude is to be (over)whelmed by the sense of gratitude. Jenny Diski's final book, *In Gratitude*, is a memoir of her early life as guest-cum-adoptee in the household of Doris Lessing, interleaved with what she underwent while losing her life to lung cancer. The book appeared in print a week after her death, and is a case study of the polarizing power of the preposition "in" when brought into close proximity with "gratitude," shadowing the word it precedes, but not yet a prefix. Diski's *In Gratitude* is alive not only to D.W. Winnicott's startling remark that dead parents are better than inconsistent ones, but alive to the example of Lessing as a writer getting on with it, demonstrating by her example that the making of literature is not the best part of living despite the fact that literature lives to realize all kinds and ways of being alive.

Alongside *In Gratitude* I could put Gillian Rose's *Love's Work*, another memoir of losing life that refuses the sentimentality that too easily arises when we might be predisposed to compassion, or too prepared to see a love-life as strictly loving. When she awoke from surgery not with the cancer excised but with a colostomy bag, she began, voluntarily, a profound meditation on human waste and wasting: "I want to talk about shit—the hourly transfiguration of our lovely eating of the sun."[10] Sententious and sensuous, this sentence binds together inside and outside; is an ecstatic, excremental vision. Rose did not go looking for her life to end this way, and did not flinch when it did. She found a way to make a work for which I am profoundly grateful out of a wasting, fatal disease. Not anger, hatred, censoriousness but indifference is the ultimate threat to our sense of gratitude. Indifference is to our sense of gratitude what pitch darkness is to our sense of sight. Our sense of gratitude begins in appreciation, in what one can't help but live for, but it lives just as well in the lucidity of dislike.[11]

---

9   Among many others I have heard Jamaica Kincaid and Linda Nochlin express, proudly and publicly, undisguised contempt and hatred for Lucian Freud.

10   Gillian Rose, *Love's Work*, introduction by Michael wood and also including "In Memoriam: Gillian Rose" by Geoffrey Hill (nyrb classics, 2011), 94.

11   The book of essays by the poet and novelist Amit Chaudhuri, *The Origin of Dislike* (Oxford University Press, 2018), is a fine anatomy of gratitude and its vicissitudes. See especially the title essay.

We owe a debt of gratitude to what we despise and to what leaves us cold; admitting our dislikes, we will see more clearly why we like what we like. To what we are indifferent might just as well be forgotten— for a time. Perhaps, and this is part of the promise literature lives to realize, later in life we might be grateful for what we couldn't in earlier times abide. Art is long, and life always feels short when there remains so much art to which gratitude might bind us. Meaning to offer a back-handed compliment to Eden, meaning to beat back a nostalgia for the edenic, E.M. Cioran wrote: "paradise is life without commentary." I doubt he had ever read Christopher Ricks.

Michael Autrey

Again I Shake Your Hand

Rereading a book you have loved in youth is a perilous thing. You may discover that what you so admired is less worthy of admiration, or, at the least, that you and the book have drifted apart. *You* may not have been infatuated or immature; *it* may not have been meretricious; it is only that time has changed you both. You are now an old man, and it is now an old book, and persons and books do not necessarily age in tandem. Encountering this old flame can be—embarrassing.[1]

I offered, for this volume, to say something about *Keats and Embarrassment*, without quite taking the measure of what I was doing. Was I lucky in my heedlessness? I don't think so; memory, too, has its intuitions. The difference between reading the book fifty years ago and reading it today is great, but not wide—not unbridgeable. Remembering the book—the circumstances in which I first read it, the lessons it taught me, the formative influence it had on me—has revived, at the same time, my sense of its intrinsic value.

Keats and Embarrassment was first published by Oxford University Press in 1974, but the book, to me, will always be the paperback edition of 1976, with Poussin's *Echo and Narcissus* on the greenish cover, and complimentary flourishes from Bergonzi, Byatt and Raban on the back. Its pages have dried out a little, and in rereading I have torn a couple. The date is significant: I had been a year under Christopher's supervision, and he himself had begun his tenure as Professor of English at Cambridge at the same time as I began my PhD. I proposed to write about Byron's influence on Robert Browning, a subject which failed to interest Christopher sooner than it ceased to interest me. But in 1976 I wrote, by chance, something that did catch his eye—it had nothing to do with my 'topic'—and which he used (I now realize) as a means of shifting the points and diverting me onto a better track. Around the same time, speaking to me gently—for he could be very

---

1   Christopher, of course, cites the preeminent instance, Arthur Clennam's meeting with Flora Finching in Dickens's *Little Dorrit* (*KE*, 166).

gentle—of his scepticism about the Byronic Browning, he asked me whether there wasn't—didn't I agree?—something equally Keatsian about Browning. And he coupled this with an acerbic rejoinder—for he could be very acerbic—to a comment I made about a line in *Sordello*. I am ashamed of the comment now, not because it was wrong (we are all wrong sometimes—even Christopher) but because of the spirit in which I made it, attempting to prove that, although I was working *on* Browning I was not working *for* him, and was perfectly capable of taking a detached, amused view of his failings. The line occurs in book 3 of the poem, in a passage which evokes (as part of an extended metaphor) the wanderings of the children of Israel in the wilderness of Zin (Exodus 16-17):

> A hungry sun above us, sands among
> Our throats, each dromedary lolls a tongue,
> *Each camel churns a sick and frothy chap.*[2]

I cited this line as self-evidently 'bad,' but Christopher demurred. Didn't the verb "churns" accurately describe the sideways-sliding motion of a camel's jaw while it chews the cud? and wasn't this action evoked by the sound and cadence of the line itself? But it was especially the word "frothy" that caught his eye, I think, because it is so congruent with the vocabulary studied in *Keats and Embarrassment*, the vocabulary of the body, its sensations and excretions: blushing, oozing, sweating, foaming. The sick camel froths at the mouth, an image both repulsive and truthful—'true to life,' and true to the life of the poem, its own way with words being an admonition and example.

The general lesson I took from this exchange—that one shouldn't condescend to 'one's' author—came home to me immediately; my particular acknowledgment of the 'Keatsian' side of Browning followed when I read *Keats and Embarrassment*, as I did soon afterwards. I know the book revolutionized my understanding of what poetry could do—not just the poetry of Keats, which I thought I knew, but Browning's, and Byron's too, for that matter. For Byron is Keats's great antagonist, yet Christopher, though Keats's partisan in this book, is generously acute about Byron, even where Byron is ungenerous and impercipient about "Johnny Keats's *p-ss a-bed* poetry." And what is true of Byron goes for other writers, some of whom Keats himself knew and relished

---

2   Robert Browning, *Sordello* iii 793-5, in *Poems of Browning*, eds. John Woolford and Daniel Karlin, Vol. 1 (1826-1840), (Longman, 1991), 580. The text is that of the first edition of 1840; my italics.

(Shakespeare, Milton), others from later times who stand at the opposite pole of sensibility (Aldous Huxley, or Samuel Beckett, who makes a scene-stealing cameo appearance in chapter 3). This, too, was a model for emulation.

The book holds up astonishingly well. A very few passages have, like its pages, dried out, and the argument is flawed in places—the distinction between *embarrassment* and *shame* is not, to my mind, sufficiently made clear, especially as regards the reasons why we blush. The practice of leaving lengthy quotations to speak for themselves—notably the Sartre quotation on pages 139-42—is sometimes questionable, though when it involves the 'primary' texts, especially Keats's letters, it reminds me of the best lectures I heard as an undergraduate at Cambridge, by A. C. Spearing on Chaucer or Gillian Beer on the eighteenth-century novel—lectures in which the superb reading aloud and 'performance' of an author's work was a means of entrusting that work to us, trusting us to 'get it' and keep it, as I have done for fifty years with *Troilus and Criseyde* or *Tom Jones*.

To love and admire an author ought not to seem strange in the world of literary scholarship, but it is still moving to witness Christopher's fearless personal advocacy, his unembarrassed embrace of what others have found embarrassing in Keats. Chapter after chapter—on blushing, on taste, on sex—asks us to look where we have flinched from looking, to take seriously what we have taken for granted as trivial or inept, to enlarge rather than shrink both the scope of human feeling and its expression in poetry. These demands on us are made, first, by general propositions, from the most basic ("that embarrassment is very important in life") to the most complex:

> that the critic, in the nineteenth century as now, was too quick to assume that there could not possibly be any point in Keats's inducing . . . a hot tingle and discomfort. Granted, there is not an immensely wide range of worthwhile effect and comprehension which lies open to such a use of language, but the effect is neither simple nor trivial, since it compacts a necessary struggle within the sympathetic imagination: its recognition, when confronted by the physicality of others (and especially of those loved by others), of a generosity to be attained without sentimentality (that is, without the pretence that there is no possibility of distaste or embarrassment) and without morbidity (which is fixated upon those possibilities).[3]

3   *KE*, 103-4.

This is from the longest, most daring chapter, "Keats, Byron, and 'Slippery Blisses,'" a masterpiece of scrupulous exposition—think what a loss the argument would suffer without the parenthetical comments, and indeed without these comments being suspended within parentheses.

Such general propositions are not weightless: they are ballasted by detailed observations on words, phrases, lines, of which these few must stand as exemplary. On the image of Niobe in *Endymion* (I 337-43):

> What animates the lines is a particular recognition about an abandonment to grief such as Niobe's: that it is embarrassing. Here is the physicality of a grief manifest in "the trembling knee / And frantic gape"; what makes the lines disconcerting indeed is the candour with which they raise a matter that a more grandly tragic manner may be prone to forget: that a great impediment to our full sympathy with frantic grief is its being embarrassing to contemplate, especially in its physical distortion.[4]

On the image of the kiss in "Isabella," "his erewhile timid lips grew bold, / And poesied with hers in dewy rhyme" (st. IX):

> The kiss is a rhyme because it rhymes (pairs) their lips . . . and doubly so because the upper and lower lips already rhyme with each other. It is "dewy" because the lips are wetted by saliva, a fact at once romantically expressed and attractive (as if the reader were either the kisser or the kissed), and also disconcerting (the reader is neither, and the saliva on lips is something which cannot but be faintly uneasy to contemplate unless one is not just contemplating it) . . . . And "poesied"?: because a kiss is a creative act, like writing a poem; like a poem, it both recognizes what already exists and brings something new into existence; it both is bred from, and breeds love.[5]

On "To Autumn" (the only poem to be quoted in its entirety in the book), taking flight from "the ambivalence of feeling" which moulds the image of the beehive's "clammy cells" or the "last oozings" of the "cyder-press":

> Pressure: the ambivalence of physical sensation is another of the strange, truthful, and bracing pressures which give poignant life to "To Autumn"— pressure downwards, loading and bending the trees; pressure inwards, filling all fruit with ripeness to the core; pressure outwards, swelling the gourd and plumping the hazel shells; the pressure of poise and movement, as the gleaner steps across the brook and yet keeps steady her laden head;

---

4   *KE*, 9.
5   *KE*, 98.

the pressure of sleep and of opiate; the pressure of the wind; the direct
and patient pressure of the cyder-press. And at one with all these, the
pressure of futurity and of approaching winter.[6]

That short summative sentence at the end is given its depth and
passion by the long sentence that precedes it. Christopher's style,
here, is fully answerable to its subject. "Depth and passion" is not my
phrase, since Christopher speaks of "the depth and passion of Keats's
poetry and letters."[7] But then of course the phrase is not Christopher's,
either, since he borrows it from "My Last Duchess," where it describes
the Duchess's "pictured countenance, / The depth and passion of its
earnest glance."[8] "My Last Duchess," as it happens, is the only poem by
Browning that Christopher writes about in *Keats and Embarrassment*,
in a passage that focuses on Frà Pandolf, the painter's, praise of the
"faint / Half-flush that dies along her throat"—a phrase which, when
the Duchess was alive, spoke of the ungraspable life of her body, but
which is denatured by her husband's appropriation of it. Christopher
finely remarks that the Duke speaks "as if his medium were Frà
Pandolf's paint rather than words," so that the half-flush "is pointedly
not conceded to be a blush." And yet the Duke unwittingly undermines
himself, as dramatic monologuists are apt to do: in alluding to the
Duchess's "earnest glance" he summons up the relation of the *glance*
to the *blush*, which, as Christopher reminds us elsewhere in the book
are primitive synonyms.[9] Here is the Keatsian side of Browning, in full
measure—just one of the moments in the book for which I am grateful,
for which I love it. For what Christopher says of a kiss, and of a poem,
may be said also of his, the best, criticism: "it both recognizes what
already exists and brings something new into existence; it both is
bred from, and breeds love."

Daniel Karlin

---

6   *KE*, 208-9.
7   *KE*, 133.
8   "My Last Duchess", ll. 7-8, in *Poems of Browning*, eds. John Woolford and Daniel
     Karlin, Vol. 2 (1841-1846), (Longman, 1991), 158-159.
9   *KE*, 87.

"Living in the Eye": Keats at Stock Ghyll Force

K eats ate a "Monstrous Breakfast" in the Salutation Inn at Ambleside on Saturday, 27 June 1818.[1] He then wrote to his brother Tom in London, describing the walk he and Brown had taken some hours earlier to Stock Ghyll Force, starting shortly after six that morning. The Force was already a tourist attraction. Wordsworth's anonymous introduction to the *Guide to the Lakes* (1810) had directed the "curious Traveller" to see "the huge breastwork of Stock-ghyll Force."[2] Keats's decision to go "tramping" in the Lake District and Scotland had been with the hope that "it would give me more experience . . . identify finer scenes[,] load me with grander Mountains, and strengthen more my reach in Poetry . . .."[3] He went, that is, with strong preconceptions of what he was to experience. As he told Tom, "The space, the magnitude of mountains and waterfalls are well imagined before one sees them." What interests me is the extraordinary freshness with which Keats describes what he calls "the first waterfall I ever saw,"[4] the sight and sound of which was to surpass his expectations.

Keats's letter gives a prefatory account of the two men's walk to the sight:

> . . . we went to see the Ambleside water fall. The morning beautiful—the walk easy among the hills. We, I may say, fortunately, missed the direct path, and after wandering a little, found it out by the noise—for, mark

---

1   *The Letters of John Keats 1814-1821*, ed. Hyder Edward Rollins, 2 vols. (Cambridge University Press, 1958), I, 302 (hereafter '*L*'). I am particularly indebted to Hermione Lee's help and advice in the shaping of this essay.
2   First published with no indication of authorship as the introduction to Joseph Wilkinson's *Select Views of Cumberland, Westmorland, and Lancashire* (R. Ackermann, 1810), 39. Much altered in 1820 by which time this description of the Force had disappeared.
3   *L*, I, 342.
4   *L*, I, 302. In fact this was not Keats's first sight of a waterfall. On 16 April 1817 he reported seeing "the little waterfall" in the Chine, Isle of Wight (*L*, I, 130-31).

you, it is buried in trees, in the bottom of the valley—the stream itself is interesting throughout with "mazy error over pendant shades."[5] Milton meant a smooth river—this is buffetting all the way on a rocky bed ever various—but the waterfall itself, which I came suddenly upon, gave me a pleasant twinge.[6]

This lively and swift-moving account of their circuitous route to the falls, only discovered by its sound buried in the trees after missing "the direct path," uses the allusion to the calm beauty of Milton's river Eden to establish by contrast the physical turbulence of Ambleside stream's ever-varying "buffeting" over its "rocky bed." But its conclusion, saying that the sudden sight of the waterfall gave him "pleasant twinge," seriously underplays Keats's early morning experience which Keats goes on to recapture.

> First we stood a little below the head about half way down the first fall, buried deep in trees, and saw it streaming down two more descents to the depth of near fifty feet—then we went on a jut of rock nearly level with the second fall-head, where the first fall was above us, and the third below our feet still—at the same time we saw that the water was divided by a sort of cataract island on whose other side burst out a glorious stream— then the thunder and the freshness. At the same time the different falls have as different characters; the first darting down the slate-rock like an arrow; the second spreading out like a fan—the third dashed into a mist— and the one on the other side of the rock a sort of mixture of all these. We afterwards moved away a space, and saw nearly the whole more mild, streaming silverly through the trees.

This account goes far beyond the "pleasant twinge" that might be evoked by a picturesque scene, and takes us into the language of the sublime (not that Keats would have used this word which he considered as one of the clichés of nature-writing).

Keats compresses his reactions to the Force itself into a mere one-hundred-and-sixty-two words. It is highly visual and its frequent dashes signal the pressure placed on Keats's syntax throughout. The language of the passage mimics the contradictory effects of the water's interplay with the rocks, forcing Keats to invent phrasal compounds ("fall-head," "cataract island" and "slate-rock") and call up violently contrasting images ("arrow," "fan," "mist") to describe its effects of height, noise, and light. The passage is full of active verbs ("streaming down," "burst out," "darting," "spreading," "dashed into a

---

5   *Paradise Lost,* iv. 239, part of Milton's description of the "river large" running through Eden (Milton has "under" for "over").

6   For this and the following description of Stock Ghyll Force see *L*, I, 300-301.

mist"), embodying "the thunder and the freshness" it describes, and in the course of doing so endows all three parts of the falls with life— "the different falls have as different characters" from one another.

That is the whole of Keats's description of the Force. He then attempts to describe its significance:

> What astonishes me more than any thing is the tone, the coloring, the slate, the stone, the moss, the rock-weed; or, if I may so say, the intellect, the countenance of such places. The space, the magnitude of mountains and waterfalls are well imagined before one sees them; but this countenance or intellectual tone must surpass every imagination and defy any remembrance.

He continues with characteristic promissory eloquence:

> I shall learn poetry here and shall henceforth write more than ever, for the abstract endeavor of being able to add a mite to that mass of beauty which is harvested from these grand materials, by the finest spirits, and put into etherial existence for the relish of one's fellows.

Keats's summary of the specific effect of the Force as being the sight of the "intellect, the countenance of such places," is promptly rephrased as "this countenance or intellectual tone." In this essentially visual experience, the natural scene takes on a character, a living personality of its own for the spectator.

Normally Keats, like other Romantic poets, uses the word "tone" to mean sound ("ditties of no tone"). Here "the tone, the coloring, the slate, the moss, the rock-weed" carries its painterly sense. This was a recent coinage. Joshua Reynolds used the word in 1790 to mean "tone of colour,"[7] and Hazlitt described the "fleshy tone'" of the husband in Hogarth's *Marriage-a-la-Mode* in 1817.[8] Keats's choice of this technical term shows that his response to Stock Ghyll Force is that of a painter.

The other word he uses allied to "tone" is "countenance" put forward as a synonym for, or equivalent of, "intellectual tone." By the end of the description Keats has moved to personifying the "different falls" as "different characters." And his use of "countenance" here parallels his earlier portrayal of Endymion's foolish mockery of "nature's holy

---

7   In his "Fourteenth Discourse" (1790) Reynolds notes that in Gainsborough's portraits, painted by candlelight, "flesh seems to take a higher and richer tone of colour" (*Works of Sir Joshua Reynolds*, ed. E. Malone (T. Cadell, Jun. and W. Davies, 1797), Vol. 1, 298). The *OED* (10a, b) dates the earliest examples of this usage as 1821 and 1825 respectively.

8   *The Round Table: A Collection of Essays on Literature, Men, and Manners* (A. Constable, 1817), Vol. 1, 82.

countenance" at the conclusion of his poetic romance (Book IV, 948). The word is used nowhere else by Keats in this near-pantheistic sense, nor are these ideas developed elsewhere. Nevertheless, they do suggest that lying behind Keats's description of the Lakeland waterfall is Wordsworth's "It was an April Morning" published in the second edition of *Lyrical Ballads* in 1800.[9]

Wordsworth's speaker also follows a "Rivulet, delighting in its strength," the morning alive with sound (ll. 2-5), all marked by "such deep contentment in the air"

> That every naked ash, and tardy tree
> Yet leafless, seem'd as though the countenance
> With which it look'd on this delightful day
> Were native to the summer ....
> (ll. 14-17)

The speaker continues upstream and, at a "sudden turning" comes across a waterfall making a song like "some natural produce of the air," and goes on to marvel at the

> ... foliage of the rocks, the birch,
> The yew, the holly, and the bright green thorn,
> With hanging islands of resplendent furze ....
> (ll. 20-33)

The collocation of morning, the following of a stream, the trees' "countenance" all looking onto the scene, and the unexpected encounter with a waterfall with rocks, trees and "hanging islands," makes a striking parallel with Keats's description of Stock Ghyll Force. It may be no more than a remarkable coincidence. But it is worth noting that Keats and Brown were planning to call on Wordsworth at Rydal Mount later that very day. It may be that Keats was conscious of Wordsworth's earlier poem. If so, he made his own version of his encounter with the waterfall. He did not follow the older poet's exploratory belief in nature as educative force.

Why did Keats introduce this overwhelming experience by calling it no more than "a pleasant twinge"? One reason is Keats's distrust of mere "description." This is not the first time he had expressed his mistrust. A few months earlier, describing Devonshire, he had

---

9   *Lyrical Ballads with Other Poems, in Two Volumes* (Longman and Rees, 1800), Vol. 2, 179-81, where it appears as the first poem under "Poems on the Naming of Places."

exclaimed, "Scenery is fine—but human nature is finer."[10] The same reservation lies behind the instructions he gives Tom as he finishes his letter: "Let any of my friends see my letters—[but] they may not be interested in descriptions—descriptions are bad at all times—I did not intend to give you any . . .." This embarrassed apology for his account of Ambleside's waterfall is not an aberration. A year later, after copying his astonishingly vivid depiction of Fingal's Cave for the George Keatses, he dismisses the whole passage as "this dull specimen of description," adding for good measure, "For myself I hate descriptions."[11] In that light, Keats's phrase "a pleasant twinge," immediately before his powerful account of Stock Ghyll Force, reads as a form of anticipatory self-deprecation.

Keats's dislike of description stemmed from a determination not to be seen as a tourist himself. Hence his mockery of the standard vocabulary used for portraying "Mountains, Rivers, Lakes, dells, glens, Rocks, and Clouds" through terms like "beautiful, enchanting, gothic picturesque fine, delightful, enchancting [sic], Grand, *sublime*" [my italics] when writing to Reynolds.[12] However, two moments in his account of seeing Stock Ghyll Force identify a deeper cause for his dissatisfaction with description. The first is his recognition that the Force's "countenance or intellectual tone must *surpass every imagination and defy any remembrance.*" That realisation is repeated shortly after when he contradicts Hazlitt:

> I cannot think with Hazlitt that these scenes make man appear little. I never forgot my stature so completely [in seeing the Force]—I live in the eye; and my imagination, surpassed, is at rest . . ..

"Living in the eye" surpasses the imagination, leaving it nothing do. "Living in the eye" gives him no way of turning the magnitude and grandeur of a Lakeland waterfall or Scottish mountains directly into poetry though he had done so in prose. There are no descriptions of *specific* natural scenes in his poetry. Even where one might be expected, as in "I stood tip-toe upon a little hill" or "Not Aladin magian," written in response to his subsequent trip to Staffa,[13] Keats makes no attempt

---

10 *L*, I, 242.
11 *L*, II, 198. Keats adds these sentiments when copying his original letter to Tom for the George Keatses (*L*, 348-9).
12 *L*, I, 322. See also I, 325 for his inability to "write about scenery."
13 See the problems of earlier texts in settling on a suitable title for this odd poem ("Fingal's Cave in Staffa—A Fragment," "On Staffa," "~~Lycidas's~~ Lines/ On Visiting 'Staffa'").

to do so. Descriptions of specific scenes are restricted to his letters. Ironically, despite Keats's real gift for the kind of description he despised, it was exactly what he had no place for in poetry.

Although he had hoped that his subsequent journeying in the Lake District and Scotland would "identify finer scenes" and "load me with grander Mountains, and strengthen more my reach in Poetry," Keats was to find as he went on from Ambleside to explore the Scottish Highlands and Mull that the writing of his own poetry became increasingly problematic. Nowhere is this clearer than Keats's contradictory reactions to his ascent of Ben Nevis on 3, 6 August 1818, at the very end of his tour. Writing to Tom the following day he starts with a long and very full description of the two men's climb through mists and clouds, of the sudden sightings of chasms, of the continually changing views, and of the mountain's immensity, a description remarkable for its altogether convincing and precise observation. But, as if overwhelmed by this serious effort at portraying natural phenomena, Keats abruptly changes his tone to the comic, once again undercutting description, by launching into a prolonged mock conversation between Mrs. Cameron and Ben Nevis ("Upon my life, Sir Nevis I am piqu'd"), a seventy-four line impromptu meant for Tom's amusement. It is only at the end of his letter that Keats turns back to copy out the "Sonnet I wrote on the top of Ben Nevis" the previous day. This, according to Brown, was written sitting on some stones a few feet from the mountain's "fearful precipice, fifteen hundred feet perpendicular."[14] The sonnet is puzzled and puzzling, and begins by asking for help:

> Read me a lesson, Muse, and speak it loud
> Upon the top of Nevis, blind in mist!

No answer is forthcoming as Keats looks into the "chasms," "vaprous" clouds, and mist spread beneath him, whose impenetrable vagueness equals that of "man's sight of himself." The poem concludes:

> Here are the craggy stones beneath my feet;
> Thus much I know, that, a poor witless elf,
>   I tread on them; that all my eye doth meet
> Is mist and crag—not only on this height,
> But in the world of thought and mental might.[15]

---

14   *L*, 1, 352-8. For Brown's comments see his *Life of John Keats* in *The Keats Circle*, ed. Hyder Edward Rollins, 2nd ed. (Harvard University Press, 1969), 2, 63.
15   *The Poems of John Keats*, ed. Jack Stillinger (Harvard University Press, 1978), 279.

At the sonnet's conclusion the speaker is in as much of a mental mist as he had been in a literal mist at its start. The grandeur of the Scottish mountains leaves him in a creative and intellectual limbo. During his Northern walk Keats found that the grandeur of mountains was not directly translatable into poetry. Instead, those experiences were to be instrumental in the creation of his epic fragment *Hyperion*, after his return to London the following autumn.[16]

John Barnard

---

16 For fuller account, see Fiona Stafford, "Keats's In-Placeness," in *Local Attachments: The Province of Poetry* (Oxford University Press, 2010), 224-71. See also "'Keats, Burns, and Scotland: 'Blind in Mist,'" in *John Keats and Romantic Scotland*, ed. Katie Garner and Nicholas Roe (Oxford University Press, 2022), 88-104.

Words, For Christopher Ricks

"Shakspear and the paradise Lost every day become great wonders to me—I look upon fine Phrases like a Lover," said John Keats to his friend Benjamin Bailey (14 August 1819), Keats himself a wonder of fine phrasings. One of his finest readers, Christopher Ricks, has an earned impatience with less than fine phrasings, especially when thoughtlessly done. Before I ever met him, I sent him one of my first publications, on Keats's letters—my own unembarrassed fan letter of sorts, from one immersed in his ever-pulsating *Keats and Embarrassment.* He wrote back, on what seemed a return-mail postcard, thanking me, but hoping I might outgrow some verbal afflictions: "strategize," when no military operation was afoot; "resonance" when nothing was being sounded; uninteresting flatliners such as "interesting"; rhetorical burps such as "thus," "in fact," "indeed," "of course." Indeed, of course I have, and in fact feel an interesting twinge every time I thus indulge myself, even provisionally.

Christopher is as generous as he is scrupulous. He sent me a recent essay, "To Put in a Word against a Word," piqued by the promiscuous use (not mine) of "debut" as a kind of faux theatricality from the social register to announce a first book: "Not a phrase, just a word; not a fine phrase . . . and damaging in ways that are not at all fine."[1] If Keats exclaimed to fellow poet J.H. Reynolds that Shakespeare's poems were "full of fine things said unintentionally" (22 November 1817), how perfectly reciprocal is Christopher's auditing of unfine things said intentionally. That's the scrupulous part. Here's the generosity. A couple of weeks after reading his essay—its opening line: "William Empson, when he felt obliged to issue a caveat . . . "— I was rereading *Milton's God* and saw this sentence about Eve's eavesdropping on Raphael's seminar with Adam: "after hearing Raphael on her future expected début, she may well want to obtain a tiny change in her experience" by working apart from her husband.[2]

---

1   *Poetry Birmingham,* spring 2024, 134-37, at 134.
2   *Milton's God* (New Directions, 1961), 150.

I sent this to Christopher in true friendship, as an arguably fine use of "début," frilly accent and all, for Eve's anticipation of society in Heaven (V:493-500). "What a delicious insistence," he replied the next day, 14 July, savoring Empson again, and elevating the word one might have expected, "instance," into emphatic "insistence." "Gusto" is what William Hazlitt called such delight: a "double relish" in the things described and "the words describing them."[3]

It's a Keatsian pleasure, too, as Ricks knows in his unembarrassed bones. "Now I shall relish Hamlet more than I ever have done," Keats tells Reynolds, 3 May 1818. Leigh Hunt recalled Keats reading, the next winter, this deliciously worded stanza (XXX) from *The Eve of St. Agnes* with "with great relish," tasting the words as his tongue shaped them:[4]

> And still she slept an azure-lidded sleep,
> In blanched linen, smooth, and lavender'd
> While he from forth the closet brought a heap
> Of candied apple, quince, and plum, and gourd;
> With jellies soother than the creamy curd,
> And lucent syrops, tinct with cinnamon;
> Manna and dates, in argosy transferr'd
> From Fez; and spiced dainties, every one,
> From silken Samarcand to cedar'd Lebanon.

In the same season, Keats coined a verb, or changed his mind halfway into writing a familiar one, to express the real effect of virtual immersion: *realish,* a sensation of "real" savored with the gusto, the taste, of "relish."[5]

The "tiny change" to which Empson refers is from Eve's always having to have Adam at her side, with her submission, subordination, and agreement to her genetic intellectual inferiority. Book IX is where she argues for this tiny, temporary, change. Then it all goes to hell. For this catastrophe, Milton's words matter, in the aggregate and in local instances and insistences. Why "change" this all-created "perfection" (V.471-72)? In the 23 December 2024 issue of *The New Yorker,* Merve Emre (Wesleyan University Professor of Creative Writing and Criticism) lectured, "There was inequality in Eden before the fall, but there was no misogyny."[6] To me, this *but* hovers over a distinction without a difference. One of the first, great, scrupulously

---

3   *Examiner,* 26 May 1816, 323-33.
4   "Mr. Keats," *Lord Byron and Some of his Contemporaries* (Henry Colburn, 1828), 1:430.
5   To the George Keatses, 2 January 1819.
6   "Occupy Paradise: How Radical was John Milton?" 74-78, at 78.

irritated female readers of *Paradise Lost* was Mary Wollstonecraft.[7] She summoned Milton into *A Vindication of the Rights of Woman* (1792) to note the misogyny of Eve's creation, not in overt invective but, more perniciously, in its praised foundation. When Milton "tells us that women are formed for softness and sweet attractive grace [alluding to IV:297-99], I cannot comprehend his meaning," she says with crafty disingenuity, unless "he meant that we were beings only designed . . . to gratify the sense of man when he can no longer soar on the wing of contemplation." Scoring *formed* as Milton's sorry fiction, she skewers the disingenuous notion of "sweet attractive grace"—*attractive* to men, that is, grace reduced from spiritual quality to docile flesh.

Ricks, unlike Emre, is acute on the way words in prelapsarian situations fall on the ears, fall in the eyes, of the fallen reader. He reads "Eve's wanton ringlets" (IV.306) not as symptom of a culpable wanton independence from her assignment (as do Harold Bloom and fellow-snipers) but as a "fallen word" unhappily, but not morally, nor proleptically, tainted by its society elsewhere: the "wanton rites" and "wanton passions" we saw in Hell (I.414, 454), then later, Satan's come-hither as he "Curld many a wanton wreath in sight of Eve" (IX.517).[8] Wollstonecraft sees a sociology of words in Satan's casing of the joint ere this approach, which she quotes for readers of *Vindication* to prick the wanton rites in his sightline on Eden's perfection, its flaws undisguised to him (and Wollstonecraft) by the gloss of hyperbole, with a polish of scripture. These are her italics on a passage in Book IV (634-38) that she finds particularly annoying:

> To whom thus Eve with *perfect beauty* adorn'd:
> My Author and Disposer, what thou bidst
> *Unargued* I obey; so God ordains;
> *God is thy law, thou mine*; to know no more
> Is Woman's *happiest* knowledge and her *praise*.

"These are exactly the arguments that I have used to children," she says sarcastically, defamiliarizing the lore and its pernicious legacy.[9] Eve's perfect beauty of body is matched by a mind that can say no more, know no more: "*Unargued* I obey." Wollstonecraft refuses such measures of perfection. Voicing the political spirit of her age, with unreformed progressives in her rhetorical sights, she quips, seriously,

---

7   Oddly, Professor Emre fails to mention any female or gender-attentive critic.
8   Milton, writes Ricks, provokes us to consider "wanton" in "paradisal state of language" when such words were not "infected" (*MGS*, 110-12).
9   *A Vindication of the Rights of Woman* (Joseph Johnson, 1792), 33-35.

"The *divine right* of husbands, like the divine right of kings, may, it is to be hoped, in this enlightened age, be contested without danger" (83, her italics).

How these elements of unfallen Eden strike a woman writing in 2024 as no "misogyny" is a puzzle to ponder. But these days women are being told as much by the Vice President of the United States. When Ricks celebrates "the life in Milton's verse,"[10] he is speaking the grammar of Wollstonecraft's lively attention. It is to Wollstonecraft's divine credit that she juxtaposes, on the same page and following (36-37), lines in which she begs to say, "Milton seems to coincide with me." This is Adam's brief to "his Maker" (VIII.381-92), where Milton seems to be speaking Wollstonecraft (her italics again) to divinely deaf ears:

> Hast thou not made me here thy substitute,
> And these inferior far beneath me set?
> Among *unequals* what society
> Can sort, what harmony or true delight?
> [...]
>   of *fellowship* I speak
> Such as I seek, fit to participate
> All rational delight—

On this angle, what do you make of Bob Dylan's line, "And there are no sins inside the gates of Eden"? Not just retro-theology, this is also a test of whether we want to see the lettering, hear the wording even, of *sins* in "sin[s ins]ide." The letter-glimpsed ambiguity is paired to a semantic puzzle in this song's bottom line: "And there are no truths outside the Gates of Eden."[11] So much depends on how you understand *outside: beyond?* or *with the exception of?* In the Edenic imaginary, it's all truth, until Satan gets there with his wanton-wreathing tongue. Dylan's poetry makes it possible for us to read "truths" as "the Gates" themselves: formidable, but not impenetrable. Are there any grating sins in Eden's gated "innocence"? Wollstonecraft thought so, nailing the word *innocence* itself: "when the epithet is applied to men, or women, it is but a civil term for weakness" (34). How deft, how trenchant, is her syntax: first a patent insult to men, then leveled for women. "Only absolute in loveliness, the portion of rationality granted to women, is indeed, very scanty," so she weighs the civil penalty (110), exasperated at Adam's report of his first swooning (VIII:547). I'll grant her this

---

10   *MGS*, Prefatory Note (np).
11   "The Gates of Eden," *Bringing it all Back Home,* 1965.

indeed (I think Christopher might, too). Are there sins of misvaluation (miss-valuation) inside Eden's gates? Notwithstanding the temptingly titled *Dylan's Visions of Sin,* Ricks's sharp eyes missed this nesting.

Yet if this kind of under-lettered nesting is not on Ricks-radar, he is blazingly attentive to word-play, to its ways and sways—so ingenious, so illuminating, so seductive, as to shift the grounds of understanding, on first pass and often in rereading. He was the first to defend Keats's double feeling about poetry that seemed to him true in the moment, and on review *mawkish.*[12] Ricks likes the risk that Keats took with this effect, "which a poem might indeed be the worse for advocating or gratifying but the better for accommodating" (this "indeed" is earned, for its literal sense of the doing).[13] Ricks knows where Keats is strong, even when seeming modest. Writing to Reynolds, 3 May 1818, Keats doubts what help metaphysical "Philosophy" may be in the physical trials of life in the world:

> among the effects this breathing is father of is that tremendous one of sharpening one's vision into the heart and nature of Man—of convincing ones nerves that the World is full of Misery and Heartbreak, Pain, Sickness and oppression . . . all leading to dark passages—We see not the ballance of good and evil. . . . To this point was Wordsworth come, as far as I can conceive when he wrote 'Tintern Abbey' and it seems to me that his Genius is explorative of those dark Passages.

"Convincing ones nerves," impresses Ricks: "it is a great phrase in its compacting of the highest understanding with the most inwardly physical experiencing." He homes in on the prepositional insight of "vision into the heart and nature of man," a phrasing in the same letter, in which Keats measures Milton's certainties against Wordsworth's progress "to dark passages": Milton "did not think into the human heart, as Wordsworth has done." "Keats," says Ricks, "was among the most magnanimous, great-hearted, of men and poets." Caught in the culture wars as *Blackwood's* Z and the *Quarterly's* Croker skewered the *Poems* of 1817 and *Endymion,* Keats wrote to the George Keatses about these slings and arrows: "This is a mere matter of the moment—I think that I shall be among the English Poets after my death" (14 October 1818). The paused *I think* strikes Ricks as "pure Keats, in its confident freedom from arrogance, as is *among the English poets,* since his poems

---

12   T Woodhouse to Taylor, 19, 20 September 1819.
13   *KE,* 146-47.

have always been among theirs, enjoying their company and having them live again in the life of his allusive art."[14]

No wonder Ricks is the greatest reader ever of Wordsworth's feeling for the force of prepositions. You could say "prepositionality," but that's the kind of word, in sound and *chi-chi* critcalese, he is likely to swat. He reads with the best of them, among the best of them. He has no use for critics who take "a lugubrious relish in trying to scotch any close criticism which might suggest that a poet's use of words is subtle, delicate, ingenious, or new." He said this in 1965 (in defense of Milton).[15] 60 years on, Christopher Ricks is not only unscotched, but continues to chide words that don't work this way, and to champion those that do.

Susan Wolfson

---

14 "Keats's Sources, Keats's Allusions," *Cambridge Companion to John Keats*, ed. by Susan J. Wolfson (Cambridge University Press, 2001), 154. This essay was soon collected in *ATTP*.

15 *MGS*, 21.

At the Breakfast Table

"There is present," Christopher Ricks has written with regard to Keats and the poetry that lodged itself in Keats's mind, "not only the imagined but the imaginary":

> It is this act of imagining *within* a work of imagination that from one point of view compounds the store set upon imagination, imagination upon imagination after all. But from another point of view, to distinguish the imaginary from the imagined must be to introduce a crucial distinction that is in its turn germane to the distinction between imagination and all else.[1]

When it imagines, Keats's poetry often compounds, in Ricks's sense. Sometimes, though, the matter seems a little simpler:

> The day is gone, and all its sweets are gone!
>   Sweet voice, sweet lips, soft hand, and softer breast,
> Warm breath, light whisper, tender semi-tone,
>   Bright eyes, accomplish'd shape, and lang'rous waist![2]

Little is left to the imagination, and perhaps too that is the point, since the delights of the day that is gone are really memories and not exactly (or merely) imagined things, "Faded" though they may be (faded four times in the next four lines) by the coming of night. What is more (for more in Keats's poetry is always more) the night to be watched through is no other than "the dusk holiday—or holinight" for "fragrant curtain'd Love," with its "darkness, thick, for hid delight." In a way, what is hid stays hidden; but the nature of the "holinight" is not all that difficult to imagine. It is, though, (at least on the face of things) *only* imagined—that is (at least maybe) imaginary—until night brings round the day once again. But at least personified "Love" is placated by the lover's night of abstinence:

---

1   *ATTP*, 173-174.
2   John Keats, "The day is gone, and all its sweets are gone!" (1819), *Complete Poems*, ed. by Jack Stillinger (Harvard University Press, 1978), 374.

But, as I've read Love's missal through to-day,
He'll let me sleep, seeing I fast and pray.

Keats's poem offers no reason to suppose (and its entire movement is in the finding of no such reason) that the coming morning will not see the sweet breaking of this night's erotic fast, when matter for the imagination can once again become a real matter.

The day's "sweets," then, are only gone for the moment, and they are not entirely 'gone' anyhow while the poem hungrily imagines them. The poem's opening ("sweet" appears three times in the space of two lines) is sufficiently insistent to set up an anticipation of further sweets to come once the fast is broken. And the assurance in that final couplet is also the conclusion of an argument successfully made—in this, the Shakespearean sonnet structure which Keats employs does its job well. The reiterated "sweet" suggests Shakespeare: the 154 Sonnets have that word 57 times, sometimes densely reiterated. In Sonnet 54, there is this:

Oh how much more doth beautie beautious seeme,
By that sweet ornament which truth doth giue,
The Rose lookes faire, but fairer we it deeme
For that sweet odor, which doth in it liue:[3]

"Sweet" both looks and smells, "ornament" and "odor"; and although "Canker bloomes" offer some resemblance to this, they cannot match the reality:

But for their virtue only is their show,
They liue vnwoo'd, and vnrespected fade,
Die to themselues. Sweet Roses doe not so,
Of their sweet deathes, are sweetest odors made:

Sweetness, that is, doesn't fade away so easily: instead, it goes from "sweet" to "sweetest." Does Keats, with his threefold "sweet" and fourfold "faded," remember Sonnet 54? Better, does his poem have Sonnet 54 as an imagined thing inside its own work of imagining? A Shakespearean sonnet, after all, mustn't pretend ignorance of Shakespeare's *Sonnets*, if only because its form carries them like a kind of metrical muscle-memory. Of the many things any such poem may be said to imagine, the Shakespearean sonnet is inevitably one.

---

3   William Shakespeare, *Sonnets* (1609), Sonnet 54, ll. 1-4 and 9-12.

It would be easy—and wrong—to become a little too clever on this point. One could say, for instance, that Keats writes Shakespearean sonnets that imagine being Shakespeare's Sonnets. But this is misleading, and possibly frivolous. For Keats—in this poem at least—is busy imagining not what he assuredly already has (the Sonnets), but what he wants, and looks forward to having when the next day comes. The hunger here may be for what is delayed, but isn't for what is unattainable, any more than it has been unattained.

Nevertheless, hunger brings the imagined into play. One of the two speaking voices in W.B. Yeats's 'Ego Dominus Tuus' holds forth on Keats and hunger, responding to his companion's assertion that "No one denies to Keats love of the world; / Remember his deliberate happiness":

> His art is happy, but who knows his mind?
> I see a schoolboy when I think of him,
> With face and nose pressed to a sweet-shop window,
> For certainly he sank into his grave
> His senses and his heart unsatisfied,
> And made—being poor, ailing and ignorant,
> Shut out from all the luxury of the world,
> The coarse-bred son of a livery-stable keeper—
> Luxuriant song.[4]

There is little "luxury of the world" about these lines, though: in fact, "Luxuriant song" comes across as something they can barely imagine. Instead, Keats becomes the subject of a thumbnail lecture of the kind that scarcely radiates generosity: "poor, ailing and ignorant" and "coarse-bred" are too certain (and snobbish) by far. Yeats knows at least some of this about the lines, and his speaker is a slightly pompous dogmatist (called—pompously and dogmatically—*Ille*) who can easily be dismissed by the poet should need arise. Rather "Luxuriant song" than this, surely, in most contexts. Yet *Ille* transcends his own limitations in an act of imagination, turning Keats into a schoolboy "With face and nose pressed to a sweet-shop window." It is here, rather than in his lines of commentary and interpretation, that the speaker makes Keats into an "imagined thing" within the poem. And Keats is imagined in the act of imagining, hungry for what he cannot have. What is in the "sweet-shop window" is tellingly close to all the sweet things in Keats's poetry—close, even, to the temper of a line like "The

---

4   W.B. Yeats, "Ego Dominus Tuus" (wr. 1915), ed. by P. Allt and R.K. Alspach, *The Variorum Edition of The Poems of W.B. Yeats* (Macmillan, 1957), 370.

day is gone, and all its sweets are gone!" It is the desire, the hunger and the lack that spur Keats into "Luxuriant song." That may be debatable in critical terms; but it is convincing in terms of imagined content inside an imagining poem.

Yeats's speaker had already been loitering in Keatsian territory. At least, his attempts at near-dogmatic pronouncements about art and life are made possible by Keats's toying with them long before:

> The rhetorician would deceive his neighbours,
> The sentimentalist himself; while art
> Is but a vision of reality.
> What portion of the world can the artist have
> Who has awakened from the common dream
> But dissipation and despair?[5]

These lines have certainly learned from "The Fall of Hyperion: A Dream," where Keats's figure of the Moneta gives her poetic petitioner a protracted and stern telling-off:

> Art thou not of the dreamer tribe?
> The poet and the dreamer are distinct,
> Diverse, sheer opposite, antipodes.
> The one pours out a balm upon the world,
> The other vexes it.[6]

Which is all very well, and may be very well put: but telling "The one" from "The other" is not so straightforward as the syntax suggests–it is the poet and not the dreamer, that is, who does this balm-pouring, but distinguishing these sheer opposites is in fact a gamble, as Keats's speaker knows. The bones of losers lie all around him; and dreamers have always, after all, been perfectly capable of dreaming that they are poets. As so often, the dream had started so well: even this poem begins by reassuring itself that "Poesy alone can tell her dreams, / With the fine spell of words alone can save / Imagination from the sable charm / And dumb enchantment" (Keats, *anno aetatis* 23; compare W.B. Yeats's "Song of the Happy Shepherd," *anno aetatis* 20: "Words alone are certain good").[7] The dream can be something quite other than what Yeats (by the time he was much older than the age Keats managed to reach) called "a vision of reality."

---

5   Ibid., 369.
6   John Keats, "The Fall of Hyperion: A Dream" 198-202, *Complete Poems*, ed. by Stillinger, 366.
7   John Keats, "The Fall of Hyperion: A Dream" 8-11, *Complete Poems*, ed. by Stillinger, 361; W.B. Yeats, "Song of the Happy Shepherd," *Variorum Edition*, 65.

Keats's—or Keats's speaker's—dream begins with the remnants of a meal:

> on a mound
> Of moss, was spread a feast of summer fruits,
> Which, nearer seen, seem'd refuse of a meal
> By angel tasted, or our mother Eve;
> For empty shells were scatter'd on the grass,
> And grape stalks but half bare, and remnants more,
> Sweet smelling, whose pure kinds I could not know.[8]

Imagined in this meal, as Keats prompts us to notice, is the picnic prepared by Eve in the fifth Book of *Paradise Lost*. But where in Milton there is "fruit of all kindes, in coate, / Rough, or smooth rin'd, or bearded husk, or shell" here the shells are empty, and the "Sweet smelling" things are "remnants"—"grape stalks but half bare."[9] It is as if somebody else has got to all the food before Keats's speaker arrived: something is left, but what is left is not all there once was. The rest, the full banquet, is something you (and he) just have to imagine. The sweet smell in this case is the smell of not quite enough, of leftovers from a feast to which the poem's speaker is a latecomer. And everyone else, as the speaker soon finds out, has perished: in reality, they were not poets but dreamers.

Of course, when Yeats grandly invokes "a vision of reality," he too (whether he or his speaker knows it or not) is also gambling, in the hope that he proves to be neither "rhetorician" nor "sentimentalist." The outcome of the bet isn't known (and can't be), but it is telling that a hope to awaken "from the common dream" issues in references to Keats. "Dissipation and despair," though? If Yeats's speaker *Ille* sees these things in Keats, he does so unselfconsciously, as though he himself is able safely to look down on them. That assumption may not itself be a safe one, and a few lines earlier, *Ille*'s confidence in the whole matter risks coming to a sticky end:

> For those that love the world serve it in action,
> Grow rich, popular and full of influence,
> And should they paint or write, still it is action:
> The struggle of the fly in marmalade.[10]

---

8   John Keats, "The Fall of Hyperion: A Dream" 28-34, *Complete Poems* ed. Stillinger, 362.

9   John Milton, *Paradise Lost* V, 341-2.

10   W.B. Yeats, "Ego Dominus Tuus," *Variorum Edition*, 369.

Ille condescends to mere "action," as Keats's Moneta certainly does not: "'None can usurp this height,' return'd that shade, / But those to whom the miseries of the world / Are misery, and will not let them rest."[11] Yet "The struggle of the fly in marmalade" is something other than condescension, in its sudden apprehension of something both commonplace and desperate, something ordinarily beneath the notice of rhetorical (or sentimental) abstraction. The fly's "struggle" is only literally a thing to be looked down on; an attraction to sweetness has turned into a life-or-death struggle to get away from the sweet thing it had craved. When, more than twenty years later, Yeats describes the poet as "never the bundle of accident and incoherence that sits down to breakfast," no pot of marmalade is mentioned; yet its presence on that table might still be imagined.[12]

Imagined, in fact, as it was when a later poet imagined Yeats inside a poem of his own, just as Yeats had imagined Keats in "Ego Dominus Tuus," and as Keats in "The Fall of Hyperion" had imagined "our mother Eve" and her open-air spread of wholesome delicacies in Milton. In his last collection, Edwin Muir has "The Late Wasp":

> You that through all the dying summer
> Came every morning to our breakfast table,
> A lonely bachelor mummer,
> And fed on the marmalade
> So deeply, all your strength was scarcely able
> To prise you from the sweet pit you had made,—
> You and the earth have now grown older,
> And your blue thoroughfares have felt a change;
> They have grown colder;
> And it is strange
> How the familiar avenues of the air
> Crumble now, crumble; the good air will not hold,
> All cracked and perished with the cold;
> And down you dive through nothing and through despair.[13]

As to the poem itself, and as to Muir, it is impossible to do better than Mick Imlah's judgement:

> Here the poet's normal procedure does not quite stick his subject in amber: what is caught is not a posture but a dying movement, whose finish is out

---

11   John Keats, "The Fall of Hyperion: A Dream" 147-8, *Complete Poems*, ed. by Stillinger, 364.

12   W.B. Yeats, "A General Introduction for my Work" [wr. 1937], *Essays and Introductions* (Macmillan, 1961), 509.

13   Edwin Muir, *One Foot in Eden* (Faber, 1956), 82.

beyond the poem. Every word of the last line, which you cannot always say with Muir, seems perfect in its place. And so the rare singleness of his writing passes into another medium: 'Late Wasp' could not be improved, rewritten in verse or prose, repeated, repointed or recapitulated.[14]

All true, to Imlah's credit as well as Muir's. (The best criticism of poetry is in the giving of credit–an act of gratitude that shows how subtly and comprehensively in poetry gratitude can do its work.) But what is "out beyond the poem" is also what the poem is able to imagine inside its own working: here, Yeats's marmalade-stuck fly that prompts thoughts of "dissipation and despair" for *Ille*. Muir corrects that fly to the more plausible wasp. This is a gain in verisimilitude (and Yeats was maybe giving the game away when he chose a fly, for his fly in the marmalade is really a fly in the ointment, as far as the poem's argument is concerned); at the same time, it is an imaginative gain, for "struggle" here is profoundly imagined–"all your strength was scarcely able / To prise you from the sweet pit you had made."

The poem's feeling for a doomed, late-season wasp might well be said to follow a Keatsian prescription for imaginative empathy ("snail-horn perception," and the like) which has tended to be more praised and recommended than successfully carried through in modern poetry. The poem's perception is wasp-y, without being in the least waspish. And Muir has somewhere in his hearing Yeats's "dissipation and despair" in that last line which Imlah praises; but now, "through" is offering something, however sticky and difficult, in the way of hope. The wasp might indeed come through this. Just possibly, William Empson is working on Muir too, with the last line of his "This Last Pain":

Imagine, then, by miracle, with me,
(Ambiguous gifts, as what gods give must be)
    What could not possibly be there,
And learn a style from a despair.[15]

Poetry can imagine sweetness in many ways, but by imagining the wasp in its 'sweet pit' Muir takes even sweetness to somewhere it has not quite been before. Just as decisively, Empson's indefinite article before "despair" takes the abstract (and too frequently abstracted) thing and makes it particular, possibly unique, even if completely

---

14   Mick Imlah, *Edwin Muir: Selected Poems* (Faber, 2008), xxii.
15   William Empson, "This Last Pain" [publ. 1932], *The Complete Poems*, ed. by John Haffenden (Penguin, 2001), 53.

unspecified. Is this "What could not possibly be there"? But there it is, and there too is Muir's wasp, which is the metamorphosis of Yeats's fly. It's likely enough that Empson came to regret that Yeatsian "by miracle" in his poem, yet it is the right phrase even so. Here Empson, like many of the best twentieth-century poets, cannot quite resist Yeats's (sometimes fatal) allure: he—and Muir, much more so—is stuck with him.

The "act of imagining *within* a work of imagination" is as delicate as it is complicated. And the fact that no poem has ever actually fed someone is a truth, but it isn't exactly "a vision of reality." For that, we need to accept that sweetness can be imagined, just as the hunger for it can be imagined; as the risks of it can be imagined, and as both the depths of and escapes from despair are imaginable, in poetry's ways and means. And poetry, too, can imagine other poetry than its own, whilst still within its own. For although the world a good poem was written in, with all its accidents and confusions and contradictions, its sweet-shop windows and its breakfast tables, may die, the poem itself has the means to live on: "Sweet Roses doe not so, / Of their sweet deaths, are sweetest odors made." At the heart of the process, for the best poetry, and the best appreciation of poetry as well, are imaginative openness, generosity, joy, and gratitude: those sweet things.

Peter McDonald

Here

For Christopher

Just up the street, past the four Evergreen Pears, now, in late February, magnificently white, despite two of them being overshadowed by two taller and aslant Paperbarks, and past the African Fever Tree, with its yellow bark and odd pairs of white thorns all along the finely foliaged branches, covering the tree, and right across the street from Brian's Queensland Bottle Tree, on the left, on Madison, is a Yucca Century Tree, which has bloomed, though century must be mythical, this kind of Yucca seldom surviving a hundred years, but it has, to everyone's astonishment and joy, suddenly bloomed, a light-lime-colored virginal tree thirty feet high growing out of the ten-foot Yucca, as if time were no longer time, but a rare, amplified present.

Harry Thomas

Querying Ricks on T.S. Eliot's "Wrong'd Othello"

I write to thank Christopher Ricks for both his friendship and his example: for many kindnesses both personal and professional; for many hours of conversation in his office and in his home; for the thousands of poems and essays that he has edited with such intelligent scrupulosity, enabling all of us to come into fuller possession of them; and for the companionship of his many critical books and essays, which have offered so many more hours of humane and bracing critical conversation.

I write also to continue that conversation by posing a series of questions to T.S. Eliot, or, practically, to Christopher as Eliot's incomparably attentive editor and expositor. These questions are about Eliot's reading of the great speech near the end of *Othello*, in which Othello proffers a summary account of the events that we have just witnessed, telling his on-stage audience how they "must" speak of his love for Desdemona and of his killing of her, and then of the subsequent judgment that he pronounces upon himself, a judgment that he carries out as the speech ends in his self-execution. Eliot attends to this passage in his 1927 essay (first a public lecture), "Shakespeare and the Stoicism of Seneca."

Here is Eliot's comment, as it frames the speech:

I have always felt that I have never read a more terrible exposure of human weakness—of universal human weakness—than the last great speech of Othello. (I am ignorant whether anyone else has ever adopted this view, and it may appear subjective and fantastic in the extreme.). It is usually taken on its face value; as expressing the greatness in defeat of a noble but erring nature.

> Soft you; a word or two before you go.
> I have done the state some service, and they know't,
> No more of that. I pray you, in your letters,
> When you shall these unlucky deeds relate,
> Speak of me as I am; nothing extenuate,
> Nor set down aught in malice; then must you speak
> Of one that loved not wisely but too well;
> Of one not easily jealous, but, being wrought,

> *Perplex'd in the extreme; of one whose hand,*
> *Like the base Indian, threw a pearl away*
> *Richer than all his tribe; of one whose subdued eyes,*
> *Albeit unused to the melting mood,*
> *Drop tears as fast as the Arabian trees*
> *Their medicinal gum. Set you down this;*
> *And say, besides, that in Aleppo once,*
> *Where a malignant and a turban'd Turk*
> *Beat a Venetian and traduced the state,*
> *I took by the throat the circumcised dog,*
> *And smote him, thus.*

What Othello seems to me to be doing in making this speech is *cheering himself up*. He is endeavouring to escape reality; he has ceased to think about Desdemona, and is thinking about himself. Humility is the most difficult of all virtues to achieve; nothing dies harder than the desire to think well of oneself. Othello succeeds in turning himself into a pathetic figure, by adopting an *aesthetic* rather than a moral attitude, dramatizing himself against his environment. He takes in the spectator, but the human motive is primarily to take in himself. I do not believe that any writer has ever exposed this *bovarysme*, the human will to see things as they are not, more clearly than Shakespeare.[1]

I read this first as a student and have never since read or seen or taught Othello without pondering it, working to bring its persuasive force into relationship with my own sense of the play and of the character. Thinking and writing about other subjects as well, I have had frequent occasion to return to the passage and, especially, to Eliot's piercing observation that "Nothing dies harder than the desire to think well of oneself." But I have recoiled from the sense that the passage diminishes Othello in stature and dignity, that its exposure of his self-dramatizing and self-exculpatory impulses does not just complicate but deny the tragic *magnitude* of his story and of this moment in the theatre. In particular, the italicized phrase, *"cheering himself up"* seems to do this work of diminution.

In his essay, "T.S. Eliot and 'Wrong'd Othello,'" published in *Along Heroic Lines* (2021),[2] Christopher celebrates and complements this instance of Eliot's critical "genius," defending it against misconstruction, laying out the precise character of its claims and of its achievement, and finding in it a resonant substructure of echoes

---

1   *Selected Essays* (Faber, 1932; 3rd edn. 1951), 130-31. I follow Eliot's practice in italicizing the passage from *Othello*. Eliot does not cite an editor or edition, but is quoting from the Folio text.
2   *AHL*, 84-105.

and allusions to the language of Shakespeare and of Eliot's own poetry. The most salient of Christopher's demonstrations, for me, are, first, those that emerge from his repeated notice of the "excruciating" specification that the weakness of character Eliot locates in Othello is not just Othello's, but "universal human weakness," a weakness that readers and viewers must acknowledge as their own even as they apprehend it in the speech. And, second, the discovery of many instances in Shakespeare of "cheering up," instances that suggest the phrase was used by Eliot, as by Shakespeare in Christopher's examples, to describe a substantial act of mind, not the idling distraction that modern ears hear in it, but something like the taking heart that prepares the mind for a great test or for death.

I am persuaded that Eliot's emphasis on universal human weakness effectively wrongfoots those critics who have felt the need to defend Othello against a presumed dismissal of his claims to our sympathetic attention. I struggle, however, to un-hear a diminution in "cheering himself up," even after Christopher's characteristically impressive gathering of relevant quotations. Beyond this, I'm eager to ask of Eliot's shade, or of his text, a sequence of more speculative questions. I offer these questions not so much in respectful disagreement as in admiring curiosity.

I'm curious about Eliot's characterization of the conventional view that the speech expresses "the greatness in defeat of a noble but erring nature." He prompts us to hear the patness of this formulation, the ways that the "but" clause skates quickly and slickly past the enormity of the error in question, which is an act of brutal murder. He doesn't cite any expressions of this conventional view, which must come in many gradations and variants. I hear (but am I mistaken?) the implication that any version of it must be in error to the extent that it allows the contemplation of Othello's nobility at this heightened moment in the drama to blot out or distract from the brute fact of his crime. The error ascribed, furthermore, feels moral as well as cognitive, as if those conventional viewers of the play were to some degree complicit with Othello in averting their eyes from things as they are. Or if not that, then insufficiently alert to the universality of that human weakness and to the way it is being here exposed to us.

But what of Othello's particular, non-universal nature, his stature and authority within the world of the play, the rhetorical and behavioral distinction that Shakespeare endows him with through its first half? To think of Othello's as a universal human weakness engages our sympathy for him but co-exists uncertainly with my own sense—does Eliot share it?—that he appears so often and so convincingly as a splendid and impressive figure. If it is a "universal human weakness" to hide from the knowledge of our own bad acts, to incorporate them too quickly into a more bearable reconstruction of our stories, is Othello more or differently subject to this weakness than he might be? Doesn't Eliot's devastating judgment of Othello, for all the invitation to see his weakness as universally shared, imply that Othello might and should have done better, might have delivered a summary account of his career that would have given us a less blameable Othello in a diminished *Othello*?

These questions lead me back to a slightly earlier moment in the final scene, to the second of the three extended speeches that Shakespeare gives to Othello as he moves from the murder of Desdemona to the wrenching recognition of her innocence and his own terrible mistake, then to the culmination of his suicide. The last scene contains much more than these three speeches. I think especially of the agonized and agonizing creatureliness of Desdemona as she faces her death; and of the perfectly modulated representation of Emilia's ordinary humanity as it is forced to extraordinary declarations of love and defiance and courage. But the three big speeches do offer themselves as high points supporting a narrative arc that moves from one sort of tragic poise, into discovery and despair, and then to the recovered poise of the conclusion—a poise too easily and self-deludingly recovered, in Eliot's view. In the opening lines of the Act V, scene ii, Othello pauses over the body of the sleeping Desdemona, relishing her apparent purity even as he laments her crime and his obligation to punish it, horribly appointing himself as the agent of "Justice" in an impersonal "cause." A longer look at this speech could only extend and reinforce the sense that Othello mistakes his own nature as completely as he mistakes Desdemona's.

But what of the speech he gives much later in the scene, when he looks again at Desdemona's dead body after having been wrenched suddenly into an entirely new and horrible understanding of his circumstances? Othello has learned at V.ii.235 that it was Emilia who picked up Desdemona's handkerchief and gave it to Iago. After an unimaginable few moments in which he must absorb all the implications of this information—Desdemona's innocence, Iago's villainy, the completeness with which he has been duped and deceived—he lunges ineffectually at Iago, who stabs Emilia and flees, leaving the stage to Othello and Emilia, who dies singing the Willow Song of Desdemona (a Folio addition) and condemning Othello's cruelty and mistake. He

has had only a few lines in these few moments, first in the lunge at
Iago ("Are there no stones in heaven/But what serves for the thunder?
Precious villain!") and then a brief, first gesture at complete surrender
to circumstance, four lines ending in "Let it go all." And then another
four, remembering a weapon that is hidden somewhere in the room.
And then this as Gratiano re-enters:

> Behold, I have a weapon;
> A better never did itself sustain
> Upon a soldier's thigh. I have seen the day
> That with this little arm and this good sword
> I have made my way through more impediments
> Than twenty times your stop. But O vain boast!
> Who can control his fate? 'Tis not so now,
> Be not afraid, though you do see me weaponed.
> Here is my journey's end, here is my butt
> And very seamark of my utmost sail;
> Do you go back dismayed? 'Tis a lost fear.
> Man but a rush against Othello's breast
> And he retires. Where should Othello go?
> Now, how dost thou look now? O ill-starred wench!
> Pale as thy smock! When we shall meet at compt,
> This look of thine will hurl my soul from heaven,
> And fiends will snatch at it. Cold, cold, my girl?
> Even like thy chastity.
> O cursed, cursed slave! Whip me, ye devils,
> From the possession of this heavenly sight!
> Blow me about in winds! roast me in sulfur!
> Wash me in steep-down gulfs of liquid fire!
> Oh Desdemon! dead Desdemon. dead! Oh! Oh!
> (V.2.260-282)[3]

Elsewhere in his lecture, Eliot has offered Marlowe's Faust as the
exceptional figure from the drama of the period, "the hero who has
reached that point of horror at which even pride is abandoned."
Might we—might *he*—say the same of Othello here? Or would he say
of Othello what he does of Baudelaire in a passage that Christopher
cites? "[I]t is possible to pass through the most terrible experience
protected by histrionic vanity."[4] I read the speech as inviting equally
a performance in which dramatic expression devolves into histrionics
and vanity, and another in which that devolution is merely a way station
to the rawest of utterances, in which those terminal repetitions and
bellowings expose a suffering unmanaged by any shaping impulse

3   *The Complete Pelican Shakespeare* (Penguin Classics, 2002).
4   From "Baudelaire in our Time," in *The Dial*, May, 1927; cited in Ricks, *AHL*, 98.

other than Shakespeare's. The opening lines feel less like a deliberate act of self-recovery than an unthinking and unsustainable relapse into his default mode of self-presentation—a mode that collides quickly with the brute and fresh-born fact of Othello's loss of self, his abject submission to a fate that he no longer imagines controlling. And then, succeeding that, a new and more bruising collision with the fact of Desdemona's betrayed and murdered body and of his own, damnable agency. Is he thinking of Desdemona here as a guilty human might who was contending more successfully to see himself as he is? This speech of Othello's, less studied and celebrated than the other two extended speeches in the closing scene, perhaps because of its rant, grows in power and interest as we read back to it through Eliot's treatment of the third speech and discern here the multiple waverings between denial and acknowledgment. At first, the denial of soldierly posturing; then later the flight from unillusioned recognition into masochistic excess. And then back in the last line as speech abandons grammar in the repetitive naming of three brute facts: Desdemona, Dead, Oh! What would Eliot have said of it?

I repeat in closing that I am not asking these questions because I imagine that they pose unanswerable—or even especially hard to answer—challenges to his reading of the great last speech. I ask them because I want what we can't have, the uniquely interesting answers that he would give in an expanded account of the play. Trying to bring this earlier speech into contact with Eliot's reading of "Soft you, a word or two before you go," I can construct a plausible critical demonstration that locates one part of Othello's human failure in the speed and completeness with which he recovers his dignity of utterance and clarity of purpose between the second speech and the third. Or perhaps in which Eliot answers other of my questions by noting that an implicit argument of his lecture/essay is that heroic drama—the Shakespearean version of it, as inflected by Senecan stoicism—necessarily exposes the ethical compromises of a secularly defined heroism.

But as Christopher reminds his readers in many different places, it is of the essence of genius that we cannot imagine for ourselves what it would say. As firmly as Christopher has rejected the title of genius for himself, it remains true of him that, again and again in his extraordinary career, he has offered to all of us marshallings of information and insight that I cannot imagine producing for myself and for which I am pleased to have this opportunity to express my gratitude.

Tim Peltason

Moral Gambling in *Hamlet*

"It fortuned (high God did so ordain) . . . "–Spenser, *Faerie Queene*, III. vii.27
"God is a witness that cannot be sworn."–Beckett, *Watt*
" . . . the devil can cite Hamlet to his purpose."–Ricks, *Allusion to the Poets*

By my count there are five gambles, literal or figurative, in *Hamlet*, or at least five that cannot be doubted. Hamlet *père* and Fortinbras *père* gamble territory on the outcome of single combat, as Horatio's speech on the motivations of Fortinbras *fils* discloses. That gamble is an avatar of the bout between Laertes and Hamlet in Act V, on which (so Osric informs Hamlet) Laertes and the King have wagered even stakes but with Hamlet being given a handicap. Hamlet assures Horatio: "I shall win at the odds," given the handicap Laertes agrees to. This contest is the antitype both of his father's bout (where the stakes were even) and of his certainty that the ghost of his father has told the truth: "O good Horatio, I'll take the ghost's word for a thousand pound" (III.ii.312-13). Hamlet's spontaneity will soon lead to the death of the fairly innocent Polonius, whose spying Hamlet calls *rash* (III.iv.38), picking up on his mother's words four lines earlier: "O, what a rash and bloody deed is this" (III. iv.34). Indeed, Hamlet sees Polonius as succumbing because of the bad bet he's made in spying on them: "Thou wretched, rash, intruding fool, farewell / I took thee for better. Take thy fortune": *his* fortune, the result of *his* gamble. Hamlet's own repetition of the formula *take thee*—I *took thee* for they better; *take thy* fortune—suggests (however subliminally) that Hamlet's own fortune, the result of his own gamble then, was killing Polonius, whose death is the first in the play, and leads to all the others. How should we think about these moments of rashness? Well, the last gamble on my list is the one in which Hamlet, again, "Rashly– / And praised be rashness for it" (V.ii.7-8) opens the commission being carried by Rosencrantz and Guildenstern.

I won't talk about all these gambles in what follows, but I list them here to suggest how much Shakespeare is thinking about moral gambling in the play.

I

The concept of moral luck would seem to imply the complementary idea of moral gambling, since luck (the way we use it now, for both good and ill), is the gambler's abiding concern. Are there any theories of moral luck that make moral gambling permissible? This question comes up in torts, where there's a distinction between *taxing the risk* and *taxing the harm*. How much should recklessness which doesn't lead to disaster be fined; how much more should it be fined if the same recklessness does lead to disaster? If a drunk driver just misses someone, should they be treated more leniently than the drunk driver who kills?

Moral luck also comes up in rendering verdicts, and in the early seventeenth century Coke quotes an old idea in canon law: that proofs of guilt have to be clearer than light. I'd draw particular attention to his chapter on false imprisonment in *The Institutes of the Laws of England* where he cites "the rule of law, Quod in criminalibus probationes debent esse luce clarioribus,"[1] i.e. clearer than light. In that chapter he argues against being too fast to conclude guilt, or even to arrest someone suspected of a capital crime, lest they not have a chance to marshal proofs of innocence. This despite the fact that they need not defend themselves at all: "The testimonies and the proofs of the offence ought to be so clear and manifest, as there can be no defence of it" (Coke, 29). This is where our concept of proof beyond a reasonable doubt comes from: you can't just gamble that the prisoner is guilty, even if the bet looks good. If the coin comes up heads three times in row, there's still a reasonable chance that it's an honest coin.

Issues of luck in cases of mortal peril come up in *Hamlet*—what if Hamlet is unlucky enough to send Claudius to heaven because it seems pretty clear he's praying? If Claudius's moral luck may send him to heaven, this would be particularly disturbing since Hamlet *père*'s bad moral luck has meant that he was

> Cut off, even in the blossoms of my sin,
> Unhouseled, disappointed, unaneled,
> No reck'ning made, but sent to my account
> With all my imperfections on my head. (I.5.83–85)

---

1   *The Third Part of the Institutes of the Laws of England: Concerning High Treason, and Other Pleas of the Crown, and Criminall Causes*, (M. Flesher, 1644), 210.

II

These are examples of the luck of the draw, of gambling on outcomes. But there's another kind of moral gambling—the kind that corresponds to the moral luck that Bernard Williams begins his essay on moral luck with: Gauguin's. Williams is interested in Gauguin's gamble on his future, a gamble that (as I read it) will harm others if he loses but not so much that such harm won't be justified if he wins. Williams contrasts this kind of gamble and the happiness that it might lead to with "the Robespierrean government to which Heine compared the Kantian system in general."[2] In the Kantian system there's no room for taking a chance, even on your own chances to do good. Williams summarizes that position (which he disagrees with) this way: "Justice requires not merely that *something I am* should be beyond luck, but that *what I most fundamentally am* should be so, and, in the light of that, admiration or liking or even enjoyment of the happy manifestations of luck can seem to be treachery to moral worth."[3] As I say, Williams disagrees with this position, as making it impossible for a person to have "a life of one's own," and he calls this "a genuine pathology of the moral life," concluding that "the limitation of the moral is itself something morally important" (53).

A happy manifestation of luck, as Williams calls it, may be found in one of the instances I've already cited, Hamlet's opening of the packet carried by Rosencrantz and Guildenstern:

> Rashly—
> And praised be rashness for it; let us know,
> Our indiscretion sometime serves us well
> When our deep plots do pall; and that should learn us
> There's a divinity that shapes our ends,
> Rough-hew them how we will—
>
> HORATIO That is most certain.
>
> HAMLET Up from my cabin,
> My sea-gown scarfed about me, in the dark
> Groped I to find out them; had my desire,
> Fingered their packet, and in fine withdrew
> To mine own room again, making so bold

---

2   Bernard Williams, "Moral Luck," in *Moral Luck: Philosophical Papers 1973-1980* (Cambridge University Press, 1973), 20-39, at 38.
3   "Moral Luck," 38.

(My fears forgetting manners) to unfold
Their grand commission . . ..

In *Hamlet* the wrong done by opening the packet is in itself trivial, a gamble that if it doesn't work out would be of no importance: He'd find something innocuous and reseal the packet. But, as for Gauguin, his gamble works out (for himself, not so much for Rosencrantz and Guildenstern), even more so after the attack by the pirates, an event of positively Spenserian convenience.

But the moral lesson Hamlet draws from this is perhaps a little surprising. You don't have to gamble at all—rough-hew your ends how you will, the heavens will punish offenders "when they see the hour is ripe on earth" (*Richard II*, I.ii.7). That's lucky! Because for the first four acts of the play Hamlet does feel pressured to gamble although the rules of justice—the requirement to find proofs of guilt so definite as to be clearer than light—preclude probabilistic judgment.

III

Unlike with Gauguin, if Hamlet gambles on an blameless Claudius's guilt, he will lose his soul and not just his time; he won't simply fail in the obligations he owes to other people (like Ophelia) but will do mortal injury to an innocent man, not simply behaving neglectfully (even if "we may suppose [such neglect] to be grim" [Williams, 23]). But let's turn back to Coke (and to his invocation of Gratianus or Gratian's twelfth century compilation of canon law, the *Decretum Gratiani*, which says that guilt requires being "provided with evidence that is indubitable and clearer than light"—*indiciis ad probationem indubitatis et luce clarioribus expedita*).[4] This is the origin of what has come to be known as "Blackstone's ratio," from his eighteenth century commentary on the laws of England: "It is better that ten guilty persons escape than that one innocent suffer." But this is of course a rhetorical ratio: he's not calling on finding someone guilty if there's less than a 10% chance that they are innocent. You need proof, to use the English formulation, to a moral certainty. The idea goes much farther back, to the highly influential Matthew Hale in the seventeenth century, and to Sir John Fortescue, Henry VI's Chief Justice, whose MS in praise of the laws of England (written for the young Prince Edward), *De laudibus*

---

4   *Decreti, Secunda Pars, Causa II, Qaestio VIII, C. 2*, 503. I think this goes back to Justinian.

legum Angliæ, saw print in the sixteenth century. Mulcaster's 1599 translation (it first appeared in 1573, about three decades after the Latin was published) reads: "I would rather wish twenty evill doers to escape death through pitie, then one man to bee unjustly condemned."[5]

Actual innocence or guilt isn't the issue, then. It's *proof* of guilt that matters. Their guilt must be "open made to justice" even if other guilty people, even those on the jury, remain free (*Measure for Measure*, II.1.19-24). Othello, in a play that could be called an inversion of *Hamlet*, demands ocular proof, but accepts something less than that: his moral luck is disastrous. But it would have been so even if Desdemona *had* been guilty, since then Shakespeare would have confronted us with a Gettier problem: "Is justified true belief knowledge?"[6] The answer is (of course) no. (Otherwise Gettier wouldn't have written the paper.) Say that Desdemona were guilty. Othello would truly believe she was guilty then. And he would be justified in that belief on the evidence of the handkerchief. But the evidence was planted, so that the truth of his belief and its justification would be unrelated.

I think Hamlet *may* have a *justified true belief* that the King is guilty. But unless he *knows* it, he would be *immorally* relying on moral luck, engaging in a moral gamble, if he were to take arms against a sea of avuncular troubles. This claim suggests a further resonance to his soliloquy at the end of Act II, when he worries that the ghost might be a devil assuming a pleasing shape. The abuse might consist in more than the King's possible innocence. It could be that the King is guilty, but that Hamlet can't say that he *knows* that the King is guilty. True belief isn't enough. Justified belief isn't enough. *Perhaps* justified true belief would be enough for Hamlet and for Shakespeare, even if that doesn't mean the same thing as knowledge. But at any rate, as soon as the thought comes to Hamlet that the ghost might be a devil, he must consider that he doesn't (yet) have a justified belief in the King's guilt, however much the confirmation bias he has noticed in himself ("O, my prophetic soul"–I.v.48) makes him wish he did.

And it seems Shakespeare takes care to indicate to the audience that *we* know something that Hamlet doesn't, and that we know we know something Hamlet doesn't. We alone hear the King's aside– "How smart a lash that speech doth give my conscience" (III.i.56)–

---

5   *A Learned Commendation of the Politique Lawes of England*, trans. Robert Mulcaster, (Thomas Wight and Bonham Norton, 1599), 62.

6   See Edmund L. Gettier's famous three-page paper, "Is Justified True Belief Knowledge?" *Analysis*, 23:6, (1963): 121-123.

in response to Polonius's repetition of Hamlet's point, just a minute or two earlier, that the devil can assume a pleasing shape. And the connection to Hamlet's speech is made still more strongly since the King seems to be confirming the wisdom of Hamlet's plan to catch his "conscience" with the Mousetrap. But the Mousetrap doesn't work, since Hamlet can't resist describing Lucianus as "*nephew* to the king" (III.ii.268), which means (as has been often noted) that the King's response to the play might be provoked by the implied threat from Hamlet to kill him rather than a guilty reaction to the representation of his own crime.

This is where Hamlet bets that his belief is justified. He's now willing to take "the ghost's" word. He doesn't call him "my father" because here it doesn't matter who the complainant is, just what it is that he reports. But *is* he justified? Horatio is the skeptical noter in the play, as when he contradicts Bernardo and Marcellus about how long the ghost has lingered at the start. Horatio is, as usual, accurate, if you rewind and do the counting. And now Horatio does not confirm Hamlet's judgment. All he says, twice, is that he noted the King's response "very well" (III.ii.314, 316). If we are looking to Horatio for confirmation that Hamlet's belief is justified, we don't have it yet.

What about its truth? Well, we get that in the King's soliloquy: "I did the murder" (III.iii.58), but (just as in the earlier aside) it is conspicuous that Hamlet does not hear this (which is why he mistakes the King's failure to pray for prayer). I think that as with the aside to Polonius, this is a clear signal to the audience that we know more than Hamlet does. And what do we know? That the King is guilty. But Hamlet *still* doesn't know this, and therefore would still be doing some morally impermissible moral gambling were he to kill the King on the basis of what he might now consider clear and convincing evidence—a lesser standard than proof to a moral certainty.

Well, what about the killing of Polonius? Of Rosencrantz and Guildenstern? What about the death of Ophelia? Hamlet is clearly responsible, in one way or another, for each of those deaths, and his hesitancy of course leads to the deaths of Gertrude and of Laertes. Six relatively innocent people die so that one guilty person may go free. But except for Ophelia's death (as it seems) they're "not near my conscience" (V.ii.65) because Hamlet's acts were not gambles but were reactions to emergent occasions, and even if we agree with what seems Horatio's explicit but typically understated misgivings about the deaths of Rosencrantz and Guildenstern (did they know what was in the packet? Is making love to their employment enough?) the point of Hamlet's response is that conscience is his concern—the King's and his own. If he's too casual about his rashness, that's because rashness isn't the considered gamble that Shakespeare is interested in here. (Thus Laertes is ready to act rashly until the King slows him down and brings him to consideration.) He wants the contrast between spontaneous and considered action, because it is the latter which brings up the deep questions about moral gambling.

IV

But what about the King? And what about our judgment? I've been accepting the common consensus that the King did kill his brother. Common because he confesses in what I would call a private and therefore, so to speak, off the record soliloquy—the equivalent in a modern court of evidence excluded from the trial. The King himself alludes to the fact that defendants (at least in Star Chamber cases) weren't required to testify—the origin of our Fifth Amendment:

> But 'tis not so above:
> There is no shuffling; there the action lies
> In his true nature, and we ourselves compelled,
> Even to the teeth and forehead of our faults,
> To give in evidence. (IV.iii.64-68)

But let's say we're the jury, or *a* jury. The Court, says Coke (in the same passage I've already cited) is "in stead of Councel for the prisoner," and thus must make sure that the legal system doesn't load the dice against the accused. Can the Court, can Hamlet, who has to stand in for the Court as a defender of the King, can *we* understand the soliloquy in such a way that the King can be defended from the charge of murder? Is it actually a gamble to find him guilty? Or is it a sure thing?

Well, consider another reason the King might have been so upset by *The Mousetrap* (or *The Murder of Gonzago*), besides its implicit threat. Here's something else that might catch his conscience. The Player Queen is firm that she won't remarry after her husband's death:

> In second husband let me be accurst.
> None wed the second but who killed the first.
>   *   *   *
> A second time I kill my husband dead
> When second husband kisses me in bed ... (III.ii.202-207)

This is clearly metaphorical, like Hamlet's sarcastic wonder that "a great man's memory may outlive his life half a year" (II.ii.140-141). But the guilt that it anticipates is real: remarriage will expunge the memory of the first husband, *retroactively* turning his death into metaphorical murder. This retroactivity might be what is now haunting the King. How could he have retroactively killed his brother dead a second time, forgetting him and causing Gertrude to forget him?

How likely is this? Not very. Off the record? yes, I'm sure he's guilty. But even here accepting that would be gambling. We should still prefer twenty evill doers to escape death through pitie, then one man to bee unjustly condemned. It's to Hamlet's credit that the quietism he displays on his return is a final refusal of the moral gambling he's been tempted by throughout. When he kills the King, he does so on certain knowledge, on the basis not only of eye-witness testimony but of what he himself witnesses and suffers.

William Flesch

Lard

When I received the invitation to contribute to this volume my first thought was to say "Yes, of course I would be delighted to join the chorus of approval. I would willingly pay tribute to the influence Christopher has had on my thinking and to express my gratitude for the kindness he has always shown me." But my second thought was to say "No: I can't possibly take on another project. I'm supposed to be writing a collective biography of the Scriblerus Club." For years I have been saying "I am writing a collective biography of the Scriblerus Club." Writing that book has involved many years of not writing. Indeed, there is a parallel between my not-writing of my biography and the group's not-writing of *The Memoirs of Martinus Scriblerus*.

The Club comprised a group of friends who used to meet in St James's Palace and plan an impressive range of satires, the centerpiece of which was the biography of a fictional learned dunce, Martin Scriblerus. The group only met regularly in 1713-1714 and the *Memoirs* was not published until 1741. Between 1714 and 1741 they made intermittent progress on the *Memoirs of Scriblerus* and published a number of squibs and occasional pieces. What makes this belated text important is that the group's members included some of the leading satirists of the day and a leading politician: Jonathan Swift, Alexander Pope, John Gay, Thomas Parnell, John Arbuthnot and Robert Harley, Earl of Oxford. Arbuthnot was physician to Queen Anne, which is why they met in his rooms in St James's Palace. When Queen Anne, the last Stuart monarch, died in 1714 and was succeeded by the first Hanoverian, George I, their political and material hopes died with her. Arbuthnot lost his rooms in St James's Palace and Swift left London without saying goodbye to his friends. The group broke up but continued to correspond, collaborate and meet when they could. Their reunion in 1726 resulted in the publication of several Scriblerian projects, including *Gulliver's Travels*, *The Beggar's Opera*, *The Dunciad* and the four-volume collection known as the *Pope-Swift*

Miscellanies. Completion of their originary work was still some way off.

Thinking about contributing to this collective work put me in mind of a letter Arbuthnot wrote to Swift on June 26, 1714, encouraging him to keep working on the *Memoirs* to distract himself from his political troubles. "Pray remember Martin, who is an innocent fellow," he urges and then sets out a series of ideas for medical satires that he is working on. He expects Swift to respond in kind.[1] He also reports that "Pope has been collecting high flights of poetry, which are very good, they are to be solemn nonsense." This collection was eventually published as *Peri Bathous: or, Martinus Scriblerus His Treatise of the Art of Sinking in Poetry* in the *Miscellanies* in 1727. The exchange reveals something about the nature of writing and especially the problems of producing jointly authored texts. Swift grumpily replied:

> To talk of Martin in any hands but Yours, is a Folly. You every day give better hints than all of us together could do in a twelvemonth; And to say the Truth, Pope who first thought of the Hint has no Genius at all to it, in my Mind. Gay is too young; Parnel has some Ideas of it, but is idle; I could putt together, and lard, and strike out well enough, but all that relates to the Sciences must be from you.[2]

Swift complains that the friends do not equally pull their weight and that they do not have equal talents both in subject expertise and writing skills. Scholars in the past have been interested in questions of attribution of chapters of the *Memoirs* and items in the Scriblerian corpus. Here it seems that Pope is concentrating on poetry while Arbuthnot is working on medicine. Yet Arbuthnot also helped Pope compile the passages of bathetic verse quoted in the mock *ars poetica* until, as Pope complained to Swift in 1727, he "grew quite indolent in it, for something newer, I know not what."[3] Similarly, both Swift and Arbuthnot satirized "all that relates to the Sciences," as evidenced by *Gulliver's Travels*, especially the third voyage.

What is more interesting to me than the question of attribution is that this passage brings together another issue which is important to an understanding of the nature of the Scriblerian collaboration. The question is not just "Who wrote what?" but, more fundamentally,

1   Arbuthnot to Swift, June 26, 1714, in *The Correspondence of Jonathan Swift, D.D.*, ed. by David Wolley, (Peter Lang, 1999), Vol. 1, 625-626.

2   Swift to Arbuthnot, July 3, 1714, *Corr.*, Vol. 1, 630.

3   Pope to Swift, [? January 1727/28], in *The Correspondence of Alexander Pope*, ed. by George Sherburn, (Clarendon Press, 1956), Vol. 2, 468.

"what are the processes involved in collaborative writing?" Because the group scattered geographically soon after it formed, Scriblerian writing involved a long gestation between initial conception and publication and other processes took place between the two. These processes might also operate in solo compositions.

Swift employs a surprising vocabulary to suggest what activities he thinks this kind of writing entails: thinking of hints, putting together, larding, striking out. I will take each in turn. By "hint," Swift seems to mean the initial spark of conception. The mostly likely match in the *OED* for Swift's sense is Hint, n. 1.a.: "A slight indication intended to be caught by the intelligent; a suggestion or implication conveyed in an indirect or covert manner." What is relevant here is not indirection but reaction: one person throws out a hint and expects another to catch it and run with it. Writing as a team sport. Swift implies that the process of Scriblerian creation is fundamentally collaborative. The noun "hint" occurs numerous times in Scriblerian correspondence and conversation and each time it means one person is passing on an idea to another to "write up." Arbuthnot and Swift were the chief hint-mongers. Here is Arbuthnot from the aforementioned letter to Swift: "I dont give Yow these hints to divert yow but that yow may have your thoughts, & work upon them."[4] And Swift to Pope: "a hint that a sett of Quaker-pastorals might succeed, if our friend Gay could fancy it . . . I believe further, the pastoral ridicule is not exhausted, and that a porter, foot-man, or chairman's pastoral might do well. Or what think you of a Newgate pastoral, among the whores and thieves there?"[5] Twelve years later, the last of these hints turned into *The Beggar's Opera*. Pope claimed that *Gulliver's Travels* also emerged from a Scriblerian hint: "It was from a part of these memoirs that Dr. Swift took his first hints for Gulliver. There were pygmies in Schreibler's travels and the projects of Laputa."[6]

Swift is dismissive about one of the writerly contributions he could make: "I could putt together," he says. This term has different meanings and connotations. The *OED* has for "Put together," v. tr. 1.: "To bring into proximity, or into contact; to place side by side; to juxtapose." Its illustrations are suggestive:

---

4   Arbuthnot to Swift, June 26, 1714, *Corr.*, Vol. 1, 626.
5   Swift to Pope, August 30, 1716, *Corr.*, Vol. 2, 177-78
6   Joseph Spence, *Observations, Anecdotes and Characters of Books and Men*, ed. by James M. Osborn, (Clarendon Press, 1966), Vol. 1, 56.

1669: When I transplant Melons from the Nursery-bed, I put commonly two roots together.
Philosophical Transactions (Royal Society) vol. 4 902.
1690: Upon the first Occasion, that shall make him put together those Idea's in his Mind, and observe whether they agree or disagree.
J. Locke, *Essay Humane Understanding* [sic], i, ii, 9.

I want to put that together with two of the second senses of the compound term:

2.a. To combine or bring together (parts or elements) to make a whole or unity.
2.c. To make or form (a whole) by the combination of parts or elements; to construct, compile, compose.

So, we can say that for Swift, putting together might mean grafting things together to create something new (a fruit, an idea), but it could also mean juxtaposing unlike things in order to notice incongruity. The first sense denotes creativity but the second implies the sort of juxtaposition that is fundamental to satire. Both of them would be productive for the *Memoirs*. The final work of putting together the *Memoirs* in the sense of compiling the various elements into a whole was performed by Pope. Yet it is likely that Swift played a role in the early stages by putting together ideas and that Pope, who was primarily a poet, learned from the way Swift constructed his prose satires.

Next, Swift admits that he could "lard" Martin. To turn to the *OED* again:

Lard n. The fat of a pig or other swine; fat bacon or pork; lardons (see *lardon*, n.). Also: the fat or fat meat of other animals.
v. *transitive. Cookery.* To prepare (lean meat, poultry, or fish) for cooking by placing small strips of bacon or other foods within or around it to add fat or enrich the flavour. Also *intransitive*.
l.c. *transitive.* To intersperse (speech or writing) *with* particular words, expressions, ideas, etc., esp. in a way that is considered to be calculated or self-conscious. c1550–
  A few modish lewd words to lard his Discourse with. *English Theophrastus* 52 1702

The verb comes from the idea that you might dress a piece of meat with fat and bacon strips. Butter up. Smear over. It is a secondary activity, not the main source of protein, but vital for enhancing the flavour.

Finally, Swift concedes that he could "strike out well enough." The transitive sense of crossing out seems to be what he has in mind:

III.11.a. *transitive.* To mark (a surface) with a line or lines. Also to strike out, through. 1539–1710
III.13.a. To cancel or expunge with or as with the stroke of a pen. Const. *from, off, out (of),* rarely †*away;* also (*U.S.*) without const., esp. in legal contexts, and *colloquial,* in the *imperative,* annulling or reversing what the speaker has just said. Also to strike (a name, a person) off or (now rarely) out of a list.

So, he could edit, perhaps for style (strike out follows "lard") or to expunge whole sections—at this stage the contents of the *Memoirs* were not fixed and Pope continued to make changes up until he published it in his prose works (the number of chapters in the table of contents does not match the text, as two were combined after the contents page was printed). The intransitive sense of "strike out" might also be in play for Swift: "I.1.a.v. To make one's way, go. In early use chiefly *poetic.* In later use, chiefly with adverb (*forth, forward, over*) or phrase indicating the direction." So, contrary actions are available for consideration, one creative, indicating a change in direction of travel, the other destructive or editorial. Indeed, the work of satire is to create a new version of reality in order to destroy the satirical target.

Anyone who has witnessed the evolution of one of Christopher's books from lecture to publication will know that his own writing practice resembles "but," as the saying goes, "in a good way," the processes described so diffidently by Swift. He frequently takes his hint from the writers he studies (one of my favorites is his essay on verse as a form of punctuation which takes a hint from Wordsworth's line "A pure organic pleasure from the lines"[7]). He puts together numerous instances of the feature that interests him, quite literally pasting scraps onto a sheet of paper to construct a new idea. I would not say he, ahem, *lards* his writing—it more a process of embroidering, riffing, fencing, pirouetting—but the result is enhanced and enriched by his interspersals. As for striking out, Christopher expunges erroneous readings and marks up books in his authoritative editions and lights out for new territory (always but most strikingly in his *Along Heroic Lines* which brings poetry and prose into new relations). The editors of this volume have put together many of Christopher's friends and former students to laud not lard him for the hints he has thrown us and we have caught from him to enrich our writing and our lives.

Judith Hawley

---

7   *TFOP,* 89–116.

Stillborn

Here, in Wolvercote Cemetery,
Beyond the chapel (always shut),
The Polish and the Jewish sections,
Past "Dictionary" Murray and Tolkien,
Is the children's section. My son's here.

You'll forgive anything in a place like this—
Soppy inscriptions, toys on the graves;
And allow yourself anything,
Like the loss of composure lowering
His short white coffin, light as balsa wood,
Unreachably deep in black earth.

Everything about him was shocking:
The heartbeat lost, his still perfection.
The need to name, and register his name,
Take clothes to bury him in.

At home we have prints of his hand
And his foot, and a wisp of soft hair.

It still unsettles that here he'll stay.
The hardest thing is to walk away.

Archie Burnett

A Good Egg

James 2:24 Ye see then how that by works a man is justified,
and not by faith only.

"What does your mother think?"

The strength of Christopher's scholarship comes from his greatest ability, in its humility, its love and its theft, to seek confirmation. He is humanly flawed, like the rest of us (a festschrift really for the rest of us), and also scholarly flawed. He grabs at flaws creatively; denies creative ability, but creativity is the crux of the genius. Sometimes derided for his punmanship, puns are among the tools that make up the awl, the all in all that gets him to the point.

He can drive a running "joke" (sometimes self-deceiving, often self-deprecating) off its axles, then carry it on his back by foot for the last mile—*Once a Green Howard, always a Green Howard*. He claims to be innumerate but calculates like the most numerate (and sums things up as the story is told); lacking in the visual arts, but laughs off some not understanding his stunning essay "The Eye's Mind" for *Collected Works Joan Goldin*, properly placed penultimately before the index in the monograph (they'll have to look at it).

He sometimes takes power from his pathological reneging, but we love him—our father called him a good egg—and will go on with our egging him on—*Look up, look up, seek your Maker, 'fore Gabriel blows his horn*—and close with this poem which he knows.

A Beckenham Boy

i.

Look left, look right the blackbirds take flight
    The Green Howards are all in green
This is *your* victory. Blood, toil, tears, might
    And God has saved your Queen

Come Sunday ride at Eastertide
    The cherry trees hung all in bloom
Take your pride and luck in stride
    One hangs high at noon

One hangs right, one hangs left
    The cherry tree blossom is white
No one should hang for love *and* theft
    But they hang you just for spite

ii.

On Easter day the children at play all around the mead
Plucked primroses there and they left them with care left them still sweet
    for dead
Down the road the boys did follow wherever the girls they lead
The meadow was green, the sun was yellow, and the sky was red indeed

The noonday Sun to air on high
Daffodils and palm are gathered to die
Under the midnight stars the poplars give sigh
To the yellow moon and the red sky

iii.

You never knew when you were young
Bostonians you live among
    And if as a boy grows older
He leaves his sweetheart true
    The one who gave her shoulder
The one he never knew
The fold long waits for you

Luck is chance and trouble sure
So hedge your bets and leave me poor
No muse will make you drunk with rhyme
Milton cannot do like wine
So dip into this copper kettle
And lie among the stinging nettle

iv.

England's last great elm
    Stands still upon your grounds
Passed by and by
By horsemen high
    And their hunting hounds

v.

The laurels are cut took to fair
Though if God is in Gloucestershire
Then He is sure to see you there

The daffodil goes as the Lent lily went
The snow hung cherry bough low bent
Tells all that was allowed and spent

The whispered heaven-heard repent
Tells of the path of ill intent
That takes you back to Beckenham, Kent

L.A. Nemrow

Julie Nemrow
Lisa Nemrow

Along the Lines of Ricks

A decade and a half ago now, I joined an MLA panel under the auspices of the ALSCW that featured a return to the convention program of Christopher Ricks, recently knighted. I was rather surprised to see in the audience an internationally renowned colleague in narrative theory from the Ivy League, who approached me after Sir Christopher's closing—and typically show-stopping— lecture on William Empson's scale of citation and analysis: "I thought he was supposed to be the enemy! He's great." Never less than great, yes, and never more so than earlier, for me, in commentary implicitly taking up Empson's mantle in the typologies of the twofold, tacitly refining the fertile terrain of "double grammar" for the bi-directional vectors of prepositions and run-on line endings in Wordsworth's masterful syntactics.

Such is the serial energy that Ricks denominates as poetry's "force," momentum as well as moment. Ready for testing in these terms is a later poet whose innovation Ricks admired without ever writing about at length. In a turn to Gerard Manley Hopkins, the allusive titles of two benchmark essays on Wordsworth (on enjambment as "A pure organic pleasure from the lines," and on prepositional stratifications as "A sinking inward to ourselves from thought to thought"[1]) trace the force, as well as pure pleasure, of poetic linearity per se—all the way down to syntactic and even phonetic sequencing—that are manifested in dappled ontological "inscapes" when taken *up* and *in(ward)* as transferred mental "instress." Featured by enjambment as well as prepositional increments, the extra notch of penetration signaled by Wordsworth's "inward to" points toward Hopkins's "over-rove" rhymes and their driven, cross-syllabic variants, whereby, in reverent attention to the Created world's inscape, "repetition, *oftening, over-and-overing, aftering* must take place to detach it to the mind."[2] The

---

1   "William Wordsworth, 1 and 2" in *TFOP*, 90-114, 115-132.
2   From a little-cited essay titled, with apt pride of place, "Poetry and Verse," in "Lecture Notes: Rhetoric," *The Journals and Papers of Gerard Manley Hopkins*,

phrasing is odd, even for Hopkins, though the procedure is intrinsic. Hopkins does not abstract from essence "to" mental understanding, but rather implies "detach ... to the mind" as if it were "dispatch to the mind": an immediately internalized instress.

Applying Ricks's pitch of scrutiny to Hopkins has a way of spotlighting the one facet of lineation—unfurled phonetic density—that tends to be downplayed in the critical tradition Ricks admires and sustains. He is on record more than once (including in a riveting video interview after his knighthood[3]) in celebrating Leavis's remarks on Keats's "To Autumn," the season personified "like a gleaner" who—with enjambment's mimetic finesse—"dost keep / Steady thy laden head across a brook." Comparing the scholar, who "knows more" than the general reader, to the critic, who simply "notices more," Ricks celebrates Leavis for noting how the assonant momentum of "gleaner"/ "keep" needs the grammar of the next line to steady the prepositional syntax. Supplemented in this, one might add, by the serial equipoise that Hopkins' extra phonetic interlacing typically features: phrasing balanced off here in the deftly tread chiasmus, twice over, of "steady thy laden head."

More immediately than Leavis on Keats, however, Empson on Hopkins models a "Ricksian" reading of the latter. In measuring the fulcrum between octave and sestet in "The Windhover," charged already in the dedication "To Christ Our Lord," Empson hears the bifold resonance of the pivotal verb, "Buckle!," transitive and intransitive at once, supported on either side. This is the labyrinthine path toward the volta:

> I caught this morning morning's minion, king-
>   dom of daylight's dauphin, dapple-dawn-drawn Falcon, in his riding
>   Of the rolling level underneath him steady air, and striding
> High there, how he rung upon the rein of a wimpling wing
> In his ecstasy! then off, off forth on swing,

The rove-over rhyme severs *king* from *kingdom* for a regal personification that sheds phonetically across chiming participles and

ed. Humphrey House, completed by Graham Storey (Oxford University Press, 1959), 289.

3   Over two hours of probing rumination with Alan Macfarlane from 2013: https:// uk.video.search.yahoo.com/yhs/search?fr=yhs-litmus-caerus&ei=UTF-8&h-simp=yhs-caerus&hspart=litmus&p=christopher•ricks•inter-view&type=1476589-vsub-2_22598_nwtb#id=1&vid=978b59a6f460deb-c5a5d1c149c970064&action=click

tandem noun rhymes (*riding/striding/wing/swing*), all propelled by enjambment. At the same time, it launches with "dom" a linear tattoo of alliteration serving to sweep "dawn" up in—and along by—"drawn" on the way to the sound rather than sight rhyme with "Falcon." The famous hyperbolic levitation of the bird's "riding / Of the rolling level underneath him steady air" is enriched by the hint of "steadier" across the swift pre-positional obtrusion of the palindrome "level" via "underneath." The prepositional enjambment of "striding / High," lifting vigorously against the inertial pressure of the coming line-drop, pauses for two suspenseful prepositions at "rung upon the rein of a wimpling wing / In his ecstasy." As if buoyed in this not-quite-said "wing/ing" by the equally unsaid but phonetically irresistible "wind" (always hovering there in "windhover"), the falcon is tracked across the prepositional swoosh of the chiastic "off, off forth" on the homophonic "(hi)s / wing."

At the point of apogee and plunge, with a double grammatic fold, comes that volta, "here / Buckle!" Bent vector and blent energy, drop and latch, collapse and clasp link the epiphanic "chevalier" of the Lord to reverential instress of a revealed aerial inscape. Hopkins is even more daring in the sequel of lowly everyday comparisons:

No wonder of it: shéer plód makes plough down sillion
Shine, and blue-bleak embers, ah my dear,
Fall, gall themselves, and gash gold-vermilion.

Yet here Empson's high flight of coruscating ambiguity runs into headwinds from his critics, on a point where precisely the collaborative dimensionality of prepositions and enjambments would have shored up his argument—and not least when supported from the phrasing's phonemic infrastructure. A discussion in *TLS* critiqued Empson's reading of this passage from a quarter century before (1930), comparing the lustrous force of airborne predation with the implicitly smoldering figures of human suffering. Empson's anticipation of the guttering fire trope of the last two lines, this protest went, had him over-reading an implicitly "harrowing" metaphysical cause, rather than the ordinary physical effect, when "sheer plod makes plough down sillion / Shine."[4] In a complaint that Empson mistakes the

4   *Argufying: Essays on Literature and Culture*, ed. John Haffenden (University of Iowa Press, 1988), 332; a correspondent in a *TLS* exchange (1955)—revisiting Empson's discussion of "The Windhover" in *Seven Types of Ambiguity* from 25 years before—wonders "Why should Mr. Empson construe so strangely 'plough down sillion shine'? True, sillion may shine, but it is the shine of

turned earth, rather than the plow, as source of the shine, one crux is the preposition's shove into enjambment. Empson's reading of *plough down,* though he didn't say so, gains force from the "transegmental" re-grooving—like "*dapple-d*awn-drawn"—that transfers instrument to result in the tacit hyphening of "Plough(e*d*)-*d*own sillion."[5] The enjambment "sillion / Shine" then takes its flow and glow from the prepositional split along vertical and horizontal lines (down into the ground, down [along] its grooved rows) to converge on the "gash gold-vermillion."

Hovering for me in this closing trope is Ricks's signature concept of the "anti-pun": a semantic suggestion that calls for notice and then has to be logically ruled out. Ricks sees this in the "fleet waters of the drowning world" in Wordsworth's dreamscape, where the primary meaning of fleet is rapid, but on the waters, a ghost of armada shimmers.[6] Hopkins tilts this dynamic. Characteristic of his subsyllabic overlaps and dispersions, "ash" is both there and not there at once—as opposed to only half there, then gone. More integrally embedded—almost in the mode of "dapple d(rawn)" or "plough d(own)"—*ash* seems shadowed in such a phantom alternative as "the last gasp of ash-churning gashes." An extreme (and this time literal) case of such oblique punning (operable cousin to the anti-pun) comes, we will find, in the conclusion of Hopkins's "The Sea and the Skylark," a poem that begins with the blithest Shelleyan spirit of cross-word phrasal play when bracketing the sounds of ocean and sky by a prepositional variant of "near and dear" in the unabashed "On ear and ear."

---

the plough the poet is considering . . .." Empson's undaunted rejoinder (336) disdains (typically enough) any *phonetic* wordplay to his defense. Though the editor of T.S. Eliot has a well-known Harvard lecture on the poet's "Auditory Imagination," Ricks, too, is interested more in represented sound and speech than any syllabic grain.

5 I refer here to a coinage of mine, based on the linguistic concept of "segmentation," developed in *Reading Voices: Literature and the Phonotext* (California University Press, 1990) and deployed in in many of my stylistic studies since, down through *Streisand: The Mirror of Difference* (Wayne State University Press, 2022). The self-exemplifying portmanteau term was an attempt to capture the skid and blur of phonetic adjacency between syllables within and across words, now by elision, now by liaison. My auditing the recurrent mimetic effects of such ligatures in Streisand's legato delivery—as well as in Hopkins's enunciative over-runs—can be taken to mark a signal difference between my approach to song "styling" and Ricks's lexical, syntactic, and thematic treatment of popular lyrics in the steadily enlightening *DVOS.*

6 *TFOP*, 99-100.

An immemorial music cued to the title is soon contrasted, however, with the downbeat of human life in this "sordid turbid time"—the very phrasing working to extrude an intermediate third, "torpid." (Wordsworth warned in "London 1802" of a spiritual "fen of stagnant waters.") Says Hopkins: "Our make and making break, are breaking, down / To man's last dust…." Our kind ("make"?) and its work (making), in the onrush of participial grammar and its prepositional hinge, are tracked in collapse (by mimetic lineation) somewhere between verb phrase and its double, either adverbial or prepositional (either breaking down per se—or decomposing [in]*to*). The poem approaches closure by flushing out, drowning out, the sounds of skysong and seabeat alike, sluicing civilization away to a primal biological muck ("first slime"). And doing so by an internal enjambing of syllables as well as syntactic spans. Within the shamed precincts of a "shallow" human "town" lurk, mired, the twin adulterated etymologies of "lime" (from Latin *limus* for mud) as well the proto-Indo-European *(s)lei* for "slimy," a condition to which pulverized limestone often reverts. In travestying the primeval clay of non-Adamic humus reductively soiled beyond renewal, more chaotic than inchoate, Hopkins has pressed the phonetic anti-pun (evoked now without being revoked) to the depths of an arche-pun in the decalcified residue of "man's fir(st *s) lime.*" In the malleable—and again transegmental—ear of so intuitively philological a poet, etymon becomes metonym.

Internal syllabic enjambments, braced by prepositions, are yet more drastic in the sprung rhythms of Hopkins's tragic masterpiece, *The Wreck of the Deutschland*. Early and late intonations speak to each other, audit each other, in the arc of catharsis. The early "leeward" drift of the fated ship ("She drove in the dark to the leeward," st. 14) finds its eccentric "rove-over" forensics across the switchback gradation of the next two lines. With the ship become passive object of the storm, the soundscape returns as the force that—over three separate *words*— "dre*w her* / D*ead*" to the shore, so that the personified ship's passive *Dead*-reckoning also evokes a collective noun for the doomed. Given a rove-over drift almost thematized there as the draw of a riptide, we read on toward the poem's climactic sprung leak in lineation at the point of redemption:

> Dame, at our d*oor*
> *D*rowned, and among our shoals
> Remember us in the roads, the heaven-haven of the rew*ard*:
> Our heart's charity's hearth's fire, our thoughts' chivalry's throng's L*ord*.

The drowned nun's compensatory "rew*ard*" slots into rhyme (corrective of that *leeward* disaster) only if the metaphoric "door" also anticipates the welcoming portal to heaven-haven: "d*oor* d/rowned" on route to(ward) rew-*ard*—or say coming "rowned" after all to solace. Such a segmental over-ride is bolstered, two lines on, with the cross-word rhyme of "shoals" with "[éngli]*sh souls*." The whole echoic schema is aimed in a propulsive *towardness* meant to settle on and affirm the resonant order of the "L*ord*," rhyme of all rhymes.

This consolatory closure has been anticipated in the sprung reason, as well as rhyme, of Hopkins's internalized over-rove when God in the fifth stanza, before being seen as "throned behind / Death"—at a hairs-breath remove, figured by that infinitesimal spread of phonemic enjambment—is manifest in the subliminal meaning beneath sublime mortal turmoil. The full pressure of "th*under*" and the "spl*endour*" of its "w*onder*" weigh upon the answering noun of its comprehension, breaking apart any facile rhyme to the self-enactive descent of "*under*/stand." Graphically allegorized in this undergirding way is the divine anchorage—resting "level underneath"—of all vicissitudes, whose strophe tails off in its own strenuous mitigation of catastrophe. Ricks's tandem preoccupations are here performed from within a single composite etymology, as the preposition defers by internal caesura to the enjambed underbite of its own grounding second syllable. Backed by the critical tradition that Ricks has for decades so magisterially channeled, reading comes to its own *under*standing. It does so in Hopkins, and with anti- and arche-puns in mind, by what we might call a simultaneously *antiphonal* poetics saturating verse lineation ("pure" and "organic") at every level of its sequencing, from exacting rhyme schemes to extravagant phonemic license in the slip-knots of syntax. If one guesses that Ricks may have shied away from analyzing at length the admired pied densities of Hopkins' over-hung, over-rung syllabic spans because this critic's "noticing" gift is keyed more to the logical shapes of phrase than to the inner turns of wording in process, this in no way discounts the burnished tools he has lent us for pursuing the latter along the armatures of the former. No one, in tuning an ear to the syllabic churning of either poetry or prose, can afford to ignore, one level up in the scale of notice, the reverberant, self-varying *force* that Ricks finds exerted by the fuller span of phrasal evocation in the poetic lineage he has for decades so stirringly illuminated.

Garrett Stewart

Ricks on Eliot on Forster on Lawrence

Each of us carries in memory dozens of moments in Christopher's writing or in his conversation that have especially helped us think about literature and life. (Also: we live with a sense of having forgotten or mentally misplaced hundreds more such moments.) So each of us is likely to feel that to present one example is to unfairly neglect countless others. But vivid specificity has a good chance of being more valuable than a cloudy try at comprehensiveness.

That's a thought in tune with Christopher's beautifully heartfelt essay "Literary Principles as Against Theory." Midway through the essay Christopher notes that while literary theorists enjoy exposing a critic's failure to test the meanings of all the terms being used in a commentary, the theorists themselves are inevitably unable to test *all* the terms they themselves wield—because "once you insist on regressive or recessive elaborations, not one of your own terms is stable." I love the illustration of this point that Christopher immediately offers.

> The death of D.H. Lawrence in 1930 moved E.M. Forster "to say straight out that he was the greatest imaginative novelist of our generation." Whereupon T.S. Eliot's recessive philosophical proclivities, which he usually resisted when writing literature or about literature, notoriously urged him to speak in the wrong regressive way: "The virtue of speaking out is somewhat diminished if what one speaks is not sense. And unless we know exactly what Mr. Forster means by *greatest, imaginative* and *novelist*, I submit that this judgement is meaningless." But the philosophical incitement was disabling, not enabling, and Forster did well to resist it and to turn the tables on it: "Mr. T.S. Eliot duly entangles me in his web. He asks what exactly I mean by 'greatest,' 'imaginative' and 'novelist,' and I cannot say. Worse still, I cannot even say what 'exactly' means—only that there are occasions when I would rather feel like a fly than a spider, and that the death of D.H. Lawrence is one of these." For the resistance to the philosophical web was no less dexterous than powerful. Eliot's "exactly" is no less open to retort than Forster's "greatest."[1]

---

1   *EIA*, 323-324.

Forster's response to Eliot's supercilious complaint brings a tear to my eye. This is intensified by my awareness that Christopher respected Eliot intensely and, in keeping with Christopher's ardent loyalty to his favorite writers, was very apt to see insight in everything Eliot wrote. I would have expected Christopher to prefer Eliot's view in any disagreement between Eliot and Forster.

So it is moving to find Christopher commending Forster in the exchange about Lawrence. Christopher could have presented any number of cases in which Eliot (or another great writer) wisely resisted theorized complications and reservations; but he chose this one. He prompts us to realize that our favorite writers can sometimes be wrong. (And I've thought forever that Christopher was wrong about Virginia Woolf.)

Having praised Forster's response to Eliot, Christopher makes clear how it applies to the potential absurdity in literary theory: "Those who stall or forestall the reading of a poem by first asking combatively what it is to *read* can themselves be asked the prior question of what it is to *to*. The existence of a problem need entail no obligation to grapple with it."[2] That assertion is memorable and helpful as we know it comes from a critic who has chosen to grapple with puzzles and mysteries in every essay he has written.

The Eliot/Forster passage is an example of Christopher's fabulous vitality in adducing. ("Vitality in adducing"—is this a phrase Christopher would approve of? You and I have asked this question about hundreds or thousands of phrases we've come up with.) I mean his dazzling ability to suddenly offer an unexpected illustration or piece of evidence in support of any idea he proposes. Are such adducements (the word is not in the dictionary but it should be) sometimes deliberately dazzling? OK, yes—but in a delightful stimulating way. They create our amazed sense of the simultaneous presence in one mind of all of literature in English—it's all available to Christopher at any moment! This is an illusion, no doubt, to *some* extent; but it has given each of us a distant ideal toward which we can happily stumble.

Mark Halliday

---

2   *EIA*, 324.

Canens for Christopher

'makes thought about literature continuous with literature'
(Christopher Ricks)

Why pause for nothing
        where Tiber's slow drag tumbles to rapids,

stopping to watch
        its long haul, wall-bound, bridged by a fall?

Or why stand, idling
        while a verb reverberates, a name rehearses

dispersals, departures
        in a watery part song, sung to riverrun:

Canens, remember?—
        the nymph who could sing to move the hearts

of heartless things,
        entreat the trees to hear, the beasts

of war to cease,
        the leaves to twitch their wind-blown ears—

then gave her living
        voice to the river's soundingness,

dissolved, unselved.
        I might hear the lyric's singing infinitive,

its self-absenting
        form in flow. Sweet Orphic girl,

your name's a story
        stored in the sound of a river flowing

to the shallows, the mouth,
        in tributaries of ravelled recall.

                    * * *

Word-tuner, player,
        you taught me to hear the wisdom and wit

of print in its singing,
        sound in its carrying. I salute you here

where Tiber Island
        cuts the drift either side of stone,

and I pause, divided
        in myself also, between thought and dream.

Christopher, bearer
        of sense, interpreter, you helped me to hear

how clerk and poet
        might sing together, critic and writer

join in the winding
        journey downstream. I read you still

for pleasure to know—
        how allusions, lies, grand style, line endings

might keep us listening
        against the fashions, the schools, the wars:

against what passes
        in favour, and soon goes. In you I hear

the ear's infinitive:
        Canens—a singer found in the singing.

For all this, thanks.
        For the rest, a pause—and the sense of sounding.

                                        Angela Leighton

In Ovid, the nymph Canens could sing to move the beasts and stones, but
having lost her beloved to the wiles of Circe she eventually lies down by the
Tiber, and her body is dissolved in its waters.

In His Element

Throughout the crop of critical essays gathered under the title *Along Heroic Lines*, Christopher Ricks alludes to the Ocean and the oceanic. The inaugural essay of the collection, revisiting his inaugural lecture as Professor of Poetry at the University of Oxford, opens with *gratitude* and the coincidence of gratitude and pleasure preserved in the word *grateful*–leading promptly to its opening instance, from Milton's *Paradise Lost*: "There are wafted," he writes,

> *Sabean* Odours from the spicie shoare
> Of *Arabie* the blest,

–"whereupon," Christopher continues,

> many a League
> Cheard with the grateful smell old Ocean smiles.[1]

In "The Anagram," an essay concerned with that figure's capacity to enact both disorder and the energies of reordering, the ocean returns as Valéry's "La mer, la mer, toujours recommencée,"[2] and, later yet, as the cause of spiritual danger and an opportunity for salvation felt in Donne:

> In what torne ship soever I embarke,
> That ship shall be my embleme of thy Arke.
> What sea soever swallow mee, that flood
> Shall be to mee an embleme of thy blood;[3]

In "Dryden's Heroic Triplets," a verbal topography comprised of "Sand," "the *Beach*," and "the *Strand*"[4] again unites the oceanic with the social and the public: "The Strand as both ancient seashore and London thoroughfare,"[5] Christopher glosses the word, before

---

1   "The Best Words in the Best Order," *AHL*, 1.
2   "The Anagram," *AHL*, 34.
3   Ibid., 44.
4   "Dryden's Heroic Triplets," *AHL*, 62.
5   Ibid.

exploring further ("E're Sails were spread, new Oceans to explore")[6] and arriving at the rich metaphoric possibilities surrounding "the cruel and cruelly suffering figure of Peter Grimes tied to his dread monotony of tidescape."[7]

The ocean shimmers in the background of essays on Henry James and T.S. Eliot, on Byron and Beckett and Carmen Bugan—writers who all left their native shores, their geographic crossings being emblems of crossings linguistic and artistic, with their perils and pleasures.

These recurrences are not idiosyncratic—but, rather, pick up on recognitions rippling across English literature. Nor do they boil down to a "thalassocratic" empire's maritime obsession. Alive in Donne's rhyming of "flood" with "blood," the figure that brings together *the ocean without* and *the ocean within* flourishes in Marvell's mind—

> The Mind, that Ocean where each kind
> Does streight its own resemblance find.[8]

It is also Coleridge's figure of praise when writing of "the unfathomable depths" of Shakespeare's "oceanic mind." ("Microcosmic" could hardly be adequate, here.) Wherever we find the oceanic metaphorically linked with Mind and Language, it speaks not just of one serving as a medium for the other, but of their reciprocal workings as one another's media. Likewise, the truism—or half-truth—that language is "a medium of communication," draws our attention to an obscure converse possibility: that, both as individual writers and collectively as a culture with developed mass media, we ourselves serve as a medium for the continued self-realization of the language.

As a medium *of* the English language, a writer achieves individuation by developing the inherent potentialities of English for things like true acknowledgement, wisdom, wit and beauty. Hence the organization of *The Force of Poetry*, Christopher's earlier collection of essays, each of which, he writes, "attends to an aspect, feature or resource of the language manifested in poetry":

Summarily: the essay on Gower gives salience to diction and formulae.

---

6   Ibid., 65.
7   Ibid., 78.
8   "Andrew Marvell: 'Its Own Resemblance,'" *TFOP*, 34.

That on Marvell, to a particular figure of speech. That on Milton, to sound and sense. That on Johnson, to metaphors dead or alive.[9]

The list goes on (to Wordsworth, Beddoes, Housman and others, via Empson), its regularity of phrase bringing forward something in the critic himself: a comprehensive sensibility of the language; an alert readiness for a richly varied display of its capacities.

One more instance: in his essay "Word Making and Mistaking," Christopher described one of his darker nights when, in the midst of marital discord, two British policemen showed up at his door. "We get a 'phone-call, sir, telling us that someone has gone beresk," was their apologetic explanation.

> Beresk! My heart leapt up when I beheld this rainbow in the night sky. What a covenant. All shall be well, and all manner of thing shall be well. On a night like this, even on a night like this, it was good to be alive. Beresk! Bereft, burlesque, grotesque, and berserk ... I felt better at once.[10]

Christopher describes the policeman's spontaneous word as "a salmon-leap of the language"—an exuberant salto from the medium's vivid depths. "I haven't forgotten," he writes gratefully,

> how hope suddenly took wing, like Marvell's very bird of a soul in "The Garden," or like The Beatles' very soul of a bird (it taking off from a flatfoot pedestrian phrase), a bird which was, the singer sings, only waiting for this moment to arise.[11]

In my first autumn of study at the Editorial Institute, Christopher asked me a bewildering question—not solely about criticism but about life in general. As he and I were walking somewhere across the Boston University campus, he asked me whether I had ever asked myself whose *contempt* I thought I would most fear. To him, he added promptly, by way of explaining, it was Empson's contempt that would have been intolerable. (Christopher was knighted the following year.)

There was delicacy in Christopher's way of enclosing the question within another question, as if to lessen its prophylactic sting: an acknowledgement that minding the potential causes of humiliation, while a good aid to navigating life, isn't in itself painless. A closely

---

9   *TFOP*, vii.
10   "Word Making and Mistaking," *The State of the Language* (University of California Press, 1990), 461.
11   Ibid.

related, though a milder thought—Matthew Arnold's—is returned to in the Prefatory Note to *Along Heroic Lines*:

> When tracing "the ideal line of study," we should (Matthew Arnold suggested) "fix a certain series of works to serve as what the French, taking an expression from the builder's business, call *points de repère*—points which stand as so many natural centres, and by returning to which we can always find our way again."[12]

Over the years of knowing Christopher, I saw him endeavor to supply his students with a choice of "natural centres" that could help us find our way both humanly and professionally, as scholars and critics. One particular conversation, though, has become for me an emblem of my student years at the Editorial Institute.

During a semester-long directed study, sometime around 2010, I would come to see Christopher in his office once a week for an hour, to talk about criticism and my own work in progress. To one of those meetings I brought a translation I was tinkering with—not of Mandelstam, my main subject, but of Nikolay Zabolotsky's poem "A Forest Lake." Composed in a suffocatingly crowded cattle-car, while tormented by thirst on his journey to a Soviet labor camp, the poem embodied Zabolotsky's heroic capacity to rise above the inhumane circumstances and to maintain his own integrity and wholeness of mind—with no helper at his side but for the Russian language.

Unhurried and broad across the page, Zabolotsky's poem flows single-mindedly towards its longed-for consolation: the vision of an incandescently conscious lake, hidden deep within a wild forest teeming with beasts. As we discussed the phrasing of my translation, Christopher suggested that I read the poem aloud in Russian: he thought that hearing its rhythms in the original might be helpful.

I began to read, but after a while my eyes wandered off the familiar page. Across the room, seated quietly on his ivory-colored sofa, Christopher was listening with his eyes closed. The room opened up to the poem's imaginative space. I was deeply moved by that moment, when Zabolotsky's sublime poem was met with Christopher's exquisite consideration. This memory sometimes visits me still, never failing to leave me thoughtful—and grateful.

Anna Razumnaya

---

12 *AHL*, vii.

Preface to *Baltics*

The dissertation I wrote for Christopher Ricks at Boston University's Editorial Institute was an annotated edition of a notebook and diary kept by the Swedish poet and Nobel laureate Tomas Tranströmer in 1952, two years prior to the publication of his first collection of poems. Parts of the diary, and the greater part of the notebook, consist of drafts of what the poet then regarded as sections, or movements, of a single "long poem in the spirit of Eliot." Eliot was, and was to remain, the foreign-language poet who meant most to him. I could hardly have hoped for better guidance than that which Professor Ricks provided, both during our discussions, and in his writings on Eliot. The most important of the latter for me was the formidably annotated edition of *The Poems of T.S. Eliot* that he and Jim McCue published shortly after I began my studies. It soon became a model for my own editorial apparatus.

That "long poem in the spirit of Eliot" proved beyond Tranströmer's powers so early in his career. Sometime in 1953 he came to feel its sections lacked sufficient unity, and he recast them as the three long*ish* poems that conclude his first slim volume. It was not until twenty years later, twenty years during which he established himself as one of the world's leading poets, that he realized his plan. Published in 1974, *Östersjöar (Baltics)*, set in the microcosmos of the Stockholm Archipelago, is his longest and most Eliotic poem. Eliotic with a difference: The "other people" Robert Lowell claimed (somewhat unfairly, Professor Ricks has argued) were absent from *Four Quartets* are central to *Baltics*, especially the poet's maternal grandfather and grandmother. This difference does nothing to disguise the poem's indebtedness to Eliot, particularly the Eliot of *Four Quartets*. Tranströmer lightheartedly and touchingly acknowledged this debt when, in inscribing a copy of the book for the critic Staffan Bergsten, he referred to himself as "Eliot's grandchild."

I don't think I have ever discussed the merits of Tranströmer's work as a whole with Professor Ricks. I do know he likes *Baltics*. During our first meeting after I began my program, he mentioned he had

73

read the poem the previous night (in Samuel Charters' translation). He was surprised, he said, by how much he liked it, going on to say how much he admired the deftness of its transitions, and how moving he found it. When I undertook the present translation of the poem for this Festschrift, I had some hopes of superseding the already existing ones (by Charters, by Robin Fulton, and by Patty Crane). I cannot claim to have done so, though I hope my version has its own merits, particularly as regards the rhythm. In any case, I offer it now to Christopher in the spirit in which I began it, one of admiration, gratitude, and friendship.

Bill Coyle

Baltics

I

It was before the time of radio masts.

Grandfather had just made pilot. In his almanack he wrote up the
    ships he piloted—
names, destinations, drafts.
Examples from 1884:
SS Tiger   Capt. Rowan   16 feet   Hull Gefle Furusund
Brig Ocean   Capt. Andersen   8 feet   Sandöfjörd Hernösand
    Furusund
SS St. Petersburg   Capt. Libenberg   11 feet   Stettin Libau
    Sandhamn

He took them out to the Baltic, through that wonderous labyrinth of
    islands and water.
And those who met onboard, and were carried by the same hull a few
    hours or days,
how much did they learn about each other?
Conversations in misspelled English, understanding and
    misunderstanding, but very little conscious falsehood.
How much did they learn about each other?

When there was thick fog: half-speed, scant clues. Out of the
    invisible came the headland in a single stride and was hard by.
Foghorns bellowing every other minute. Eyes reading right into the
    invisible.
(Maybe he had the labyrinth in his head?)
The minutes passed.
Shoals and rocks committed to memory like hymn verses.
And that feeling of "just-here-is-where-we-are" that had to be held
    onto, like when you're carrying a brimming vessel and mustn't
    spill anything.

A look down in the engine room.
The compound engine, long-lived as a human heart, labored with
    big, supple, rebounding movements, acrobats of steel, and the
    scents rose like from a kitchen.

II

The wind moves through the pine woods. It sighs heavy and light.
The Baltic sighs in the middle of the island, too, deep in the woods
    you are out on the open sea.
The old woman hated the sighing in the trees. Her face stiffened in
    melancholy when the wind blew up:
"We have to think of those who are out in the boats."
But she heard something else in the sighing, just like me, we're related.
(We walk together. She has been dead for thirty years.)
It sighs yes and no, misunderstanding and understanding.
It sighs three children healthy, one in a sanitorium, and two dead.
The great draft that blows life into some flames while blowing out
    others. The conditions.
It sighs: Save me, Lord, the waters have come in unto my soul.
I walk a long while and listen and arrive at a point where the borders
    are opened
or rather
where everything's a border. An open place sunk in darkness.
    The people stream out from the dimly lit buildings around it.
    Murmurings.

A new draft of wind and the place lies deserted and silent.
A new draft of wind, whispering about other shores.
Concerning the war.
Concerning places where the citizens are under control,
where thoughts are constructed with emergency exits,
where a conversation among friends really becomes a test of the
    meaning of friendship.
And when you're together with those you don't know very well.
    Control. A certain degree of candor has its place
provided you don't lose sight of what's drifting at the conversation's
    edges: something dark, a dark fleck.
Something that can come drifting in
and destroy everything. Don't lose sight of it!

What to compare it to? A mine?
No, that would be too tangible. And almost too peaceful, since on
    our coast most stories about mines have happy endings, the terror
    limited in time.
Like in this story from the lightship: "Autumn 1915, slept uneasy ... "
    etc. A drift-mine was sighted
drifting slowly toward the lightship, lowering and lifting, at times
    hidden by the whitecaps, at times just caught sight of, like a spy in
    a crowd of people.
The crew, in their dismay, tried shooting at it with rifles. In vain. In
    the end they put out a boat
And fastened a long line to the mine and towed it in slowly and warily
    to the experts.
Afterwards they set up the dark shell of the mine in a sandy garden
    plot as an ornament
together with the shells of *Stombus gigas* from the West Indies.

And the sea wind moves through the dry pine trees farther off, it
    hurries across the cemetery's sand,
past the leaning stones, the pilots' names.
The dry sighing
of great doors being opened and great doors being closed.

III

In the half-darkened corner of the Gotlandic church, in an aura of
    mild mold
stands a sandstone baptismal font—from the 1100s—the stonecutter's
    name
is still there, shining out
like a row of teeth in a mass grave

HEGWALDR

the name still there. And his pictures
here and on the walls of other basins, swarms of people, forms
    emerging from the stone.
Their eyes' kernels of evil and goodness are swollen to bursting there.
Herod at table. The roast rooster flies up crowing "Christus natus
    est"—the waiter was put to death—

close by the child is born, beneath bunches of faces dignified and
   helpless as young monkeys'.
And the fleeing steps of the faithful
echoing over the mouths of the dragon-scaled drains.
(The pictures more vivid in memory than in the moment, most vivid
when the font rotates in a slow rumbling carousel in memory.)
Nowhere calm. Everywhere risk.
As it was. As it is.
Only inside there is there peace, in the basin's water no one sees,
but on the outer walls the struggle rages.
And peace can come in drops, maybe in the night
when you're unaware,
or like when you're lying on a drip in a suite in a hospital.

People, beasts, ornaments.
There isn't any landscape. Ornaments.

Mr. B***, my traveling companion, affable, in exile,
released from Robben Island, says:
"I envy you. I feel nothing for nature.
But *people in a landscape*, that says something to me."

Here are people in a landscape.
A photo from 1865. The steamboat lies by the pier in the sound.
Five figures. A lady in bright crinoline, like a bell, like a blossom.
The men look like extras in some rustic production.
All of them are beautiful, uncertain, on their way to being erased.
The go ashore a short time. They are erased.
The steamboat is of a model now extinct—
a tall chimney, sunshade, slim hull—
it's utterly unfamiliar, a UFO that's landed.
Everything else in the photo is shockingly real:
the ruffles on the water,
the other shore—
I can run my hand over the rugged faces of the rock,
I can hear the sighing in the pines.
It's close by. It's
today.
The waves are contemporary.

Now, a hundred years later. The waves come in from no-man's water

and beat against the stones.
I walk along the shore. It isn't like it was, walking along the shore.
There's too much to digest, too many conversations to carry on at
    once, you have thin walls.
Each thing has gotten a new shadow behind the usual shadow,
and you hear it dragging along, too, when it's altogether dark.

It's night.

The strategic planetarium turns. The lenses stare in the darkness.
The night sky is full of numbers, and they are fed
into a blinking cabinet
an item of furniture
housing the energy of a swarm of locusts that strips bare acres of
    Somalia's earth in a half hour.

I don't know if we're in the beginning or the final stage.
A summary can't be made. A summary is impossible.
Summary is the mandrake—
(see the Big Book of Superstitions:

                    MANDRAKE

                                        wonderworking plant
that let out such a horrible scream when it was pulled from the earth
you'd fall down dead. They got a dog to do it ...)

IV

From the lee side,
closeups.

Bladderwrack. In the clear water shine kelp forests, they are young,
    you want to emigrate there, stretch out full length on your
    reflection and sink to a certain depth—kelp that keeps itself afloat
    with airbladders like we keep ourselves afloat with ideas.

Four-horn sculpin. The fish that's a toad that wanted to be a butterfly
    and made it a third of the way, hides itself in the seagrass but
    gets drawn up with the nets, snagged on its pathetic spines and

warts—when you untangle it from the threads of the net your hands
shimmer with slime.

Rockfaces. Out on the sun-warmed lichens scurry little bugs, they
hurry like second hands—the pine tree casts a shadow, it wanders
slow as an hour hand—inside me time stands still, there's no end
of time, the time needed to forget every language and discover
perpetual motion.

On the lee side you can hear the grass grow: a faint drumming from
below, a faint roaring of millions of small gas flames, that's what
it's like to hear the grass grow.

And now: the expanse of water, without doors, the open border
that grows ever wider
the further you stretch out.

There are days when the Baltic is a still, endless roof.
Dream then, naïvely, of something that comes creeping on the roof
and tries to unravel the flag lines,
tries to raise
the rag—

the flag that has been so rubbed by the wind and smoked by the
chimneys and bleached by the sun it can be everyone's.

But it's a long way to Liepāja.

V

30 July. The bay has turned eccentric—today it's teeming with
jellyfish for the first time in years, they pump along calmly, gently,
they belong to the same shipping line: AURELIA, they drift like
flowers after a burial at sea, if you take them up out of the water,
their form disappears completely, like when an indescribable
truth is lifted up out of the silence and formulated to dead jelly,
yes, they are untranslatable, they have to stay in their element.

2 August. Something wants to be said, but the words won't cooperate.
Something that can't be said,

aphasia,
there aren't any words, but maybe a style . . .

It happens that you wake in the night
and throw a few words down quickly
on the nearest piece of paper, in the margin of a newspaper
(The words radiate meaning!)
but come morning the same words say nothing anymore, scribblings,
    misstatements.
Or fragments of the great nocturnal style that went past?

Music comes to a man, he's a composer, is performed, has a career,
    becomes head of the conservatory.
Circumstances change, he's condemned by the authorities.
As chief prosecutor they appoint his pupil K***.
He's threatened, demoted, sent away.
After a few years the disfavor lessens, he's reinstated.
Then comes the stroke: right-side paralysis with aphasia, can only
    grasp short phrases, says the wrong words.
Is therefore beyond the reach of advancement or condemnations.
But the music is still there, he continues to compose in his own style,
he becomes a medical sensation for the remainder of his life.

He wrote music to texts he no longer understood—
in like manner
we express something with our lives
in the humming chorus of misstatements.

The Death Lectures went on for several terms. I was present
together with classmates I didn't know
(Who are you?)
—afterwards everyone went their separate ways, profiles.

I looked at the sky and at the ground and straight ahead of me
and since then have been writing a long letter to the dead
on a typewriter with no ribbon, only a horizon-line
so that the words pound in vain and nothing fastens.

I stand, hand on the doorhandle, and take the house's pulse.
The walls are so full of life.

(The children don't dare sleep alone in the upstairs room—what
    makes me secure makes them uneasy).

3 August. Out there in the wet grass
glides a greeting from the Middle Ages: the Burgundy Snail
the subtly yellow-grey glimmering snail with its house asway,
introduced here by monks who liked escargot—yes, the Franciscans
    were here,
quarried stone and burned lime, acquired the island in 1288, a
    bequest from King Magnus
("Þese almes and othre ilyke / Þei meten hym nou in Heuenryke")
the woods fell, the ovens burned, the lime was shipped in
to build the monastery . . .
                         Sister snail
stands nearly still in the grass, eyestalks drawn in
and rolled out, interference and uncertainty . . .
How it resembles me in my searching!

The wind that has blown so thoroughly all day
—on the outermost islets every blade of grass is counted—
has lain down to rest in the middle of the island. The match flame
    stands up straight.
The maritime painting and the woodland painting darken together.
The five-story trees' greenery, too, fades to black.
"Every summer is the last." These are empty words
for the creatures in the late summer midnight
where the crickets are sewing like mad on their machines
and the Baltic's nearby
and the solitary water-faucet rises among the wild rosebushes
like an equestrian statue. The water tastes of iron.

VI

Grandmother's story before it's forgotten: her parents die young,
her father first. When the widow senses the sickness will take her too
she goes from house to house, sails from island to island
with her daughter. "Who can take care of Maria?" An unfamiliar
    house
on the other side of the bay takes her in. There they can afford it.
But the ones who could afford it were not the good ones. The mask of
    piety cracks.

Maria's childhood ends ahead of time, she lives as a servant without
    pay
in a constant chill. Many years. The constant seasickness
during the long trips by rowboat, the ceremonious terror
at the table, their looks, the pike skin crunching
in her mouth: Be grateful, be grateful.
                                        She never looked back
but for that very reason she was able to see The New
and grab hold of it.
Ringed in, she broke out!

I remember her. I pressed myself against her
and at the moment of death (the moment of transition?) she sent out a
    thought
so that I—the five-year-old—understood what had happened
a half hour before the phone rang.

I remember her. But in the next brown photo
is someone unknown—
dated by the clothing to the middle of the last century.
A man around thirty: the bold eyebrows,
the face that looks me right in the eyes
and whispers: "Here I am."
But who this "I" is
there is nobody now who remembers. No one.

TB? Isolation?

Once upon a time he stopped
on the stony, grass-perfumed slope up from the sea
and sensed the black blindfold over his eyes.

Here, behind thick bushes—is it the island's oldest house?
The low, cross-jointed, two-hundred-year-old fisherman's shack with
    its shaggy grey timbers.
And the modern brass lock has clicked shut on it all, shining like a
    ring in the nose of an old bull
that refuses to rise.
So much huddled timber. On the roof, the ancient brick tiles fallen
    crosswise onto each other

(the original pattern disturbed by the rotation of the earth through
    the years)
it reminds me of something ... I was there ... wait: It's the old Jewish
    cemetery in Prague
where the dead live closer than in life, the stones crowded close,
    close.
So much love lies ringed in there! The brick tiles with the lichens'
    characters in an unknown language
are the stones in the islanders' ghetto cemetery, the stones raised and
    fallen.
The hovel shines
with all of those borne by a certain wave, a certain wind
out here to their fates.

Tomas Tranströmer
Translated by *Bill Coyle*

Translation as Strange Music[1]

D uke Ellington warned, "It don't mean a thing if it ain't got that swing." Using this quip as a guide to the translation of poetry, I'll consider one sentence from "Conte" (Tale), a prose poem by Rimbaud: "La musique savante manque à notre désir." Rimbaud's statement acts out the failure written into translation as a quest for original music, that "swing."

For the moment I'll leave the sentence untranslated because the whole point is that it defies translation. The French verb *manquer* points to a spectrum of meanings: to miss someone, to miss a target, to lack, to spoil, to fail, to need, to be absent. Since those words almost invariably also are used to characterize literary translation—critics point out how the translator missed, lacked, spoiled, failed the original—Rimbaud's sentence leads us into the heart of the matter. A further complication is built into the reverse electrical polarity of *manquer*: it flips its direction between French and English. "Tu me manques" in French means, not "You miss me," but "I miss you." But in considering the ways in which translators seek, and often fail, to "get that swing," I don't counsel despair. The failed quest for "une musique savante"—a knowing music? a cunning music? a wise music? a scholarly music?—prompts an argument not for futility, but for discovery, an opening into the very nature of translation and of language.

Deformation is built into literary translation. In *Translation as Citation: Zhuangzi Inside Out*, Haun Saussy points out, "No language actually has a border or a center"; languages are hybrid and always changing and exchanging, "importing" and "loaning" words and ideas.[2] As an example, he examines the Chinese poet Xu Zhimo's translation, in 1924, of Baudelaire's "Une Charogne," which assimilates

---

1   Presented originally as a talk at Boston University, at which Christopher Ricks was present.

2   Haun Saussy, *Translation as Citation: Zhuangzi Inside Out* (Oxford University Press, 2017), 5.

the French poem to the Chinese Daoist classic, the *Zhuangzi*, of the 3rd century BCE. "Une Charogne" provides a corollary to Rimbaud's "musique savante." The lover and his lady, out for a stroll, encounter the decomposing corpse of an unnamed animal, and in the processes of decay, the poet hears "une étrange musique"—a strange music. Xu Zhimo translated that music by a phrase from the *Zhuangzi*, *tian lai*, which alludes to "the piping of heaven." In decomposing Baudelaire's music into Daoist music to make a 20th century Chinese poem, Xu Zhimo adopts decomposition itself as a model for translation, and the strangeness of its music, for Saussy, isn't a failure, but a hybrid richness added to the Chinese.

What about Rimbaud's strange music? "Conte" is a prose poem. It's one of the *Illuminations*, the marvelous collection of prose poems composed between 1872 and 1874. It has eight paragraphs, the last one consisting of just one line, the sentence about "la musique savante." Since Rimbaud, in these poems, is experimenting with the Baudelairean prose poem, and in the case of two poems ("Marine" and "Mouvement") pressing the evolution into the newer form of *vers libre*, we have to attend to the presence, or absence, of paragraphs, and their relation to what might become *lines* of free verse. Some of the *Illuminations* are chunks of prose with no paragraphs; others break so often the paragraphs seem like amphibious creatures ready to crawl up on shore as verse lines.

"Conte" is clearly prose. I used the shopworn adjective "marvelous" to describe *Illuminations*. It applies accurately to "Conte," since this is a tale of marvels: a murderous Prince meets a Genie; they love, fuse, and annihilate each other. Yet both survive, and what survives of them is the grim final statement about the impossibility of satisfying desire or art: "La musique savante manque à notre désir." "There is no sovereign music for our desire," in Louise Varèse's translation. Or as the Rolling Stones put it, "I can't get no satisfaction."

We recognize this oscillation between ecstasy and the recognition of limits as a feature of Romantic poetry; one thinks of the swerve in Keats's "Ode to a Nightingale," ". . . forlorn. // Forlorn! the very word is like a bell / To toll me back from thee to my sole self!" The oscillation is essential in Rimbaud. Time and again, his expansive vision violently contracts; the Drunken Boat's deliriums shrink at the end to a black, cold puddle back in Europe.

Also essential to Rimbaud are the destruction and reconstitution of beauty. *Une Saison en enfer*, written in the midst of, or in a hiatus in, the composition of *Illuminations*, traces an arc from the insult to

Beauty on the first page to the substitution of Truth for Beauty at the end: "And I shall be free to *possess truth in one body and soul.*"[3]

The Prince in "Conte" tries just that. He starts with the massacre of beauty, his harem. There follows the massacre of his exotic beasts, the burning of his palaces, the murder of his subjects—all miraculously resuscitated. This adolescent fantasy of destruction seems to call up a Genie. Rimbaud, who had proclaimed in *Une Saison en enfer*, "Love has to be reinvented," imagines here "the promise of a complex and multiple love" which also seems to represent the poet embracing his own daemon, his genius-genie. But instead of heralding a triumph of Romantic imagination, this fusion falls back into individuation and into the failure of poetic language to translate mystic experience: "La musique savante manque à notre désir."

Which brings us to the mysterious sentence. The more manageable obstacle is the verb *manquer*, but if we look at six different versions, we see a wild variety of solutions. "La musique savante" creates even more trouble. *Savante* could mean "knowing," "scholarly," "wise," "cunning." "La musique savante" also means Classical Music as opposed to pop. And for Rimbaud, the epithet suggests his vision of himself as a magus, an initiate into occult mysteries: "Je suis le savant au fauteuil sombre" ("I am the scholar of the dark armchair), he announced in "Enfance" in *Illuminations*.[4] All of this magic has to flow into the English word for *savante*. Let's see how our translators cope.

Louise Varèse: "There is no sovereign music for our desire."[5] This strikes me as pretty good. The construction "There is no" for *manque* catches the sense of incommensurability: the desire is vast, the music non-existent. "Sovereign" for *savante* is clever: what it misses in semantic range, it makes up for (partly) in phonetics, the almost Joycean kinship in sound.

Enid Rhodes Peschel: "Masterly music disappoints our desire."[6] "Masterly" goes some way toward meeting *savante*, but "disappoints" turns the statement on its head by suggesting that there *is* such a thing as that masterly music, but that the desire doesn't approve of

---

3 Arthur Rimbaud, *Collected Works*, tr. Wallace Fowlie, revised by Seth Whidden, (University of Chicago Press, 2005), 305.
4 Arthur Rimbaud, *Illuminations*, tr. Louise Varèse, (New Directions, 1946, 1957), 13.
5 Ibid., 16.
6 Arthur Rimbaud, *A Season in Hell, The Illuminations*, tr. Enid Rhodes Peschel, (Oxford University Press, 1973), 117.

it. Rimbaud's situation is more dire: the masterly music so urgently needed *doesn't exist,* and is therefore "missed."

Paul Schmidt: "Our desire lacks the music of the mind."[7] "Music of the mind" tries to accommodate something of the range of *savante.* But the construction in English feels less idiomatic than Rimbaud's French, and doesn't sufficiently communicate the pathos. The problem is not so much that the desire falters, as that the music isn't there.

Wallace Fowlie/ Seth Whidden: "Our desires are deprived of cunning music."[8] Whidden revised and updated Fowlie's translation of *The Complete Rimbaud* from 1966. It does no harm to the singular French *désir* to make it plural in English, and "deprived" expresses the feeling of loss, with the gratifying surplus of alliteration. "Cunning," however, diminishes the power of *savante.*

Wyatt Mason: "Our desires lack an inner music."[9] With "inner music" Mason has taken a big step in interpretation, straying far from anything coded into *savante.* What's the pay-off? I don't see what's gained by this Rilkean claim of inwardness when the wisdom and magic suggested by *savante* point to a more objective search for truth.

John Ashbery: "We have no desire for complex music."[10] This version is a shocker. Ashbery knew French well. But he turned Rimbaud's statement completely around. I protest: "we"–the "we" of this poem, suddenly precipitated out of the union and separation of Prince and Genie –have all too great a desire, but the music is out of reach. "Complex music"–well, maybe. (I quoted that sentence from the bound galleys of Ashbery's *Illuminations*; he corrected it in the published text: "Wise music is missing from our desire.")

This catalogue of attempts leaves us in the situation Rimbaud describes: deprivation. We lack a music adequate to this sentence. But pondering the lack can bring us closer to perceiving Rimbaud's power even if we cannot seize it.

Turning now to the larger question of Ellington's "swing," let's look at the question of form as it plays out between prose poem and verse poem.

Here are two provocative cases:

---

7   Arthur Rimbaud, *Complete Works,* tr. Paul Schmidt (Harper Perennial, 1975), 177-78.
8   Arthur Rimbaud, *Complete Works, Selected Letters,* tr. Wallace Fowlie, revised by Seth Whidden (University of Chicago Press, 2005), 313, 315.
9   Arthur Rimbaud, *Complete Poetry,* tr. Wyatt Mason (Modern Library, 2002), 227.
10   Arthur Rimbaud, *Illuminations,* tr. John Ashbery (W.W. Norton, 2011), 35.

Paul Schmidt translated the so-called *Complete Works* of Rimbaud by breaking up the collection of prose poems, *Illuminations*, and scattering them through his own volume. There is some warrant for that; Rimbaud left his manuscripts in disorder when he went to Africa; Verlaine arranged for the publication of a group of *Illuminations* in the journal *La Vogue*, and the piecemeal state of the manuscripts has engendered controversy ever since. But the notebook pages containing the drafts show a continuous if not entirely coherent group of poems. Since their first publication in several issues of *La Vogue* in 1886, and then in the posthumous *Poésies complètes* in 1895, *Illuminations* has held its place in French literature as a whole work. Schmidt's dislocation of the collection seems gratuitous.

But Schmidt reserved his most radical treatment of Rimbaud for the *form* of the poems. He turned "Conte," a prose poem, into free verse. Here is where Ellington's swing matters.

By the age of sixteen, Rimbaud had mastered traditional metrics. He could unroll mellifluous verses in the styles of the masters, but he was also testing those constraints with jolting enjambments and outrageous rhymes. His metrics simultaneously bind in and explode out. So his decision in 1872-1874 to compose prose poems, rather than verse, matters. It matters to our understanding of his artistic development; it matters also to the history of modern poetry, as the prose poem and free verse were emerging, in uneasy relation to one another, in just this period. There's debate about whether Rimbaud's free verse "emerged" from his prose poems, or from his experimentation with verse proper. I won't go into those arguments here, but a lot rides on the distinction between free verse and prose poetry, and Schmidt has muddled it.[11]

Why would he do such a thing? Schmidt noticed, he says, that "contemporary American poets have developed a sense of equation between the syntactic unit and the line of verse." (A debatable claim.) He asserts that a major "formal characteristic" of Rimbaud's prose poems was "the arrangement of syntactic units on the page." That description could apply to any writing. Rimbaud's "arrangement" seems to him "so close in intention to the form of most modern American poetry

---

11   André Guyaux, the most recent editor of the Pléiade Rimbaud, rejects the idea of *vers libre* emerging from Rimbaud's prose poems: see *Oeuvres complètes*, ed. André Guyaux, the note on "Marine," 969-970. I disagree.

that I have tried to make an equation between sentence and line the major formal device of my translation of these poems."[12]

Observe the consequence:

Tale

A Prince was annoyed that he had forever devoted himself
Only to the perfection of vulgar generosities.
He foresaw astonishing revolutions in love,
And suspected that his wives were capable of more
Than an agreeable complacency ... [13]
(and so forth).

What poetry could Schmidt have been thinking of when he lined up these clauses like cans on a supermarket shelf? He mentions Frank O'Hara and John Ashbery, but his lines have nothing of their dynamism. Nor do they resemble the verse of William Carlos Williams or Marianne Moore, neither of whom would have signed Schmidt's mortician's contract to "make an equation between line and sentence." He has completely lost Rimbaud's subtle, irregular pacing. His version is neither a prose poem nor a verse poem, but that irritating counterfeit, a prose text masquerading as verse.

Recalling Baudelaire's "strange music," we may consider an opposite case, Keith Waldrop's turning Baudelaire's lyric "Une Charogne" into a prose poem. This, too, is a radical move: Waldrop reformed many of *Les Fleurs du mal* into prose. Baudelaire will survive. As is well known, he rewrote some of his own verse poems into prose poems as he explored new forms of consciousness and art.

In a draft of a preface for *Les Fleurs du mal*, Baudelaire succinctly described the art of verse: "Rhythm and rhyme satisfy the three immortal human needs, for monotony, symmetry, and surprise."[14] In verse, surprise is created by contrast with the narcotic powers of monotony and symmetry. In prose poetry, narcosis and surprise have to be engineered differently.

"Une Charogne" is a poem about decomposition of the flesh and recomposition in art. Waldrop certainly decomposed the poem. Gone are the sculpted quatrains alternating alexandrine and octosyllabic lines; gone are the rare enjambments that act out the spill-over of

---

12   Schmidt, xviii.
13   Ibid., 177.
14   Charles Baudelaire, *Oeuvres complètes*, ed. Claude Pichois (Bibliothèque de la Pléiade, Gallimard, 1975), 182.

verminous life agitating the corpse. Gone is the lulling swing of this sinister love song, not to the woman, but to the art that will survive the woman.

Waldrop translated Baudelaire's tight quatrains into the loose prose poetry of verset, explaining that he took his model from the biblical versets of the Psalms:[15]

> Recall, my soul, the thing we saw that fine mild summer morning:
> there at a bend in the path, loathsome carrion on a bed sown with cobbles,
> Legs in the air, like a lewd woman, scorching and sweating poisons,
> reeking belly split open nonchalantly, cynically . . .[16]

I take Waldrop's exercise to be deliberately provocative, an attempt to de-lyricize the lyric, like pouring weed-killer on a garden to see what will be left. *Something* is left—the bare stalks of argument and image, and, perhaps, a document of the aesthetics of an era suspicious of closure, symmetry, and song—suspicions which Baudelaire himself planted, long ago.

Waldrop's translation joins hundreds, probably thousands of other versions of this celebrated poem. He doesn't turn Baudelaire into a Daoist, like Zu Xhimo with his *tian lai*, piping of heaven. But Waldrop creates his own "strange music" for Baudelaire's "étrange musique." I conclude that literary translation inevitably creates a "strange music," not only strange, but estranged and estranging, and that to appreciate and judge translation we must learn to live in a state of devotional estrangement. However we think of it—and for me, translation is a shamanistic art involving a state of possession, even sacred cannibalism—translation turns decay into new forms of life. Like theater and magic, it's an art of illusion that understands itself as illusion.

Rosanna Warren

---

15   Charles Baudelaire, *The Flowers of Evil*, tr. Keith Waldrop (Wesleyan University Press, 2007), xxiv.
16   Ibid., 42.

Emily Dickinson and Revision

Whenever I teach Practical Criticism—though at my place, UCL, it's less freightedly known as Commentary and Analysis—I think of Christopher and the pleasure he brings to, and derives from, poems, and try to work in his spirit. This essay is a small offering to express my gratitude for many things, but particularly for the twenty-six single-spaced pages of bracing commentary he magnanimously sent me about the MS of my book *Henry James and Revision* (1990). I can't think of revision without thinking of Christopher.

Some comparisons of poems—comparison being central to the exercise—work exceptionally well, and others flatter to deceive. It's only a good road test, going to and fro with some actual students, that generally shows the mettle of any particular conjunction. So when I find one that really works I tend to stick to it.

Teaching the same exercise repeatedly, year after year, risks boredom (for the teacher) but can have its advantages: when you know it so well, it can become a familiar multi-purpose tool. When a student asks a question, or raises an issue, you have generally encountered it before and have something in your locker. Not that a brilliant student won't occasionally reveal something to you that you hadn't seen yourself. The passage, poem or poems, when intimately explored, becomes an emblematic object, a case of language at full stretch that can tell you, or suggest, all sorts of things.

I don't even remember when I started to teach Emily Dickinson's "Safe in their Alabaster Chambers,"[1] but know that I was drawn to it because it is a challenging case of revision, revision pre-publication as everything, almost, is with Dickinson, but presenting some serious questions about our attitudes to writing. And for a decade or two it's

---

1   It's numbered 124 in *The Poems of Emily Dickinson; Variorum Edition*, edited by R.W. Franklin (Belknap Press, 1998), 3 vols, I, 159-164. Hereafter F124 and *Variorum*. I owe thanks to Dave Isaacs, Neil Rennie and Peter Swaab for their help with this piece.

been the first thing I present to freshman English students on their arrival—without attribution and without attaching dates to show the relative order of the four texts which are bracketed under that title.

*

I don't want to foreclose the question of how to describe the four texts of "Safe in their Alabaster Chambers," so I offer them to the students as "four poems, or four versions of a poem." I start the discussion with a sometimes hilarious party-game, of a sort: the four previously unseen texts are presented with no paratextual information, and I ask students both to be ready to say in what chronological order the texts were produced, and to rank them in order of their preference, revealing the known chronological order only at the end. Once they've had a chance to look closely at the texts, I go round the class and record what each student declares to be their guesses about the order and their preferences.

Then, looking at what they've said, I try to tease out the differences between those who have thought the earliest version is preferable, those who think the last, and variations in between. For some—though they may not have formulated this to themselves—there is a story of continuing improvement, with Dickinson making the poem better and better. For others, there is a cut-off, occurring immediately after the production of the first version, after which the poem seems only to get worse—maybe because they feel the initial flow of inspiration can rarely or never be recovered. Sometimes the students' decisions suggest a process of amelioration halting after the second or third version, in which, like a painter who doesn't know when to stop, the poet starts to add unhappy touches which carry the poem away from what, at least for a proportion of viewers, it was to have been or could have been. These seem to me differences worth exploring.

Although there *are* some interesting variations (one of wording, one of lineation) between the versions of the first stanza of this two-stanza poem, or these poems, the attraction of this as a case for investigation is that Dickinson writes four distinct second stanzas, each with a different relation to the first, construing it in a different way.

Firstly, then, we should examine the opening stanza, almost the same in each of the versions or poems.

> Safe in their Alabaster Chambers—
> Untouched by morning
> And untouched by noon—
> Sleep the meek members of the Resurrection—
> Rafter of Satin,
> And Roof of Stone. (F124B, *Variorum* I, p 160)

"Safe" implies some danger, but it turns out "morning" and "noon" are
the threats these expensively protected subjects don't have to worry
about. "The meek members of the Resurrection," the elect in this quite
Protestant world (and "the meek" will inherit the Earth according
to the third beatitude (Matthew 5.5)), seem to be very comfortably
ensconced in their expensive tombs, described as "Chambers,"
suggesting bedchambers. In the earliest text, of late 1859, they "Sleep,"
a theologically sanctioned euphemism for death, pledging that they'll
awaken at the Resurrection; in subsequent versions, the difference
being a small matter of life and death, they more noncommittally "Lie"
(F124C, F124E, *Variorum* I, pp. 161, 162). This is not a pauper's grave.
Nothing but the best for these "meek members": "Rafter of satin, /
And Roof of stone" (in all subsequent versions these two short lines
are combined). They are "Safe" enough, but twice here "Untouched"
seems to hint that they are also rather blankly failing to feel or
respond to the light of day, failing to feel its beauty and warmth. A
thought that might seem monstrously unfair, if it means criticising
the dead for their failure to show an alert responsiveness to life. That
suggestion is perhaps only an undercurrent; but it *is* reinforced by the
unsettling mismatch between "Alabaster," "satin" and "stone" on the
one hand and "meek" on the other. These meek brethren and sistren
seem to have done very nicely for themselves, and to be enjoying the
privileges of their membership "of the Resurrection."

Having some prior knowledge of Dickinson's resistance to the
religious revival in Amherst that had claimed the rest of her family
I was, I confess, primed and on the lookout for this reading of her
introduction of "the meek members" as quietly dissentient;[2] but I
want to think I would have got there, without external prompts, by
examining the second stanza of the first known version of the poem:

---

2   "They are religious, except me—and address an Eclipse, every morning—whom
     they call their 'Father.'" Letter 338, 28 April 1862, to T.W. Higginson, *The Letters
     of Emily Dickinson*, edited by Cristanne Miller and Domhnall Mitchell (Harvard
     University Press, 2024), 358. (Hereafter *Letters*.)

Light laughs the breeze
In her Castle above them—
Babbles the Bee in a stolid Ear,
Pipe the sweet Birds in ignorant cadence—
Ah, what sagacity perished here! (F124B, *Variorum* I, p 160)

It's now explicitly said that "the meek members" are "stolid"; they were "Untouched" by the light and warmth of "morning" and "noon" in the first stanza, but "Light" (as an adverb) qualifies what "the breeze" and "the Bee" and the "Birds" do here, laughing, babbling, and piping, which sounds much more fun than being stolid. I take the "Castle" belonging to "the breeze" to be the tomb beneath which the meek so unresponsively lie; this second stanza picks up and continues the first's temporal momentum from "morning" to "noon," and its vertical impetus from "rafter to Roof," taking us into the light and warmth of afternoon and raising us a few feet "above them," above the earth which the meek have inherited, to celebrate the vivacity of a summer day.

Dickinson offers us in the third and fourth lines some judgmental adjectives, drawing more on Latinate diction, which brings along with it an implication of class, education, authority and at times pomposity, than on the plain directness, simplicity and possible reductiveness of the Anglo-Saxon alternatives. The birds are "sweet" (Anglo-Saxon) but then their cadence is "ignorant" (Latinate): there's a clash. The adjectives seem to reveal a conflict or debate the poem is obliquely engaged in. We find restrictive language ("stolid," already-quoted and Latinate) on the one hand characterising "the meek members" as lumpish and deaf to whatever "Babbles the Bee" in their ear; but then on the other hand (the Latinate "ignorant") sounding dismissive about untutored nature, devaluing the piping of the "Birds," though we mightn't have expected birds to be very learned in any case. The mixed signals make us suspect an irony.[3]

---

3 Another possible reading comes to mind as I reread: that "Light," "Babbles" and "ignorant" may all imply that nature isn't to be taken seriously, by comparison with the "sagacity" which has been lost. The whole poem would thus read as uttered in the persona of some pompous mourner, following Dickinson's declaration to T.W. Higginson in July 1862 that "When I state myself, as the Representative of the Verse – it does not mean – me – but a supposed person." (*Letters*, 366). (In Dickinson's poems before this time bees, birds and breezes all figure as emblems of nature, two of them in Franklin 23, a brief pantheistic-seeming version of the church's Trinitarian formula: "In the name of the Bee – / And of the Butterfly – / And of the Breeze – Amen!" (*Variorum*, 81).)

In these first four lines, then, we have three aspects of non-human nature in their full expressiveness, marking or celebrating the beauty of the day that "the meek" are "Untouched" by. Syntactically, as we read, Dickinson has let us understand the verbs to be intransitive: "laughs," "Babbles," "Pipe" can all be sufficient activities unto themselves. But the last line of this version of the poem, following the dash—"Ah, what sagacity perished here!"—throws that intransitivity into doubt. We can read "laughs," "Babbles" and "Pipe" as transitive verbs and "Ah, what sagacity perished here!" as their object: what they are all uttering, what nature in chorus is saying. Or, indeed, that final line can be imagined as an epitaph inscribed on the tomb of "the meek members." Either a lamenting one, sorrowful for the loss of their great wisdom, or a somewhat mocking one, where, despite all the wise airs they gave themselves, they are now a quintessence of dust.

The final line is of course also susceptible of a slightly more probable reading as Dickinson's, or her narrator's, direct voicing of a conclusion, coming in with a summary comment on the contrast between the meek sleepers and the joyous wakeful birds and bee and breeze. This comment *could*, moreover, just possibly, be genuinely sorrowful, a lament for the loss of so much wisdom, perhaps inflected by the way "perished" seems to imply an eternal extinction that denies "sleep" in the first stanza—implying that the eschatological expectations of "the meek members" were delusive, and they're simply gone for ever, an immitigable loss. It's more likely, though, given the implicit satire on the plushness and grandeur of the tombs in the first stanza, and in particular "stolid" in the second, that this closing exclamation is less generous-minded, that it amounts to a simplifying sarcasm: the members thought themselves to be "meek," and to embody "sagacity," but in fact they lived in denial of breeze, bee and birds, of laughter, babble and piping, in the hope of a resurrection to which they feel themselves entitled but which will never occur ("perished").[4]

That then is the earliest version, dated to 1859.[5] Dickinson evidently showed it subsequently to her sister-in-law and close friend Sue,

---

4   Another possible additional reading, less likely but not easy to rule out, is that Dickinson *includes herself* among "the meek members." This would entail her seeing her own relatively complacent and luxurious life as exposed in essentially the same way to the vast forces of mortality in the cosmos, and so identifying with them and their fate. Her family's wealth would have bought her an alabaster chamber.

5   Miller and Mitchell state that "1) ED bound 'Safe in their Alabaster Chambers' in Fascicle 6 in 1859; 2) sometime between 1859 and spring 1861, ED sent

Susan Huntington Gilbert Dickinson, and Sue appears to have been unhappy with the second stanza. About 1861 Dickinson sent Sue a second version, with a startlingly different second stanza, with a note saying "Perhaps this verse would please you better—Sue":

> Grand go the Years – in the Crescent – above them –
> Worlds scoop their Arcs –
> And Firmaments – row –
> Diadems – drop – and Doges – surrender –
> Soundless as dots – on a Disc of Snow – (F124C, *Variorum* I, p 161)

Whereas the 1859 second stanza moved from the first vertically up a few feet into the summer day, and temporally no more than a few more hours into the afternoon, this 1861 version moves far up into the cosmos and sweeps forward onto a scale of interstellar time where vast movements of human history, revolutions and changes of régime, seem as imperceptibly tiny and quiet as a snowflake falling on snow. Students often don't notice how closely this opening line is modelled on its predecessor ("Light laughs the breeze"), with its alliteration and its inversion and even the capitalised C for "Crescent" as for "Castle"; "the Years," "Worlds" and "Firmaments" stand in for "breeze," "Bee" and "Birds." ("Firmaments – row" I take to mean they voyage through the aether, or maybe follow an elliptical path like that described by an oar—the rhyme with "snow" suggests that sense, as opposed to the just-possible different-sounding "row" as in quarrel.) But whereas in the first version we build to a sententious ending, a punch-line probably tinged with sarcasm, here the whole world of human events, on a much grander scale than that just of "the meek members," is imagined in a Pascalian way as becoming infinitesimally tiny in the grand vastness of the universe. (The beautiful patterning of d's and s's in those two final lines, where the intricately wrought repetitions and mirrorings of the sounds seem to suggest that by comparison with the universe the human scale is barely perceptible, a microscopically shrunk-down miniature, is wondrously wrought.)

One reason why Dickinson might have thought "Grand go the Years" would please Sue better than the very possibly satirical "Light laughs the Breeze" is that its quite a different kind of movement from

---

Susan the poem; 3) in June 1861, Susan gave that copy to Bowles, who visited Amherst about June 17th; Bowles apparently passed it on to the newspaper [*The Springfield Republican*], where it was published almost a year later, on March 1, 1862, dated June 1861; 4) ED sent the poem with a new second stanza to Susan in 1861." (*Letters*, 336 n.)

first to second stanza is more complex and perhaps in a sense more generous-spirited. The movement culminating in "Ah, what sagacity perished here!" seems to mock "the meek members" and their "Sleep" (henceforth revised to "Lie"), happy to taunt them with the delights of a summer afternoon—even though summer afternoons will, as we know too well, inevitably give way for all, wise and foolish, to evening, night, autumn, winter. By contrast, the movement in "Grand go the Years" opens up a vast perspective, *sub specie aeternitatis*, in which no human consciousness could be felt adequate, a vision so huge that infinite forces and stretches of time shrink human concerns to the size of a speck.

What perhaps drives Dickinson's revision is a moral reassessment: the sense that "Light laughs the breeze" disturbingly takes advantage of the dead, celebrating the life of nature they failed to grasp and enjoy, and not acknowledging sufficiently the extent to which any human consciousness is parochial, restricted for all its efforts to what in the perspective of the universe are tiny, blinkered concerns. The conversion to "Grand go the Years" would in this reading involve a self-correction, a return on the self, a recognition that point-scoring against priggish members of the community risks its own version of the complacency for which it makes fun of "the meek members."

Dickinson's private name for poetry, or one of them, is "Thought";[6] here we see the thinking, and imagining, taking a giant step further, and further away—though returning at last perhaps to an image of the New England winter, where specks of snow drift silently onto a snowy surface (the disc may suggest the roundness of a planet). "Soundless" (picking up and reworking "a stolid ear") together with "above them" we could say partly connects all this back to "the meek members" in their obliviousness, missing the "grand" events of history, continuing the line of mockery into the infinite. But thus to pull it back to satire would be to miss the way in which "Grand go the Years" transcends the original occasion, with its initial caricature of "the meek members," and concludes with a cosmic vision in which the vast movements of human history register no more with the universe than does the falling of a snowflake in the midst of a region-wide snowfall with us as humans. The desolation is not just theirs; it affects all of us.

---

6   "My Mother does not care for thought" (To TWH, 25 April 1862, *Letters*, 358); "I smile when you suggest that I delay 'to publish' – that being foreign to my thought, as Firmament to Fin – " (To TWH, 7 June 1862, *Letters*, 362); "Thought belong to Him who gave it – " (F788 ("Publication – is the Auction / Of the Mind of Man"), *Variorum* II, 742).

Nonetheless, the demanding Sue was not pleased.

> I am not suited dear Emily with the second verse—It is remarkable as the
> chain lightening that blinds us hot nights in the Southern sky but it does
> not go with the ghostly shimmer of the first verse as well as the other one—

It is certainly true that if unity is one's leading poetic criterion, "Light
laughs the breeze" follows most closely the first stanza of "Safe in
their Alabaster Chambers"—in physical proximity, in time, in season,
and in its final reference back to what we might read as a pomposity,
an affectation of "Sagacity," in "the meek members." Sue goes on to
issue a challenge to Dickinson:

> It just occurs to me that the first verse is complete in itself it needs no other,
> and can't be coupled – Strange things always go alone – as there is only
> one Gabriel and only one Sun – You never made a peer for that verse, and
> I *guess* you[r] kingdom doesn't hold one – I always go to the fire and get
> warm after thinking of it, but I never *can* again.[7]

Dickinson answers in fact by producing *two* more second stanzas, in
a demonstration of virtuosity, attempting to "couple" a second stanza
more intimately to the first. The third version (Is *this frostier?*):

> Springs – shake the Sills –
> But – the Echoes – stiffen –
> Hoar – is the Window – and numb – the Door –
> Tribes of Eclipse - in Tents of Marble –
> Staples of Ages - have buckled – there – (F124D, *Variorum*, pp 161-2)

Here we stride across the gap between stanzas from a summer's day to
the end of some succeeding winter, or rather the ends ("Springs") of
an indefinite series of winters: the first line dramatizes the attempts by
nature to attract the attention of "the meek members" in their tombs,
their stone houses. "But – . . ." the rest of the stanza clamps shut any
possibility of responsiveness in opacity and fixity ("stiffen," "hoar,"
"numb," "buckled"). Where "Light laughs the breeze" has four lines
of cheerful nature trying to get a response from "the meek members,"
followed by one line devastatingly implying their persistence of
stolidity, "Springs – shake the Sills –" reverses the proportions: it only
gives one line to nature's efforts and then four lines to their denial. The
image in the final two lines is exceedingly compressed and puzzling
for most readers: "Eclipse" seems a private reference to Dickinson's
name for Protestant religion (quoted above), so a modern typological

---

7   Quoted in Franklin, *Variorum* I, 161.

equivalent to the tribes of Israel seems in question; perhaps "Tents of Marble" refers to carved folds of cloth surrounding the tomb, and "Staples of Ages" to metal attachments on the tomb; maybe "Tribes of Eclipse . . . have buckled" aims at contriving a pun conveying the collapse of "the meek members" as well as their hardness and fixity. But these are only my best guesses. Here, I would say, the reader is baffled, lost, distracted. Christopher approvingly quotes Larkin on Dickinson's endings: "Only rarely . . . did she bring a poem to a successful conclusion. Too often the poem expires in a teased-out and breathless obscurity."[8] "'A teased-out and breathless obscurity" would certainly be a fair description of these last two lines.

Which might be why, as a later copy made in the second half of 1861 bringing together all the attempts hitherto reveals, Dickinson felt a need to have yet another go, at first only with small tweaks, then with startling new perspectives which, I would judge, lead to another "successful conclusion":

> Springs - shake the seals -
> But the silence - stiffens -
> Frosts unhook - in the Northern Zones -
> Icicles - crawl from polar Caverns -
> Midnight in Marble -
> Refutes - the Suns - (F124E, *Variorum*, p 162)

The "Springs" now shake not "sills" but "seals," as if for the Day of Judgement, and as if the members of the resurrection are finally to be awakened into eternal life (Revelation 8.1: "And when he had opened the seventh seal, there was silence in heaven about the space of half an hour.") And now it is "the silence" that "stiffens," not "the Echoes." But whereas the movement in the previous version from stimulus to non-response became fixed in the second line and everything thenceforth stated and restated the rigidity of marble, here Dickinson injects intensifying life and movement through cross-cutting, by going back to nature's attempts to penetrate the untouched interior of the "Alabaster Chambers," first where "Frosts" govern an active verb and "unhook," second where, even more actively, "Icicles - crawl." Surely if that's what spring does to such epitomes of frozenness, "the meek members" might ease up a little? But no, with an alliteration looking back to "Diadems - drop," "Midnight in Marble -/ Refutes -

---

8   "Philip Larkin: 'Like something almost being said,'" *TFOP*, 274.

the Suns –."[9] "Refutes" here goes beyond the obliviousness of "stolid" to the absoluteness of disproof: "Suns" refuses to give the satisfaction of quite rhyming with "Zones"; the stony enclosure of the tomb seems to deny the existence not only of our own solar system but of all Suns anywhere.

And with that conclusive gesture Dickinson—as far as we know—ceases to proliferate versions, leaving us not just four free-standing poems, but, if we want to attend to it, a poetic and moral adventure, a small drama of infinite interplay with an audience and with a restless conscience and imagination. Dickinson seems to keep discovering in that retained first stanza reserves of stored energy, as it were, which generate a succession of movements of thought, forward in time and up and away in space, dynamic extensions which still finally freeze back into deathliness at the close, to thrilling effect. It's perhaps less a story of indecision than of a series of decisions, each justifiable, and most of them giving rise to piercing, daring insights. If we think every beginning contains the seeds of its ending, this case shows how dazzlingly the possibilities can multiply.

Philip Horne

---

9   The capitalisation of "Refutes … Suns" satisfyingly picks up the pattern es-
     tablished at the close of the first stanza, with "Rafter of Satin, / And Roof of
     Stone."

THEOCRITUS: IDYLL I (l. 29f)

—a pastoral cup for Sir Christopher Ricks

Imagine a goblet, its burnished lip so freshly inscribed
    With blossoming vines you can almost smell them
Unfurling. Now picture every shoot of that spreading ivy
    Filigreed with so many gold berries
That just by holding the empty, burgeoning cup in your hand
    You've tasted the fruit of sheer delight—
Even before the vessel is brimming with dark red wine.

Around and around the sculpted cup those dangling vines
    Extend by design until the flowing
Outline of a woman steps from the ivy: her features so lovely
    You'd swear the gods had fashioned her
And tied back her hair with a fillet to show their handiwork.
    And speaking of long luxurious curls,
There's a tall young man on either side of her, and they're caught

In some heated exchange, it seems, by the look of their earnest gestures.
    And as long as they argue back and forth
The woman turns her attention to one, now to the other,
    Smiling at both—though nothing they say
Appears to touch her very deeply. Her heart isn't in it.
    But the hollowed-out eyes of those handsome young men
Remain transfixed, reflecting their futile ordeal with Eros.

Now turn the cup again, and see how that aging fisherman
    Crouches down on a jutting outcrop,
And with great intensity grips the sinewy mesh of his net;
    As if he was gathering strength to make
The cast of his life, the one he's now too weak to make,
    Though the bulging veins engraved on his neck
Belie that graybeard's age, and pulse with a youngblood's vigor.

Just past that old man, his back as beaten by molten waves
    As the rock he stands on, there's a vineyard
Whose gorgeous intaglio of grapes is staked on a child's
    Vigilance, and this little boy sits
On a low stone wall that's warmed by the sun. Around and about him
    Go two foxes, one of whom flashes
Between the vine-rows, devouring all that's ripe for the picking,

While the other fox is trying every trick in the book
    To snatch the kid's breakfast, his satchel that's full
Of bread and cheese, and won't give up until she succeeds
    In sending him home on an empty stomach.
But the boy is busy constructing a tiny intricate cage
    He hopes to catch some crickets with,
Interlacing the stems of rushes with tendrils of asphodels.

The boy is so carried away by the joy of weaving his trap
    He doesn't have a care in the world, oblivious
Both to the vanished grapes and his meal a trail of crumbs.
    Around and around the acanthus vine
Continues to flower, and no matter how he turns the cup
    In his hand, a goatherd's glazed eyes will never
Get to the bottom of it, spellbound as he is.

I chose to use my translation from Theocritus's Idyll for its meshing
of music and reason, its trust in the primacy of literary allusion
(Homer's Shield of Achilles), its quick-witted foxes, and everywhere
in the Greek original the felicitous play of measured discrimination:
definitive qualities and generous energies that put me in mind (and
heart) of our dear honoree. And also, because Tennyson, too, had his
Idylls. And Beckett his brand of singing shepherds. Milton his Lycidas.
And Dylan his crickets—still talking back and forth in rhyme.

George Kalogeris

"Song on Porcelain": The Lyric and the Lyrics

I first heard Czesław Miłosz's "Song on Porcelain" (Piosenka o porcelanie, 1947) in an underground cabaret in Kraków. It was July, 1981, and I was studying Polish at the Jagiellonian University. Someone sung it—a student maybe?—while strumming a guitar. I don't remember who took me to the cabaret. I don't remember what else was said or sung. But the song's refrain has been with me ever since: "Niczego mi, proszę Pana, tak nie żal jak porcelana."[1] I even remember that snippet of melody. I only had one year of Polish under my belt back then, and I understood exactly two phrases: "Proszę Pana," or "Sir" (more or less), and "jak porcelana," "like porcelain," the rhyme words in the refrain. Most of Miłosz's poems had yet to appear in English—it took a Nobel Prize to get that ball rolling—and this lyric came out in Miłosz's and Robert Pinsky's exquisite translation only several years later. Who was this "sir"? And why was someone complaining to him about porcelain? I didn't have a clue. But it was worth learning Polish to find out.

I had experienced something similar a few years earlier in Leningrad, in the fall of 1977. It was yet another study abroad program, this time with state-sponsored field trips in place of student cabarets. At one point, we were collectively transported to a movie theater to see a popular romantic comedy, a Soviet meet-cute called "An Irony of Fate" (Ирония судьбы," 1976): two attractive young citizens end up in the wrong apartments in the wrong cities, since all the housing blocs look the same. But what struck me most were the songs, which were set to the poems of Marina Tsvetaeva, as I discovered. I didn't know Tsvetaeva back then. I'd been forcefed a couple of her poems in class by an overeager Russian teacher, but none of us understood them. One song in particular stuck in my mind, so I went out and bought the album, issued on the Soviet Melodiia label. "Мне нравится, что Вы больны не мной/Мне нравится, что я больна не Вами": "I'm glad that

---

1   Czesław Miłosz, *Wiersze*, Vol. 2, ed. Jan Błoński, Aleksander Fiut, Marian Stała (Wyd. Znak, 2002), 10.

you're not sick with love for me, I'm glad that I'm not sick with love for you," or something along those lines. That much I understood. And that bit of the melody is still with me too.

A romcom with lyrics by Marianne Moore: this might give some sense of the project's oddness. But not all of it. The vocally anti-Soviet Tsvetaeva was verboten in the USSR back then. A few tiny print runs, carefully expurgated, came out in the sixties and seventies, but I have no idea who had access to them. I certainly didn't. I bought my much-abridged Soviet edition of Akhmatova—no "Requiem" of course—in a state-run shop for foreigners with dollars. My Soviet-era Tsvetaeva came later, from a bookshop in Cambridge, MA. So how on earth did Tsvetaeva end up on the soundtrack to a Brezhnev-era comedy? I wish I knew. Regular Soviet citizens could buy the soundtrack with her words in normal shops with ordinary rubles. This must have been an event back then, though I didn't realize it.

And I couldn't possibly have understood what "Song on Porcelain" sung in a Kraków basement meant back in 1981. I've done some homework in the interim though, and I've filled in a few blanks. Its composer was a young student, Stanisław Klawe, now a renowned "Polish bard," so one website informs me.[2] Miłosz had been banned, both in person and in print, from his native land since 1951—the year of his defection from People's Poland—and returned in triumph only three decades later, in 1981. He'd just received the Nobel Prize in Literature and it would have been embarrassing to keep him out.

But the song apparently predates his rehabilitation. Klawe first heard the poet's name mentioned in a high school Polish class: "I was interested in poetry and couldn't stop wondering: who is this Miłosz?" he says in an interview. It took a trip to London after graduation to find out. The eager student rummaged through archives and bookshops to discover unofficial publications of Miłosz's poems. But he couldn't just buy the books and take them back with him. They'd have been confiscated at the border: "I'd have lost my money and my Miłosz," he explains. So he recorded dozens of poems on cassette tapes, and copied others into school notebooks. It worked. When he picked up his guitar back home, "the melodies just came by themselves," Klawe recalls.[3]

---

2   https://bardowiepolscy.pl/stanislaw-klawe/.
3   https://www.cultureave.com/miedzy-cyrylica-a-szwabacha-stanislaw-kla-we-2/.

One of his first efforts was the song I heard so many years ago in Kraków. It had been circulating underground for several years by then, so perhaps another underground bard was simply passing it along. Or it may have been Klawe himself. The Cellar Under the Rams, where the cabaret took place, was apparently a legendary venue for off-the-record performers. In any case, by the time "Song on Porcelain" reached me, it was already a clandestine classic.

Is this why Miłosz violated his own principles of translation when it came to this particular poem? He resisted rhyme and meter in his anglicized work: his long-time co-translator Robert Hass still recalls Miłosz's reaction to a rhymed version of his wartime masterpiece "The World: A Naive Poem" (1943): "A mouse? Why a mouse?" he protested when Hass produced an animal to rhyme with "house." Yet he allowed Pinsky to recreate, beautifully, the form of his postwar "Song." Why? Perhaps because it was already a song, as Miłosz certainly knew by the time he and Pinsky set to work on it. And as a song it had reached a young audience who might otherwise not have known its author's name. I suspect the English version could be sung to the same tune, though I haven't actually tried it:

> Rosecolored cup and saucer,
> Flowery demitasses:
> You lie beside the river
> Where an armored column passes.
> Winds from across the meadow
> Sprinkle the banks with down;
> A torn apple tree's shadow
> Falls on the muddy path;
> The ground everywhere is strewn
> With bits of brittle froth—
> Of all things broken and lost
> Porcelain troubles me most.[4]

So runs the first stanza in their impeccable translation. The poem takes its inspiration from the "the small sad cry/Of cups and saucers cracking," tiny emblems of all the perishable forms that shape and are shaped by human lives. "Not many works escape the sands and fires of history," Zbigniew Herbert reminds us.[5] Poems too can fall prey to history's depredations. Miłosz's little verse survived its maker's

---

4   Czesław Miłosz, *New and Collected Poems: 1931-2001* (Ecco, 2003), 81-82.
5   Zbigniew Herbert, *Barbarian in the Garden*, tr. Michael March and Jarosław Anders (Harcourt Brace Jovanovich, 1985), 101.

exile at least in part because it could be sung—as one intrepid student recognized in People's Poland over forty years ago.

"The Beatles didn't shout. They sung." A friend recently quoted these phrases to me from memory when I said I was writing something to honor Christopher Ricks. He'd read Rick's review of Philip Norman's *Shout! The True Story of the Beatles* (1981) back when it first appeared in the *London Times*. He misquoted only slightly: "Shout!? But they sang, they didn't shout, even when they sang 'Twist and Shout'" (*R*, 329).

Ricks got it absolutely right, my friend said. He'd been a first-year graduate student in English, he told me, when the author of *Milton's Grand Style* was invited to Harvard and lectured on, of all things, Bob Dylan. Others may have been shocked—Harvard was notoriously unhip back in the seventies. But my friend was delighted. He too knew poetry when he heard it. Such unhipness still persists in some pockets of the academy today. One of my colleagues was peeved when the Nobel Prize in Literature went to Dylan: He's not a poet!" he snapped. "You can't read him on his own." "Don't tell that to Christopher Ricks," I shot back. That shut him up.

Songs and poems may not always coincide. But sometimes they do. And the results can be electric. I was reminded of this recently when I went to see the Dylan biopic "A Complete Unknown"—not once but twice—partly to hear the astonishing words of "Like a Rolling Stone" blasting at me from at least eight speakers. It is, as Ricks says of another Dylan song, "a masterpiece of regulated hatred" (*DVOS*, 56). Which can be, as it turns out, exhilarating. I may go again. And then I'll return once more to *Dylan's Visions of Sin* (hardcover, I couldn't wait for the paperback) to find out why I love the songs so much.

"It clearly is an amputation of a song to reduce it to its words," Ricks remarks in an interview. "But if the words are really very, very good, then there's plenty of reward in them."[6] Well, he's proven that many times over. And sometimes the reverse is true: a poem can be unexpectedly amplified by music, given new life via song. Miłosz, Tsvetaeva—I'm living proof.

Clare Cavanagh

---

6   Susan Seligson,"In the Service of Bob Dylan's Genius," "Bostonia" (Winter-Spring 2015) (https://www.bu.edu/bostonia/winter-spring15/in-the-service-of-bob-dylans-genius/).

Here is a poem to honor Christopher, a redraft of an already published poem from *The Greek Anthology, Book XVII* (entitled *Book Seventeen* for the US edition) and by one Christophorus Silentiarius, who you all know here. "The Third Voyage" is for the famous Bobysseus Dylanus, who Christophorus greatly admires. My translation is somewhat playful, yet serious nonetheless, or perhaps all the more, and is in sync with all the poems of *The Greek Anthology, Book XVII* (of which Christopher graciously wrote the book's back-cover summary, though characteristically did not want to be named). I am all too aware of the quandary others must have also of not being able to say enough about all Christopher's done and for so many.

The Third Voyage
For Bobysseus

Exhausted, we arrive in a humble fishing village,
    the shabby hotel has the feel of a houseboat.
A trawler passes in the dark with its lit tilly lamps,
    and for a moment we think
that it is we who're heading out to open sea,
    not the night-fishing crew. In such a place
I fancy Odysseus planted his oar, tired of drifting.
    All he wanted was to be left alone, to settle
in such a foreign harbor, still have the illusion
    of being on water, of voyaging.
The best of both worlds, finding himself relieved
    from the demons of constant attention,
of fame, giving himself up to glorious anonymity.

Greg Delanty

Gists

.

From Benjamin Disraeli, who matters much to Christopher: "Youth is a blunder; Manhood a struggle; Old Age a regret." Written by Disraeli between blunder and regret, one of dozens of his sayings collected in *The Oxford Dictionary of Quotations*, to which Christopher has resorted since youth.

*

Asked what book influenced him most, Christopher looked down momentarily; then a slight smile as he replied, "Boswell's *Life of Johnson*. Birkbeck Hill's, L.F. Powell's edition, obviously."

*

Driving on Commonwealth Avenue early one Friday evening, my wife (in the passenger seat) saw Christopher briskly walking to Kenmore Station. "We should give him a ride home," she said. I pulled over the car, my wife lowered the window: "Christopher! Do you need a ride home?" The sun had already set and it was difficult to see. "Yes, please," he replied. And then, squinting: "Who are you?"

*

With plans to travel to England in Summer 2016, I asked Christopher for Geoffrey Hill's address. I wanted to know more about the founding and early history of the Editorial Institute at Boston University. My travel plans fell through. Hill died in June. In the Fall, meeting to discuss the progress of my dissertation on William Carlos Williams, I mentioned that Hill died before I could see him. "That was rude of him."

*

Double-parked outside 143 Bay State Road, I rushed up the stairs to Christopher's office on the second floor. (I needed his signature on a time-sensitive form related to my dissertation). He was soon to leave for a seminar, so I handed him the form and a pen. "I just need you to sign and date this, and I'll be out of your hair." He paused. "That's not funny."

*

"When you are writing," he said, "imagine I am looking over your shoulder, ready to take issue with each word you put down. More: have Eric Griffiths looking over the other."

*

Christopher has taught for over 60 years. One afternoon, I walked into his office; he was visibly agitated. "A student fell asleep during class today. Laid his head down and slept. Has that happened to you?" More than I like, I said. "That's never happened to me before."

*

After a lifetime of buying books, at 91 he has started thinning his shelves: to Balliol College, his collections of Samuel Beckett and Geoffrey Hill. To friends, colleagues: "You should have this. I have copies elsewhere." "I won't get back to this at my age." Over the past year, he has been bringing bags (and suitcases full) of books to Commonwealth Books in downtown Boston.

While the bookseller looked through the haul, Christopher browsed the shelves. After twenty minutes or so, Christopher placed on the counter the folio Dryden, *Of Dramatick Poesie*, prefaced by T.S. Eliot's *A Dialogue on Poetic Drama*. "I ought to have this," Christopher said.

"You want this back?"

"What do you mean?"

"This was among that large Eliot collection you brought us several months ago."

"Is it?"

*

Disraeli, once more, with a sense of an ending: "When a man fell into his anecdotage it was a sign for him to retire from the world."

Jeffrey Gutierrez

Gratitude and Grace

Gratitude is among those human accomplishments literature lives to realize," Christopher Ricks said in his inaugural lecture as Professor of Poetry at the University of Oxford in November 2004. "Art enjoys the power not only to voice gratitude but to prompt it, even to restore us to a state in which *grateful* might come again to mean at once *feeling gratitude* and *feeling pleasure*—as though it once was, and ought always to be, impossible to be granted something gratifying and not be grateful for it."

At the time I paid little attention to that lecture. I was then an undergraduate English major at Boston University, and was at best vaguely aware that Professor Ricks—as I thought of him in those years—had received some important honor, and that it was connected to his occasionally jetting off to England. But Professor Ricks was always jetting off to England. He was *from* England. This significant recognition of his work as a literary critic, like Icarus's fall in W.H. Auden's "Musée des Beaux Arts," bounced right off my thick undergraduate skull. For me it was not an important success.

Likewise, I inquired not at all about the details of the $1.5 million grant that Christopher—as I think of him now—received from the Andrew W. Mellon Foundation around that time. That grant would go on to pay for my tuition and even a small stipend while I completed a master's degree in Editorial Studies. The stipend was modest, but the fact that students at the Editorial Institute were able to earn our MAs without taking on loans was little short of a miracle. That the respect and esteem in which Christopher Ricks—soon to be *Sir* Christopher Ricks—was held by his peers around the world was directly responsible for smoothing our paths at the start of our scholarly careers in this manner was, again, utterly unnoticed and unappreciated by me at the time.

Instead, here's what I *do* vividly remember: Christopher walking into class on what Wikipedia tells me must have been September 18, 2003, and announcing, "I turn seventy today and I feel like death." This statement scandalized me, because I was then twenty years old and had never seriously contemplated mortality before that moment. It puzzled me, too. He didn't *look* like death. He looked like someone brimming with life and good humor. Two decades later, he looks exactly the same to my eyes.

Another vivid memory: one weekend evening another graduate student and I were studying in the Editorial Institute library while, down the street, Bob Dylan played a concert at an arena on campus. Afterwards, Christopher must've needed to fetch something from his office and seen the light on in the library. Inside, he found Stephen Sturgeon and me, reading Ezra Pound and Wyndham Lewis and Betty Wahl. Christopher promptly handed us $40 and told us to get out of there. At the time, I would've been scarcely more astonished if he had handed us $1,000, if he had emptied out a whole wheelbarrow full of cash. A glass of wine and an appetizer at Eastern Standard in Kenmore Square! That was a big deal in those days!

Christopher Ricks hardly needs anyone to boast about his professional and academic accomplishments. And he is far too modest to enjoy me boasting about his human qualities here. But when I think of Christopher, his two great achievements—first, his remarkable contributions to literary criticism and scholarly editing; second, his magnanimity and the way that it pours out good things on anyone fortunate enough to be near him—are inextricably connected.

By magnanimity, I mean the word as Aristotle defined it. "His judgments are true," Aristotle writes of the "great-souled" man in the *Nicomachean Ethics*. "He is also open about his hating and his loving (for concealment implies fear, and shows less care for the truth than for one's reputation), and he talks and acts openly (for he is the sort to speak his mind, since he tends to look down on people, and tell the truth, except when being self-deprecating with ordinary people)."[1]

That's Christopher alright.

Here is another moment I remember: a prominent BU faculty member gave a lackluster lecture to second-year undergraduates in the Core Curriculum. Maybe it was just an off day. But I watched closely as Professor Ricks telegraphed his unmistakable displeasure and his growing, visceral impatience that John Keats's beautiful words ("beaded bubbles winking at the brim")—and a roomful of fourteenth-graders encountering the music of Keats for the first time—should be treated so shabbily. From my vantage point I could

---

1   Aristotle, *The Nicomachean Ethics*, trans. Christopher Rowe (Oxford University Press, 2002), 150–151.

not see Christopher's face. But the back of his head communicated quite enough.

Years later, when a crying baby interrupted Christopher's own lecture at Houghton Library, it was a very different story. Christopher stopped everything to express delight in the child's voice and presence, and to ensure that his mother knew how welcome both she and he were. That sort of thing happened regularly. Every once in a while, a former student would turn up at the Editorial Institute with a small child in tow and always, *always* the pair's arrival would be heralded with great joy. Years later, when my own child was born, a daughter named Evelyn Josephine, Christopher met her as a young toddler on Zoom. Afterwards, he told me it was clear that I had made Evelyn "confident of welcome."

I'm not sure I've ever received a more meaningful or wise compliment in my life. Often since I've wondered whether making other people "confident of welcome" is not only the ultimate aim of parenthood, but also of teaching. Perhaps even the aim of human existence itself. When I think back to those little ones with names like Dante who kept popping up at the Editorial Institute to disrupt our laudable pursuit of higher learning (as it seemed to me at the time), that may have been a lesson I learned rather late and from Christopher's own example.

A week ago I asked Evelyn what she likes best about Christopher Ricks. Instantly, she replied, "I like that he has a big teddy bear." For Christopher—the grandfather of several children around my daughter's age—has, indeed, always greeted her on calls with a stuffed animal friend to hand.

At last, it isn't lost on me what a gift Christopher Ricks is and has been, for me and for many others. Neither probability nor merit explains why a knight should have made my daughter smile, and it is impossible not to feel grateful.

As for Aristotle's other claim about the great-souled man, that "his judgments are true," it seems to me to capture the essence of what the Editorial Institute accomplished. There, Christopher and his co-founder Archie Burnett taught students to weigh and sift; to estimate and appraise; to select and decide; so that they and others might gain experience in recognizing and affirming the truth, which is often a great deal more complicated to discern and difficult to pin down than we are in the habit of acknowledging.

In practice, editorial studies are humbler than the preceding paragraph makes it sound. No one was walking around that beautiful brownstone on Bay State Road making grand pronouncements like, "My judgments are true." What we *were* doing was collating texts; finding and making lists of the resulting textual variants; and then painstakingly recording those variants in critical apparatuses with word-processing software that then as now was not designed with critical-apparatus construction in mind. We added appropriately informative, *not* interpretive, contextual annotation. In short, we were apprentices making scholarly editions of our chosen texts, whether the world wanted such editions or not, simply because Christopher and Archie believed that future generations ought to know how to do such things. Or at least be given the opportunity to know.

Have *you* ever collated a text? It involves comparing however many extant copies of a work there are, scanning them two at a time, eyes darting back and forth from one text to the other, roughly four words and accompanying punctuation at a glance (best I could ever do, anyway), and dutifully noting all possible changes. It was a slog at times. But the best words in the best order proved inexhaustible. Their shine, their resonance, never faded: even on a fourth read, even on a twelfth, my eyes would crinkle or widen involuntarily, the corners of my mouth would turn up or down, depending, in the presence of something sacred.

Another of the antiquated trades they taught at the Editorial Institute, however, turned out to be a bridge too far. Even when I was energetic and young and had everything to prove, indexing gave me the jimjams. In truth, so did Christopher's Bob Dylan listening parties, where he invited all comers to sit in his sunlit, book-lined office and detect minute changes to Dylan's lyrics in bootleg live performances. I went only once. But it warmed my heart that such listening parties were held weekly for a time: coffee and tea, silent people straining their ears for a moment then arguing about what they had heard, chairs pulled up around a stereo, everyone sitting alert and attentive and happy, buoyed along by a mix of curiosity, admiration, and love—for Christopher, for Bob Dylan, for the truth of what had, in any particular moment, been uttered.

Flipping through an old syllabus and folder of readings for *EI 501/701: The Theory and Practice of Literary Editing*, one finds an embarrassment of riches. Sheer superfluous goodness. Excerpts from Samuel Beckett's *Company*, Ben Jonson's "Love Restored," Percy Bysshe Shelley's "A Lament," Alfred Lord Tennyson's "Semele"; letters from Lord Byron and Henry James; manuscript facsimiles for some of the above—and that was just one Tuesday's class, "on intention." Week after week, considerations of emendation and errata, plagiarism, intellectual property and copyright, electronic editions, editing film, editing fragments, annotation, satire and blasphemy, and, my personal favorite, "neurotic oddities in editing" were placed before us in a kind of feast.

At, sadly, only infrequent intervals on these handouts, I recorded Christopher's *bons mots* as marginalia. Next to a creepy drawing in Tennyson's "Tithonus" manuscript: "A fascinating reminder of how weird poets are." On the final examination prompt for the end of the course: "This isn't an exam to prepare for; just use your wits."

Indeed, the throughline connecting these varied strands of critical inquiry may, in retrospect, have been Christopher's unflagging conviction that people *have* wits and that they ought to be *put to use*. He has presented generations of students with a way of looking at both words and the world that is rooted in the strict, rigorous, and unrelenting application of human judgment to whatever is placed in front of one—and also a way of looking at the world with a gaze animated by humor, gratitude, and love. A greatness, as Aristotle puts it, of soul.

Often enough, Christopher's *joie de vivre* and what one might call his *joie de penser* meant that even the wrong words in the wrong order, or the somewhat right words in the somewhat right order, could become a source of delight and instruction. Tennyson's exquisite poem and his clumsy, baffling drawing alike both repay close, sustained attention. Anything with human or divine fingerprints on it may well be a bottomless mystery.

It has been twenty-two years since I sat in EI 501 as an undergraduate and began the long, slow process of facing up to my own inadequacy in matters of perception, cognition, expression, diligence. It's not always easy or pleasant to start sounding the depths of one's own ignorance, nor to begin trying to dispel those blank spaces within and without by learning to notice, to deliberate, to decide. But somehow Christopher has always made using one's wits seem like great fun. He makes it seem like such a compelling and joyful thing to do that, once you realize you *have* wits, it becomes impossible to imagine forfeiting their use ever again.

Perhaps there's a message to shout from the rooftops in the Year of Our Lord 2025, as smarts are allegedly, gleefully transferred to phones and intelligence to a variety of artifices: *The present moment, howsoever it finds you, isn't an exam to prepare for; just use your wits.*

Christopher and I disagree on matters of God and the eternal. But we agree about the necessity of faith. In a lecture on "Eliot on Faith" given sometime around Christmas 2008, Christopher quoted the father of the stricken, mute, convulsive child in Mark's Gospel: "Help thou mine unbelief" (9:24). It was from that lecture, rather than any homily, that I first learned faith without doubt and trial is no faith at all. His memorable formulation, as recorded in an undated entry in my commonplace book: "The Christian who *knows* there is a God is destined for a particular circle of the hell I don't believe in." Hopefully I, who *trust* but do not *know*, will avoid such a fate.

Christopher and I agree, too, that idols are worthless and best smashed. St. Augustine writes of the simultaneous "necessity of ignorance" and the "necessity of judgment" in matters of law.[2] Though not omniscient, even those of us who don't preside over courtrooms must decide, must make decisions all day long, to do one thing and not another, and to do it this way and not another. It's no good replacing one false representation of reality, one idol, with another. (From Christopher's lecture on plagiarism: "I shall argue that this dishonesty is too often exculpated by dishonesties, by evasive banter, and by slippery history."[3])

Too often today we are encouraged—in universities, in homes, in our leisure time, at work, and maybe other places besides—to dart from presumption to presumption, from prejudice to prejudice, from one half-conscious and half-hidden love or hate to another, our minds preoccupied with reputation and negligent of truth. Any ability on my part to resist such temptations toward unthinking cowardice or false faith is owing, in no small measure, to Christopher Ricks. The Editorial Institute is where I and many others learned to be faithful in a very little—faithful down to a single comma, a single letter of the alphabet—and where, in matters of gratitude and grace, we were given so much.

Cassandra Nelson

---

2   St. Augustine, *The City of God (De Civitate Dei): XI–XXII*, trans. William Babcock (New City Press, 2013), 361.
3   *ATTP*, 220.

Call Me Prufrock

"At night the adjectives come back, *en masse*"
Roland Barthes[1]

Christopher Rick's' book *T.S. Eliot and Prejudice* (1989) is full of shrewd, subtle, troubling writing and I have long taken a particular section of it as a parable of critical hubris. Of prejudice precisely, meaning preconception, bias, a set of assumptions, and above all preemptive judgement too sure of its ground. Ricks draws our attention to one of the sources of the unstable, dangerous life of the word: "the components of 'prejudice': the premature prefix and the ill-judged judging."[2] The section I'm thinking of is a reading (and a reading of readings) of two lines from "The Love Song of J. Alfred Prufrock." A larger framing of the topic would include roads not taken and the sound of purely mental footsteps. When we learn, as we shall in a moment, that we are to pay equal attention to prejudice and to "what will be called prejudice," we know we are in for an interesting ride. "Will be" (as distinct from "is" or "has been") is eerily exact.

The lines appear twice in the early parts of the poem:

> In the room the women come and go,
> Talking of Michelangelo.

John Crowe Ransom calls the repetition a refrain and Ricks quickly challenges the definitional ground.

> Those two lines . . . had indeed seemed set to be the poem's refrain, and then the poem refrains from them, most unexpectedly; the two lines come and go, and then come and go, to come no more in all the further ninety-five lines [12-13].

Ransom also thinks the poem treats the women "with some contempt" and asks, "how could they have had any inkling of that glory which

---

1   *Roland Barthes by Roland Barthes*, translated by Richard Howard, (Hill and Wang, 1977), 115.
2   *TSEP*, 81. Further references are taken up into the text.

Michelangelo had put into his marbles and his paintings?"[3] Ricks
identifies a consensus that perhaps doesn't surprise us enough, as
other critics line up with Ransom. Grover Smith writes "And the
women meanwhile are talking, no doubt tediously and ignorantly, of
Michelangelo."[4] Helen Gardner alerts us to "the absurdity of discussing
his giant art, drifting through a drawing-room . . . ."[5] Gardner also
includes a disapproval of the women's "high-pitched feminine voices,"
inviting Ricks to suggest that the women's voices, "for all we hear,
could be as honourably gruff as those of a stereotyped woman don"
[16].

What is happening here? Well first, as Ricks says, the critics are
not recognizing the element of prejudice in their reading. "Their
sense of the lines . . . is . . . not therefore to be discounted but not
to be counted upon" [14]. Or to adopt Ricks's marvelous gloss on
the word "Observations" in the title of the book in which "The Love
Song" appeared, they are neglecting "the claims of the perceptive eye
against those of the wise mind" [1]. They know what the poem says,
but they have forgotten that it doesn't "say" it. And they might miss the
irony in the word "wise."

And then a host of interesting formal properties, like rhythm,
rhyme, grammar, and how to pronounce foreign names, is lost in the
rush to a desired meaning. It is quietly striking that in the poem the
women earn no adjectives, that their talk is only talk (not "prating"
or "prattling," as Rick suggests it could be [16] and no adverbs target
their behavior). Ricks makes an eloquent plea for a practical critical
response to this work and many others that mean a lot and seem to say
little.

Against Kenner's use of the phrase "our feeling," he says

> I wish to urge the claims not only of a plural (our feelings about these
> women), but also a further range of feeling: our feelings . . . not only about
> what we have been moved to feel, but about how we have been moved [20].

Eliot said that he often felt "The Love Song" was a swan-song, and in
thinking about why it wasn't, Ricks takes us a long way into Eliot's
later work, and indeed into whatever moral life we may think we have.
The following sentence is not easy to parse, but it is very precise. "One

---

3   In *T.S. Eliot: The Man and His Work*, ed. by Allen Tate (Delacorte Press, 1971),
      139.
4   Grover Smith, *T.S. Eliot's Poems and Plays* (University of Chicago Press, 1956), 18.
5   Helen Gardner, *The Art of T.S. Eliot* (Faber, 1968), 84.

reason is the continuity of the poem with Eliot's creative sense of not only the perils of prejudice but the indispensabilities of what will be called prejudice" [22]. Eliot's poems, Ricks says near the end of his section called "Prejudice," contextualize their contents in a way that "has the effect of implicating the reader in just such 'prejudicing strategies' as are at work within the world of the poem . . .." They engage both prejudice itself and our attitudes to it.

> It is this which makes Eliot's poems grow in interest and stature so that they incriminate both such prejudice as does not acknowledge that it would be justified only in an emergency *and* such credulity about prejudice (as to its easy distinguishability from indispensable prejudgment, for instance) as constitutes a prejudice about prejudice [121].

Michael Wood

Geoffrey Hill "On Education"

None of these three pieces by Geoffrey Hill was intended for publication, although two were delivered publicly. In each of them, Hill addressed an audience which he had no special reason to suppose would be sympathetic to the study, or even the reading, of literature. Such addresses, and the very question of address, were topics recurring throughout his critical writings. He was keenly interested in the strains that are exposed when a literary expert, a poet or philosopher or other writer, attempts to address a lay audience. On several occasions, for example, he argued that William James and Josiah Royce, in their non-professional writings, became estranged from their own intelligence, succumbing to the pressures exerted by the unspoken pledges that constitute public decorum. T.S. Eliot's public addresses and later poetry became a kind of negative touchstone for Hill, supposed instances of dereliction by failing to challenge the terms of the approbation one foresees. The first address below was made to high school students and teachers, the second piece was directed to university administrators, and the third was a lecture delivered to the top scholarship students in all fields of study at Boston University.

Kenneth Haynes

On Learning (1989)[1]

Any small boy who, reigning supreme in the kingdom of his own daydream, has woken to the dread realization that he has lost his dinner-money or his bus-pass, may be said to have received a lesson in the rudiments of philosophy or indeed of theology. In a brief but enduring moment he perceives that he simultaneously inhabits two distinct domains: one in which he seems to be the king of his own inner landscape, and another in which he is seen as a rather miserable little specimen in the landscape of another person, possibly a person in authority. Such moments, once experienced, are not only *not* forgotten, but are likely to recur at traumatic moments throughout life. It is for this reason that I cannot subscribe to that currently fashionable phrase that speaks of the "generation gap." How can there be any such thing as a "generation gap," when we all necessarily and individually exist, by a simple inexorable process, within a continuum of hours and days and years in which the child is father of the man in such a haunting way? That there are tragic, indeed hideous differences of belief and attitude and allegiance rampant in contemporary society I would be the last to deny; but to attribute such differences to the mere accident of birth-days and birth-years seems to me to be fanciful in the extreme. Let us, if you like, talk about a sensibility gap, where people can of different generations can be allies, and people of the same generation at odds with each other. There was an undeniable sensibility-gap between Sir Thomas More, who laid his head on the block for the sake of an unflinching principle, and his erstwhile master, Henry VIII, who laid other people's heads on the block at the dictates of his own immediate whim. There was a sensibility-gap, shall we say, between Henry Ford and George Santayana. Henry Ford, of whom everyone has heard, said once that "History is bunk." George Santayana, of whom very few have heard, said once that "Those who do not remember the past are

---

1   Address to Bromsgrove County High School. I have supplied brief notes and
    short titles for the pieces.

condemned to relive it." The irony is that Ford *made* history, of a kind, and we, of necessity, inhabit it. It may be a half-truth to say that we are the historical creatures of a man who despised history, but there are enough grains of truth in that half-truth to stick. Faced with such a world we are faced with something that philosophers call the I-It domain; and our human endeavour, through our relationships, our family life, friendships, religious belief, political allegiance, response to natural beauty, to literature, to painting, to music, is to transform the I-It world into the I-Thou sphere of relationship. I left one term out of that catalogue in order to emphasise it the more: education. It would be a large, but not wholly unjustifiable claim to suggest that one of the prime aims of education is to *e-ducare*, to lead forth, the spirit from the I-It into the I-Thou kingdom.

At the same time it would be sentimental and indeed a little hypocritical to pretend that education has always been, throughout its long history, a purely liberating force. There is education into servitude as well as education into freedom. And those little Board School children of the late 1870s may well have wondered, as they chanted their three Rs, wherein their alleged new freedom lay. This did not prevent such children, such men and women, young Bromsgrovians of a century ago—like my dear grandmother, to whose memory I am proud to pay public homage in this town where she lived and died—from leading lives of dignity and purpose and value. But at what cost to themselves in toil and attrition which they might well have been spared. So it would ill become me, thinking of those courageous, careworn lives, to speak lightly or idly of the material advantages and the increased opportunities for personal betterment which our contemporary society offers to a substantial proportion of its citizens. Of course we can, with reasonable good faith, offer our young people a future of opportunity and self-fulfilment denied to all but a tiny minority even half a century ago. I say only this: do not let us confuse true advancement, which is most often an arduous, tentative thing, with the empty rhetoric of incessant progress. Much of the overconfident verbiage of the sixties has already a dated, somewhat pathetic air.

Some of the most releasing pages on the aim and function of education—I would not expect them to command universal assent, but they have helped me—are to be found in a brief essay by the French Jewish writer Simone Weil, who died in 1943 at the early age of thirty-four. In her short "Reflections on the Right Use of School Studies," she wrote:

If we concentrate our attention on trying to solve a problem of geometry, and if at the end of the hour we are no nearer to doing so than at the beginning, we have nevertheless been making progress each minute of that hour in another more mysterious dimension. Without our knowing or feeling it, this apparently barren effort has brought more light into the soul.

This essay seems to have been written in April 1942. I entered this school in September 1942, to begin my own long purgatorial encounter with mathematics (physics, chemistry, biology, woodwork). At mathematics I was so bad as to be, in an inverted way, perfect. I was the perfectly bad student of mathematics. My algebraic equations were so illogical as to acquire their own surrealist logic; my theorems were like the sketch-plans of some awe-inspiring catastrophe. Despite the devoted care of my instructors, I could not conceal from myself that I was, so far as maths was concerned, a rather miserable little specimen. And of course I suffered. I did not belong to that world and therefore, to some extent, I felt I did not belong to myself. And yet, how strange, all that time, the words which might have consoled me were in existence and I did not know of them. How could I? Written in the year that I entered this school they appeared first in print in the year that I left it. But perhaps if I had seen those words in 1942, I would not have understood them. Perhaps it was right for them and for me that it took so long for me to discover them.

I have said that, in its long history, education has not always been a purely liberating force. I have also spoken approvingly of the importance of self-realisation and of the advancement of the I-Thou relationship. And you may well wonder: do I stand here as an advocate of self-expression at all costs, of doing-your-own-thing regardless? I hope it will have become apparent, from what I have already said, that I am no advocate of such clichés. I disown them (a) because they are clichés and (b) because my respect for Weil's argument forbids me to admire something which she would have deplored. Weil does not say: if you have extreme difficulty with (let us say) maths or English literature, drop the books in the trash-can, and your soul will blossom. She says, if you are having a very rough time with maths or English literature, give attention to what may seem to you personally a hopeless and arid cause, and your spirit will blossom when you least expect it. I do not like to see the art to which I am personally dedicated, the art of poetry, which is as rigorous as the art of mathematics, currently associated with the cult of instant blossoming or a merely trendy self-expression.

I evoked in the opening sentence of this talk a little daydreaming boy with no dinner-tickets. It was a fair description of a true emotion, but I would not therefore suggest that it should be one's aim in life to daydream and lose one's possessions. When we go to a boy or girl and say "The prison-doors are open: be yourself," we need to be very careful that what is released is a true selfhood and not vapours of an unrealizable daydream. And perhaps the real wickedness of the mass-media world of communication entertainment is that it confuses, perhaps unintentionally, perhaps wilfully, these two states. We are sold daydreams in the name of selfhood; and it would be difficult to think of any sector of our national life which is untouched by that falsity.

Of course there can be no easy recourse to the notion of traditional standards and values. We all know that some people are not to be trusted with such powerful concepts as traditional standards and values. Where they should be resolute, they are merely obstinate and inflexible. Their appeal to traditional values is just another way of saying "I do not wish to be disturbed." But the fact that some people cannot be trusted with them does not invalidate the values in themselves.

To ask these questions about order is not to be an advocate of permissiveness. Permissiveness is a parody of true freedom. The world we inhabit is one which has swung too often between the extremes of repression and permissive daydream; and of course the one exacerbates and excites the other. Perhaps it is a legitimate function of education not only to point to that exercise of the disciplined imagination, which is the arduous middle way between the easy extremes of repression and license, but also to preserve the memory of those human beings who could, and can, be trusted with the all-important concepts of order and freedom. In his essay "Tradition and the Individual Talent," T.S. Eliot wrote these words:

> Someone said: "The dead writers are remote from us because we *know* so much more than they did." Precisely, and they are that which we know.

Geoffrey Hill

On Teaching (c. 1997)[1]

I have been teaching for more than forty years and would be hard put to say that I have a philosophy of teaching. I do, however, have a method, or methods, arrived at through trial and error. My teaching has changed over the years, and continues to change, perhaps never more than in the nine years since I came to Boston University. Some things, however, have remained the same, and they are to be found in the area where method and goal join together. My method is to pay attention to the text under discussion and to every word my students might have to say about it. If they use a turn of phrase I happen to agree with strongly, or with which I happen to disagree, I ask them to consider the implications of their response and to incorporate what they discover in the group discussion. I ask them to consider the possibility that being able to listen to your own words may be a necessary stage towards the humility appropriate to the task of listening accurately to other people's words.

I am continually reminded of R.L. Nettleship's dictum: "the consciousness which we express when we have found the 'right word' is not the same as our consciousness before we found it; so that it is not strictly correct to call the word the expression of what we meant before we found it."[2] It so happens that in class discussion I am as much a learner as a teacher; I feel constantly an obligation and a desire to extend and deepen my knowledge of the public contexture in which the personal utterances we are studying took shape. Every student contribution to discussion, if offered with good will, must be treated with the utmost courtesy. There are ways of pulling the peripheral or tangential comment into the center for a debate. No idea need go to waste.

My thinking from day to day, as I acquaint myself with authors and texts I have not read before, reread texts I have known all my

---

1   From a report prepared for administrative review at Boston University.
2   Richard Lewis Nettleship, *Philosophical Lectures and Remains*, ed. by A.C. Bradley and G.R. Benson, (Macmillan, 1897).

life, finds its way into classroom discussion; it is in the classroom that I hear the idea "sounding" for the first time. My students test and temper my thinking; to a large extent I judge the value of my critical perceptions by my ability to articulate and defend them in my classes and seminars. To that degree, my students and I are engaging in the same enterprise. What I offer and expect from them is essentially the same as what I offer and expect from myself: a sustained act of attention. For this reason I am not tempted to make a topic more appealing by proffering "accessibility." What we read is always still to some degree undiscovered country for me. I ask of my students what Coleridge asked of the subscribers to a journal which he founded and edited: he said that he required "the attention of my Reader to become my fellow-labourer."[3]

Geoffrey Hill

---

3   Samuel Taylor Coleridge, *The Friend*, ed. by Barbara E. Rooke, (Princeton University Press, 1969), part 1, 21 (Vol. 4 of *The Collected Work of Samuel Taylor Coleridge*).

On the Study of Literature
and Language (c. 2000)[1]

R.R.K. Hartmann and F.C. Stork, in their *Dictionary of Language and Linguistics* (1972), describe "linguistic semantics" as the study of "meaning more in terms of the connexions between speech acts and the physical and intellectual environment of the speaker."

If you understand "connexions" to mean that public and private speech is determined by the physical and intellectual environment of the speaker, then I am not semanticist because I am not a determinist. I do not think that individual works are written by the Zeitgeist or by the peer group or dictated by the environment in which you grew up, or failed to grow up. Individual works are created, for the most part, by individual men and women who merit praise for their achievements and who ought to bear the censure for their failure. If you understand "connexions" in the sense of contingent forces that will unavoidably put pressure (of great variability) on each individual intelligence, imagination and conscience, without in any way overriding or extinguishing the exercise of individual intelligence, imagination, conscience, then I think I may describe myself as a linguistic semanticist, adding at once that linguistic semantics, so understood, go back a long way: at least to the mid-seventeenth century and the work of Thomas Hobbes (*Leviathan*, 1651) and probably further, to Augustine or earlier.

I have been researching, during the past twenty years or so, the interrelation of theological, political, and literary language in England (and in a limited way in the United States) from the start of the Lutheran revolution in the early sixteenth century to the present day. The principal papers which I have published in various places since 1991, particularly in the *Times Literary Supplement*, are variously committed to an investigation of material (speech acts in the context

---

1   Lecture to Trustee Scholars, Boston University.

of physical and intellectual environments) somewhat cryptically referred to as "Words, Contexture, and other Circumstances of Language" in the subtitle of my book *The Enemy's Country* (1991). I took those seven words straight out of Hobbes, though from a smaller and less celebrated treatise than *Leviathan*. I take Hobbes' words to mean, within a seventeenth-century register of inference and implication, very much what Hartmann and Stork in 1972 summed up as "the connexions between speech acts and the physical and intellectual environment of the speaker." It is difficult, I concede, to determine an exact picture of Hobbes' word "contexture" (whereas "other circumstances of language" may be understood as extrinsic, that is "Due to external circumstances; not inherent or essential; accessory, adventitious"). As with his contemporaries, Hobbes' term "contexture" applies both to the continuity or contiguity of things and to the structure and composition of mental artifacts. One could, in seventeenth-century educated England (an extremely compact environment compared to the public domain of the intellect at the end of the twentieth century) refer to "certain Fortuitous Concretions and Contextures of Atoms," or to "a regular Contexture of continued Policy," or to the "Contexture of sentence with sentence." In these three citations, chosen by the *Oxford English Dictionary*, the word "contexture" was thought adequate to cover both chance ("certain Fortuitous Concretions and Contextures of Atoms") and design, including grammatical construction ("Contexture of sentence with sentence").

I pause at my use of the word "adequate" in order to observe that the adequacy or inadequacy of words in such circumstances cannot be separated from the adequacy or inadequacy of individual human capacity to take, or to fail to take, the strain of what I, following Hobbes, called "contexture" and what Hartmann and Stork referred to as "the connexions between speech acts and the physical and intellectual environment of the speakers." The *Oxford English Dictionary* preserves at least one linguistic-contextual crux dating from the middle years of the seventeenth century. In the second edition of the dictionary, the word "sensuous" is introduced by the following editorial note: "Apparently invented by Milton, to avoid certain associations of the existing word *sensual*."[2] It also notes the lack of attestations for

---

2   The third, online edition of the *Oxford English Dictionary* is more explicit about "certain associations," writing instead "Apparently coined by Milton in an attempt to avoid the sexual connotations of *sensual*."

the word in the seventeenth and eighteenth centuries, apart from Milton (and Samuel Johnson's dictionary). It awaited Coleridge to be re-introduced in 1814.

To see what Milton has done, look up "sensual" in the *Oxford English Dictionary* (2nd edn, 1989). Until Milton's invention, as we suppose, of "sensuous" in 1641, the word "sensual" was a semantic sign meaning

> 1a: "Of or pertaining to the senses or physical sensation; sensory"
> 1b: "Perceptible by the senses"
> 3: "Of appetites and pleasures: Connected with the gratification of the senses
> 3a: "In neutral use: Sensuous, physical"
> 3b: "In pejorative use, implying the notion of something base or vicious. Now often, Lewd, unchaste."

On the basis of the evidence assembled by the *Oxford English Dictionary*, speakers and writers from the mid-fifteenth century until Milton found that the word covered both neutral and pejorative uses. Why is it Milton who first (so far as we know) sensed the word's inadequacy to the double task, or felt its inadequacy so keenly, that he found he needed two words, while around him—and for a century and a half after him—speakers and writers continued to manage to their satisfaction with the one term "sensual"?

I suggest that Milton found the use of the one word insupportable precisely because his religious, ethical, and political thought was fixed for a very great part of his creative life on that narrow, sometimes barely perceptible line across which the innocent, licit apprehension of the world through the senses shades into the use of the senses to enjoy illicit gratification through debauchery. This, we may say, is the line crossed by Adam and Eve in Book IX of *Paradise Lost*. It is the line *not* crossed by the character called "The Lady" in Milton's earlier work, the aristocratic masque (words with music and dancing) that goes by the name *Comus*. The Lady represents all that Milton invests in that idea, which rings so strangely in our twenty-first-century ears, of "the sage / And serious doctrine of Virginity" (ll. 786-7). Comus, the presiding genius of anarchic or vicious permissiveness, pleads with a powerful seductive eloquence for a freedom which Milton, with the use of theatrical symbolism, shows to be in truth bondage: Comus is Circe's child and, like her, changes human beings into brutish forms, even while they, his victims, believed themselves to be "more comely than before":

> And all their friends, and native home forget
> To roule with pleasure in a sensual stie (ll. 76-7).

If we ask why Milton found it necessary to invent "sensuous" for innocent or neutral senses, when so many before and after him found "sensual" entirely adequate for both neutral and pejorative use, the vehemence of these two lines is probably the most cogent answer to the question. Once you have "heard" them with the mind, not simply with the ear but through the ear, the negative force is so locked into the word that for Milton (and in an oblique sense for us reading Milton, reading Milton's mind) it ceases to be a term of convenience. It is drawn into one moral regiment and finds itself facing its erstwhile accommodating sibling across a line of demarcation, a line of confrontation.

I have deliberately cast my metaphor in an archaic form, as if in Milton's hands, if no one else's, "sensuous" and "sensual" had come to push of pike in some skirmish of the English Civil War, in order to stress that that was how Milton, to a great extent, saw the connection between speech acts and the physical and intellectual environment of the speaker (though he would probably reject our linguistic jargon).

Two words, etymologically unrelated but semantically associated, "liberty" and "licence", are also opposed to each other by Milton: "Licence they mean when they cry libertie" (Sonnet XII); but in this case, unlike his "sensuous"/"sensual" confrontation, his distinction derives from ancient authority by way of Machiavelli, as J. S. Smart pointed out in his edition of Milton's sonnets. "The distinction between *Liberty* and an irregular and pernicious freedom called *Licence* was familiar to Roman political thought," he wrote, giving examples of the antithesis from Cicero and Livy.[3] Machiavelli's *Istorie fiorentine* was translated into English by the courtier Thomas Bedingfield in 1595 as the *Florentine History* and dedicated to Sir Christopher Hatton, one of the chief councillors to Queen Elizabeth. In his translation, the exordium to Book IV begins:

> All Cities (and chiefly they which be well governed under the name of Commonweales) doo often alter their state and government: not by meanes of libertie and subjection (as many imagine) but by meane of servitude and lycentiousnesse. For onely the name of libertie is honoured of the people, who are the ministers of lycentiousnesse, and servitude still sought for by

---

3   John S. Smart, *The Sonnets of Milton* (Maclehose, Jackson and Co., 1921), 68-9.

the Nobilitie: so as either of them do studie not to subject themselves, either to lawes or men.[4]

This is paraphrased by Smart:

> Machiavelli argues that true liberty exists only in a state in which good laws and good order are firmly established; but such states are rare; and most Republics alternate between servitude and licence. The name of liberty is used alike by the ministers of licence, who are the popular party, and by those of servitude, who are the nobles, both desiring to escape from obedience to laws and rulers.

Of all late sixteenth- and seventeenth-century semantic cruces, I would rate the liberty-license mêlée one of the most significant, in that it is rhetorically effective in suggesting a resemblance between public and so-called private behaviours. Comus attempts to seduce the Lady by proffering licentiousness in the guise of the moral freedom which, if she had succumbed, would have revealed its true tyranny; his seductive eloquence is resisted by the Lady who opposes to his licentiousness the knowledge of true liberty which can only be preserved by self-containment (continence).

The manner in which language, the language of ethics and the emotions, is integrated with the language of ethics and politics in such works manifests itself in a style of wit which is incomprehensible, almost, to the intelligence of the early twenty-first century:

New Presbyter is but *Old Priest* writ large.

Milton again, the final line of the sonnet "On the new forces of Conscience under the Long Parliament." It is an etymological, one might say a semantic, joke. "The words *Presbyter* and *Priest* are both derived from πρεσβύτερος, the latter being the contracted form through the French."[5] So "presbyter" literally is "priest" writ large—it is larger (longer) by three letters (nine to the six of "priest").

A historical-political-semantic paraphrase of the line would take longer to spell out. Essentially, the Presbyterians, the victors in the first stage of the English Civil War fought between Royalists and Parliamentarians, are now revealed as even worse tyrants than the "priests" of the Royalist Church of England whom they had supplanted. They are "writ large" as persecutors as they are "writ large" in taking up more room on the page. This ability to be at once

---

4   Machiavelli, *The Florentine History*, tr. Thomas Bedingfield, (D. Nutt, 1905), 177.
5   Smart, *Sonnets of Milton*, 132.

precise and broadly suggestive, erudite and vulgar, is a quality of the mind scarcely existing in our own time.

It is a quality of intelligence, not so much *logopoeia* ("the dance of the intelligence among words") as the pacing and tracking of the intelligence through words, which is manifest even in those masterful arguers of that century, Bacon, Hobbes, to some extent Dryden, even Locke, all of whom put the case that English oratory needed to be purged of semantic over-proliferation, deliberated and undeliberated obscurities, unnecessary ramifications of style, vices which, these proponents argued, had been inherited from the degenerate Latin of the late medieval "Schoolmen," the pre-Reformation Catholic Scholastic philosophers and theologians. Hobbes is particularly sardonic at the Scholastics' expense: "When men write whole volumes of such stuffe, are they not Mad, or intend to make others so?" (*Leviathan*, part one, chapter 8) But the power of Hobbes's scorn is itself conveyed by and through the arts of eloquence. And notwithstanding that he saw himself as the absolute antagonist of Milton, Hobbes's style of reasoned and founded contempt works not dissimilarly to Milton's rhetoric of contempt:

> men give different names, to one and the same thing, from the difference of their own passions: As they that approve a private opinion, call it Opinion; but they that mislike it, Haeresie: and yet haeresie signifies no more than private opinion; but has onely a greater tincture of choler. (*Leviathan*, part one, chapter 11)

The whole pitch of this, entirely characteristic, passage is relatable to the semantics, the semantics of approval and disapproval. How is the value of a word determined, objectively or subjectively? Does "objectivity" have any effective status when religious and political issues are the matter of debate? Is Hobbes, in so objectifying the semantic consequences of subjective approval and misliking, evolving a finer semantics ("finer" in the sense of with more finesse), or is he merely expressing his own misliking, but with the kind of powerful and persuasive cynicism that some are able to derive from a species of self-knowledge?

I venture the suggestion that a significant number of semantic issues and questions are basically questions of intrinsic and extrinsic value, of simple and compound error, and of bad faith. Bad faith, or rather the semantics of bad faith, is the easiest to demonstrate at an elementary level; in the long term it proves to be both elusive and perplexing to follow through.

In 1529, the Erasmian reforming Catholic, Sir Thomas More, attacked the English Lutheran William Tyndale for tendentiousness in his 1526 translation into English of the New Testament. Tyndale was also Erasmian; he worked from Erasmus's new edition of the Greek New Testament. More argued that Tyndale had deliberately mistranslated crucial Greek words, rendering *presbyteros* not as "priest" but as "senior," *ekklesia* not as "church" but as "congregation," *agape* not as "charity" but as "love"; and that these mistranslations were all made in order to further the "damnable heresies" of "Luther and his felowes," as More calls them, among English readers. More cites Tyndale's literal word choices, but he neglects to point out that Erasmus himself, who remained loyal to the Catholic Church, in the Latin text facing the Greek in his edition of the New Testament, had anticipated Tyndale by translating *ekklesian* as "congregationem," and had added a note stating that he preferred "congregation" (*congregationem*) to "church" (*ecclesiam*) because "church" was liable to cause the ill-educated to think only of the building rather than of the "meeting of Christians." The Catholic editors of the modern Yale edition of the works of Thomas More scrupulously point out these details (*A Dialogue Concerning Heresies*, vol. 1, pp. 286-90 and vol. 2, pp. 680-3).

Where was More's faith in this? He was a devout son of the Catholic Church and died for his faith with great courage a few years later. But in his accusation that Tyndale mistranslated the Greek in order to pack the evidence in favor of Luther's "damnable heresies," was More writing out of simple ignorance, or error, in that he did not know that the loyal Catholic Erasmus had anticipated the Lutheran heretic Tyndale in using those same words; or was he writing out of a fully informed bad faith? More had praised Erasmus's translation, and they were on terms of intimate friendship. Moreover, he was a wide and deep reader across the whole range of political-theological writing during these years, as well as a trained and skilled disputant and apologist. We are forced back again upon a question at once elementary and insoluble. What is "bad faith"? Is it Tyndale's Lutheranism, as More alleged, or is it More's duplicitous defence of the One True Faith? That is, *if* the defence was duplicitous, and not simple error. So one treads the moral-semantic circle.

I am interested in "serious" contemporary music. (How much bad faith is embodied by my use of the word "serious," and by my putting it in quotation marks?) More than a decade ago, I was reading in *Tempo: A Quarterly Review of Modern Music* a review of a performance in Salzburg of Schoenberg's *Moses und Aron*. It was a laudatory review, and the reviewer praised in particular the producers' decision to present the narration and action as if the events took place during the Nazi terror. The production

> symbolized the persecution of the Jews by re-enacting some of the Nazi atrocities in a silent mime which preceded the opera. SS men rushed in, beat Jews, desecrated graves, and smashed up the giant Menorah, the candelabrum of Jewish religiosity, which dominated the stage (*Tempo*, no. 163, 50).

When I read it, I immediately thought that *Tempo* would have to apologize; and that if no one could see why they should, then that would be worse than the original offence. I was not surprised to find in the next issue of *Tempo* a distressed and bewildered editorial insert:

> It has been pointed out to us that the phrase "the candelabrum of Jewish religiosity" which appeared in [the] review of the Salzburg Festival production of *Moses und Aron* is open to interpretation in a pejorative, and therefore anti-Semitic sense. The Editors of TEMPO take this opportunity to state that the phrase was neither understood by them in that sense, nor was it so intended by [the reviewer]; and we apologize to any of our Jewish readers to whom it may have given offence (*Tempo*, no. 164, p. 45).

I think that their bewildered recognition that they had somehow said something that could give offence to their Jewish readers was absolutely genuine and that the words "neither understood by . . . nor intended" came straight from the heart. The crux is the word "religiosity" in the phrase "Jewish *religiosity*." As a gentile I would have been offended by the phrase "Christian *religiosity*." To me, as I read the review in 1987 in the United Kingdom, aged fifty-five, Midlands English born and bred, the word "religiosity" meant only one thing: the display of, the affectation of, religiousness; the pretence of religion; the outward gestures of religion conducted in a false or effusive manner. It clearly struck others among *Tempo*'s readership in precisely the way it struck me. But I have no doubt that to the reviewer and to the editorial board who passed it without a qualm, the word "religiosity" meant "Religiousness, religious feeling or sentiment," without any sense of a pejorative implication. Since my arrival in the United States in December 1988, I have heard the word used a few times a year, in Episcopal sermons, in academic lectures by distinguished scholars; I have noted it from time to time in learned articles and reviews; and not once, to the best of my recollection, have I heard "religiosity" used to in any way other than in the sense of genuine, sincere religiousness. The entry in the *Oxford English Dictionary* finds that the non-pejorative use is very old—it is first found in 1382 in the first Wycliffite translation of the scriptures—and continues to be in use. The pejorative sense is comparatively modern, first recorded in 1799, and well exemplified in 1829 by a phrase of Robert Southey, "A feverish state of what may better be called religiosity, than religion."

This question of the right reading of the word "religiosity" strikes me as precisely representing the nature of the connections between speech acts and the physical and intellectual environment of the speaker. Born in 1932 in a small town in the English Midlands, I had instilled into me (I have no idea how) the unshakeable intuitive acceptance that to speak of another person's religiosity, rather than of their religious feeling or practice, is to insult them. It is evident that such a response to the word is by no means unique to me, but it is not, as ten years ago I unreservedly believed it was, the general understanding among English or American English speakers that "religiosity" is a word that has only a pejorative sense.

The great *Oxford English Dictionary* in twenty volumes (2nd edn, 1989) is not a prescribing or proscribing work. It records impartially the vacillations, incertitudes, prejudicates of human thought and action as they are implanted or embedded, bedded down, in the speech-contexture, the linguistic medium. That "religiosity" should be both "religiousness, religious feeling" and "affected or excessive religiousness," since 1799 on parallel tracks, in some contexts clearly meaning the first and other contexts clearly meaning the second, speaks to me of a kind of wandering adumbration of bad faith, a confusion of contradiction at the heart of the process of expression and reception, of communication, that the semantics of one language have recorded, passively and actively, rather as the inked stylus on the old seismograph moved to record the measurable earth-tremors.

Geoffrey Hill

A Note on the Conclusion of *The Waste Land*

Except for the point, the still point,
There is only the dance. (66–67)

T.S. Eliot, "Burnt Norton"

I met Christopher Ricks over fifty years ago when he came to the University of Chicago to deliver a lecture that later became the chapter "Lies" in *The Force of Poetry* (1984). The day of his talk I joined him beforehand with a few of my fellow graduate students in English for a lunch at Hutchinson Commons. Within that admiring replica of the great room at Christ Church, Oxford, under the University of Chicago's bell tower modeled after Magdalen's, we encountered our own version of Eliot's time past meeting time future in a moment we did not, and could not, fully grasp. In one sense it was an encounter with the living history of our discipline and our prospects within it. In another, we were at table with a formidable agent of that history and discipline who proved to be genuinely curious about our scholarly interests and ambitions, however half-formed and vaguely wondering they might be. My friends and I had signed up to meet the speaker without much of an idea of how we would be received, or what we would say. Yet we were invited to speak by our visitor's keen openness. One of us quickly confessed her worry that she had arrived in the field of literary studies too late, after the most important scholarly work had been done. The history of the discipline weighed on her as she reached for a way to contribute. What was left to do? What were we now all doing? It was, to say the least, not the most scholarly question to ask on such an occasion. It was an attempt to open what by habit or anxiety it foreclosed. Whether we believed it was our leading question, it surfaced a collective doubt. My fellow graduate student was likely thinking of her still inchoate dissertation project, and feeling those intimations of insufficiency that harrow many graduate students' imaginations. She was also showing justified deference to the magnitude of what had already been accomplished in English scholarship and by the scholar in our midst. But what prompted her most of all, I believe, was our esteemed guest's extraordinary and unexpectedly welcoming attention to our halting efforts to converse.

Although I do not recall the greater part of the conversation that followed, I have never forgotten the manner or the weight of what Christopher Ricks said in his immediate reply. *You are new readers,* he told us, *and therefore in a unique position to contribute original observations and insights. There are others who want to hear from you.* He responded to what we said, or did not say, what we implied or feared. What developed from there was the kind of conversation we wanted to experience in our scholarship, our classrooms, and through the rest of our lives. In later decades, as our many academic environments became resistant to the spirit and substance of such mutually exploratory and deeply informative exchanges, we could return to the memory and spirit of that table at Chicago.

Reading Ricks's work, we are reminded that the nature of a poem, and the nature of great poetry, resists reduction even as the best work of interpretation, line by line, word by word, phrase by phrase, invites our greater attention to its sense and sensibility. Ricks reads the poet's making for the sweet and bitter fruits of close attention. To plodding schools of close readers, he offers refreshment and insight. In his focus on the thing made and its maker, including the elusive qualities that draw us deeper, *his* "sheer plod makes plough down sillion/ Shine." Hopkins' line in "The Windover" takes on new meaning. In the glow of this occasion of tribute, inspired in part by the encouragement Christopher Ricks provided me and my young friends more than fifty years ago and since, I here presume to plow a furrow of my own.

It is not at all a new thought to observe that in the "The Waste Land" Eliot deflects and attracts analysis. Ricks's readings turn on how the poem shifts its course and yet dwells in displacement, how it strangely surprises with lyrical release that is almost dispirited, and yet speaks through others, one or many, including in some fashion the poet himself, sometimes as though orphic in its ventriloquizing. Its allusions are often wandering ghosts that become haunting fragments. In its evocations, myths precipitate and crystallize anew. Vernacular swings between acts of humiliation and a bar's closing ritual give way to an aspiring plainness circling a Sanskrit chant—its wisdom deflected yet swirling by—then to a madman's raving, a sentence of deathly isolation, the whispered summons of a raging hero, and other evocations of noble debris. In this disintegration there is a makeshift yet provisioning recovery: "These fragments I have shored against my ruins."

Given this context, I am drawn toward a still relatively unnoticed set of lines (416-417) in the last section:

We think of the key, each in his prison
Thinking of the key, each confirms a prison
Only at nightfall, aethereal rumours
Revive for a moment a broken Coriolanus. (WL 414-17)

The first two lines have received the most attention, starting with Eliot's note referencing Dante's *Inferno* and the poet's encounter with Ugolino, a victim of his persecutor and his own hatred, a man condemned to starving with his children in a locked tower. These lines are followed by what might be an enlarging echo and association, despite the strange leap of phrasing and subject: the faint and nightly evocation of a "broken Coriolanus." The tragic Roman hero is whispered forth, trailing memories of his own self-enclosing hatred toward an ungrateful Rome. His once-famous name and story, here brought furtively into the poem by faint and unidentified, unreliable tales, reclaims a certain undefined authority. He, like Dante's victim, was imprisoned by his hatred, relenting only when his wife, mother, and son came forward to beg his mercy and his whole being breaks:

All bond and privilege of nature, break! (V.iii.25)

In Plutarch's life and Shakespeare's play, Coriolanus relents and makes peace, then falls victim to assassination by his anti-Roman allies.

Here again, the nature of Eliot's reference eludes a plodding scholar's gloss, as "The Waste Land" itself escapes it. Like voices coming and going, the aethereal rumors that admit him are neither certain nor dismissible. They occur only "at nightfall," when the light is going, during the hour of percipient dreams, perhaps of visions. The rumors are such that his example is unarticulated in the poem, and yet those same rumors are striking: they "revive a broken Coriolanus." In the poem's sensorium of distortions and echoes, the rumors intimate the possibility of recovery, perhaps of the hero's triumph along with the memory of his brokenness. And all this is "for a moment"—only for a moment and so a merely ephemeral instance, or is it only for a particularly charged moment in the sense that Coriolanus is an exceptional instance, revivable in some new sense, perhaps seconding the poem's turn toward a primordial Sanskrit chant: give, sympathize, and control?

Coriolanus indeed embodies that ideal, if imperfectly, in most of his speeches and actions after his submission to the family embassy. He negotiates a truce and a peace favorable to his allies that yet protects Rome from attack. He returns to the Volscians in assurance of his good faith with his anti-Roman allies. In his brokenness—his break from his ruthlessly martial past—he gives peace, shows his deep sympathy with the plight of his mother, wife, and son, and controls his notorious temper for the sake of a diplomatic settlement of the chronic conflict between Volscians and Romans. For his actions, Coriolanus expects fatal consequences from the Volscians, but Shakespeare focuses instead on the jealousy of the Volscian leader Aufidius, who takes advantage of old Volscian grudges to ensure Coriolanus does not supersede him. It is most immediately a personal grudge, not the treaty, which leads to Coriolanus's death. With a humiliating insult, Aufidius provokes the hero in order to unleash his temper and undo his life. The diplomatic accomplishment of the Roman-Volscian peace—doubly impressive because of the history and volatile temper of the man who brings it about—is as worthy of being remembered as it is momentary.

Coriolanus's legacy for the concluding stage of "The Waste Land" seems doubly apt because of his reputation as a hero who spoke truth to the ungrateful and dispiriting Roman rabble ("rabble" being Eliot's label for what he considered to be, in a sweeping generalization, modern democracy's often wayward masses).[1] The entire population of the poem and indeed its speaker seem to partake of the wasted land's illness. *Coriolanus*, for Eliot, presents in some sense a different world, artistically coherent and in Coriolanus's case suggestive of different human possibilities. The poet's famously contrarian assertion, made in the era of "The Waste Land's" composition, that *Coriolanus*, unlike *Hamlet,* is one of Shakespeare's greatest, most artful plays, should elicit more interest than it does.[2] For whatever reason, the play's completeness—its coherence, by Eliot's lights—made it a worthy recollection in modernity. It made the hero's brokenness an

---

1   " ... [T]he tendency of unlimited industrialism is to create bodies of men and women—of all classes—detached from tradition, alienated from religion, and susceptible to mass suggestion: in other words, a mob. And a a mob will be no less a mob if it is well fed, well clothed, well housed, and well disciplines." *The Idea of a Christian Society* (Faber, 1982), 21.

2   See "Hamlet and His Problems" in *Selected Essays* (Harcourt, Brace and Co., 1919).

ill-fitting yet haunting fragment of something that might be revivable in a time of waste.

Whatever the meaning of Coriolanus's brokenness, it haunts "only at nightfall." Or does the word *only* here mean, more colloquially, something like "except for": *except for* what happens at nightfall, when intimations of Coriolanus's revival come to the fore? And what is the meaning of that process of reviving? In Eliot's formulation, it is a furtive, ongoing action (it is only the rumors that "revive" it), not something completed. Yet in the moments of nightfall, rumors proverbially revive the undead ideas and ideals evoked by the broken hero.

Eliot's choice of verb in his surviving drafts provides an enticing if fragmentary history of revision. In Valerie Eliot's facsimile and transcript edition of the poem (page 78), the handwritten line shows three different choices working toward a particular idea:[3]

> Revive ~~the spirits~~ of
> ~~Repair/Restore for a moment~~ a broken Coriolanus
>   for a moment

The final, published version emerges from numerous changes in the verb and one restoration of the phrase "for a moment." (The facsimile edition misses the lining out of "the spirits," which I have restored here.) The result is the more compact and lucid line we know now:

> Revive for a moment a broken Coriolanus

In the handwritten draft Eliot has made at least four changes:

1. Replacing "Repair" with "Restore," over-writing the first word with the second in a way that retains the first two letters of the first;
2. Replacing "Restore" with "Revive;"
3. Eliminating "the spirits" and "for a moment;"
4. Re-inserting "for a moment" below the line to cancel change #3.

Most importantly, the changes in the verb move from relatively mechanical metaphors to the organic, perhaps also spiritual "Revive" and the notion of new life. If the poem had retained "the spirits" to make the phrase "Revive the spirits," that meaning might have been clearer. Rejection of the second choice of verb, "Restore," suggests

---

3   Valerie Eliot, ed. *T.S. Eliot*, The Waste Land: *A Facsimile and Transcript of the Original Drafts Including the Annotations of Ezra Pound* (Harcourt Brace Jovanovich, 1971).

the discarding of any idea as well of merely material or narrowly biological restoration. The poet is choosing to suggest a coming back to life, a reviving recovery from brokenness—in Coriolanus's case, a recovery, however momentary or doomed, from the brokenness of dishonor and death. Is this change "for a moment" or longer? The poet hesitated, left out the phrase, then returned to the tentative. Into this dispiriting and faintly enlivening predicament the poem summons the Sanskrit chant "give, sympathize, and control," in strained harmony with poetic glimpses of each command, broken by resistant voices. Coriolanus's broken control of Rome is momentarily set beside the "controlling hands" of an "expert with sail and oar" who might have won a lover's obedient heart but did not.

To the degree one seeks to read Eliot's poem from within, illuminated by scholarship though not presuming to see it from the heights of grandly presuming commentary, Eliot's editorial hesitations and revisions here offer an exemplum of "The Waste Land's" elusive and intriguing sense, as well as its method. Coriolanus's brokenness shadows forth the entire poem's wholeness: its fragment-shored ruins.

John Briggs

Eliotic Vexation in C.S. Lewis

C.S. Lewis's poetic response to T.S. Eliot's "The Love Song of J. Alfred Prufrock" captures what Christopher Ricks calls "the profound vexation which Eliot pristinely inspired."[1] Eliot's first book, *Prufrock and Other Observations* (1917), opens with a tranquil romantic scene before a strange simile disrupts the atmosphere:

> Let us go then, you and I,
> When the evening is spread out against the sky
> Like a patient etherised upon a table . . ..[2] (1-3)

Lewis responded to these lines in a 1954 poem widely known as "A Confession" but originally titled "Spartam Nactus,"[3] a Latin phrase that befuddled the editor of *The Collected Poems of C.S. Lewis: A Critical Edition*.[4] The phrase is an abridgment of *Spartam nactus es*, which appears in a Latin translation of the Greek playwright Euripides, though scholars point to Edmund Burke's *Reflections on the Revolution in France* (1790) as the intermediary link between Euripides and Lewis. Burke had used the Latin phrase to criticize the revolutionary impetus, which he considered hostile to true reform: "There is something else

---

1   *TSEP*, 197. Ricks proceeds to consider the example of Lewis's malicious remarks about Eliot in a 1935 letter to Paul Elmer More. See *TSEP*, 197-98. For further background and commentary, see Lee Oser, "Was C.S. Lewis a Christian Humanist?" *Christianity and Literature* 72.2 (June 2023): 193-207.

2   *The Poems of T.S. Eliot* [henceforth *PTSE*], 2 vols, ed. Christopher Ricks and Jim McCue, 1:5. All subsequent citations of Eliot's poetry refer to this two-volume edition. Line numbers are cited parenthetically.

3   Walter Hooper, in his editorial notes to Lewis's essay "The Idea of an English School" (orig. pub. 1939), annotates Lewis's use of the phrase *Spartam nactus es*: "This is a Latin translation of a fragment from Euripides's lost play *Telephus*. Agamemnon is speaking to Menelaus: 'Sparta has fallen as your portion (the phrase continues: *hanc exorna*)—therefore, it is yours to provide for.'" C.S. Lewis, *Image and Imagination*, ed. Walter Hooper, 328n14.

4   C.S. Lewis, *The Collected Poems of C.S. Lewis: A Critical Edition* [henceforth *CPCSL*], ed. Don W. King (Kent State University Press, 2015). All subsequent citations of Lewis's poetry refer to this edition. Line numbers are cited parenthetically.

than the mere alternative of absolute destruction, or unreformed existence. *Spartam nactus es; hanc exorna* [Sparta is yours; adorn her]. This is, in my opinion, a rule of profound sense, and ought never to depart from the mind of an honest reformer."[5]

Having glossed Lewis's Latin title, we may ask why he chose it. The one-sided answer is that Lewis was mimicking an aspect of Eliot's stylistic perversity, namely, his excess of foreign phrases. Eliot, in his landmark 1921 essay "The Metaphysical Poets," defended himself: "We can only say that it appears likely that poets in our civilization, as it exists at present, must be *difficult*."[6] In a riposte to the modernist poet's being *difficult*, Lewis was being difficult too. His alternate title, "A Confession," suggests the personal element in Lewis's literary counterattack:

> I am so coarse, the things the poets see
> Are obstinately invisible to me.
> For twenty years I've stared my level best
> To see if evening–any evening–would suggest
> A patient etherized upon a table.
> In vain. I simply wasn't able.[7] (1–6)

Met with Eliot's obscure comparison of an "evening" to a "patient etherized upon a table," Lewis poses as two parts dullard and one part dunce, constructing a less intellectual mask than Eliot's Prufrock. Where Prufrock's "table" rhymes with nothing, Lewis's "table" rhymes with "able"–a reactionary insistence on foursquare common sense. With Socratic guile, Lewis pleads his limitations, professing to be unpoetical and "coarse." But Lewis is no fool and he understands Eliot better than he lets on. He understands that Eliot's poem is a dramatic monologue, a genre that amplifies the question of the poet's relation to his persona. Likewise, Lewis understands Eliot's penchant for unusual conceits that evoke the metaphysical poets. Lewis doesn't dismiss Eliot's poem as gibberish, as if Prufrock were proposing that two plus two equals five. By recognizing Eliot's game and answering in kind, he sparks a serious conversation.

Behind his mask of naivete, Lewis rejects Prufrock's simile on philosophical grounds. Relevant is Lewis's *Abolition of Man* (1944), where Lewis observes that, in the modern world of "the aeroplane or

---

5   Edmund Burke, *Reflections on the Revolution in France*, ed. by Conor Cruise O'Brien, (Penguin, 1968), 266.
6   *CPTSE*, 2:381, Eliot's emphasis.
7   *CPCSL*, 388.

the wireless, Man is as much the patient or subject as the possessor." Man, Lewis explains, can be the "patient" who is acted upon, or he can be the one in possession of power, he who conditions or annihilates others. This dark choice is illuminated by a further comment from *The Abolition of Man*: "It is in Man's power to treat himself as a mere 'natural object.'"[8] For Lewis, Prufrock's simile puts man (the "patient") on the same table of operations as physical nature (the earth revolving on its axis), a level where force and matter join seamlessly to foreclose human freedom.

To clarify Lewis's point, let us take a closer look at Prufrock's simile. Prufrock's "patient etherised" is like the evening because (1) both are physically "spread out"; because (2) the "patient etherised" is not fully present to himself, inhabiting a liminal state of consciousness comparable to twilight; and because (3) the patient is, in an alarming reversal of the agency that Prufrock voices in his opening line ("Let us go . . .."), entirely subjected to physical and mechanical laws, like any other object in the universe of matter, including the earth. Being excellent Latinists, Eliot and Lewis were sensitive to the etymology of *patient*, which is cognate with *passion*, both deriving from the Latin verb *patior*, which, like all deponent verbs, is passive in form but active in meaning. The word *patient* thus opens realms of philosophical and theological inquiry.

Back to Lewis's poetical counterattack, where Lewis capitalizes on the early Eliot's signature debt to the French poet Jules Laforgue (1860-1887).[9] Eliot's Clark Lectures (1926) present Laforgue as a latter-day metaphysical poet whom "we can compare . . ., with very great differences, to Donne."[10] Lewis opens the third and last of his ten-line stanzas by quoting Laforgue's "L'hiver qui vient" ("The Coming of Winter"):

> Never has the white sun of a winter's day
> Struck me as *un crachat d'estaminet*.
> I am like that odd man Wordsworth knew, to whom
> A primrose was a yellow primrose, one whose doom
> Retains him always in the class of dunces,
> Compelled to offer Stock Responses . . .. (21-26)

Laforgue's line, *Un soleil blanc comme un crachat d'estaminet*, translates as "a sun white as spit in some cheap dive." Lewis, who, like Eliot,

---

8   C.S. Lewis, *The Abolition of Man*, 66 and 80.
9   For Eliot and Laforgue, see editorial commentary in *PTSE*, 1:355-61.
10 See *CPTSE*, 2:746.

began French as a boy, manages the tricky feat of keeping the onomatopoetic *crachat* and rhyming *estaminet* with "winter's day." A familiar maneuver, this rhyming of Laforgue's French with English: Eliot had done it himself in "Rhapsody on a Windy Night": "Regard the moon, / La lune ne garde aucune rancune . . .."[11] The reader must work hard to follow this war of wits, indicating that Lewis is fighting on modernist territory.

Deep behind enemy lines, Lewis fires off one final shot with the name of William Wordsworth (1770-1850), the greatest of the English romantic poets. The battle comes down to this: Eliot's modernism is a reaction against Wordsworthian romanticism; Lewis's counterreaction is a defense of it. The "odd man Wordsworth knew" is not a real person but Wordsworth's fictitious character Peter Bell. In the much-mocked poem of that name, Peter Bell is a barbaric "hawker of earthenware" whose raw view of life lacks poetry: a "primrose by a river's brim" is simply a "yellow primrose" and "nothing more." It carries no rich associations. By comparing himself to Peter Bell, Lewis again plays the "dunce." He plays it artfully, rhyming "dunces" with "Stock Responses."

Lewis's allusions show him aligning Eliot with Cambridge professor I.A. Richards (1893-1979), champion of Eliot, founding father of modern English studies, prominent atheist, and, in his skepticism toward custom and habit, a veritable anti-Burke. Lewis observes, "By a Stock Response Dr. I.A. Richards means a deliberately organized attitude which is substituted for 'the direct free play of experience.'"[12] Richards had connected Stock Responses to "critical traps."[13] Eliot befriended Richards, but Lewis stood his ground: "In my opinion such deliberate organization is one of the first necessities of human life, and one of the main functions of art is to assist it."[14] Accordingly, Stock Responses keep us from descending into the dehumanized terrain of physical objects ruled by physical laws: they guard against the abolition of man. Peter Bell, whose lack of civilizing habits eventually catches up with him, must learn to make the best of a tough world. He must adorn the bleakness of Sparta—no doubt with yellow primroses.

---

11 *PTSE*, 1:19.
12 C.S. Lewis, *A Preface to Paradise Lost*, 54-55. See also Ricks's brief summary of the disagreement between Lewis and Richards about "stock responses," *TSEP*, 88.
13 I.A. Richards, *Practical Criticism: A Study in Literary Judgment* (Routledge and Kegan Paul, 1929), 15.
14 Lewis, *A Preface to Paradise Lost*, 55.

He is an outcast who is transformed by a kind of shock therapy to learn to appreciate the wisdom of Nature. Wordsworth, a close student of Burke, would have appreciated Lewis's argument. For Wordsworth, capital "N" "Nature" was a seat of moral authority, not primal nature in the lower case, but a dwelling for our second nature, developed over the course of generations.

Lewis's vexatious response to Eliot reveals meaningful differences. Defending Stock Responses, Lewis hones a Burkean perspective where "deliberate organization" is hard to achieve and easily squandered. To Lewis, Richards's devotion to an ideal of artistic freedom invited a loss of freedom. Likewise, the Eliot of "Prufrock" was a poetic agent of destruction who went too far in his rejection of mental habits. From our own vantage point, we may warm to the argument, and respect its intensity, as a civilized conversation that is natural and necessary. Eliot to my mind needs no defending, but Lewis's attack is not unprincipled. Ever since Mnemosyne, the goddess of memory, gave birth to the Muses, bad poets have thought in clichés and good poets have dealt with them carefully, snapping us out of our doldrums, reawakening our sense of beauty and our appetite for life. But how do we distinguish good from bad, and what is the difference between meaningful avant-gardism and revolutionary bomb-throwing? In the decades after Eliot and Lewis, no one has answered these questions with greater discernment than Christopher Ricks.

Lee Oser

"You Talk Like That Without Meaning It":
Virginia Woolf and T.S. Eliot

"Missing trains is awful."
"Yes. But humiliation is the worst thing in life."
"Are you as full of vices as I am?"
"Full. Riddled with them."
"We're not as good as Keats."
"Yes we are."
"No: we don't write classics straight off as magnanimous people do."
"We're trying something harder."
"Anyhow our work is streaked with badness. Compared with them, mine is futile. Negligible. One goes on because of an illusion."
"You talk like that without meaning it."

This edgy, tense exchange could be a piece of dialogue from a modern play. In fact it's a conversation in a closed car between Virginia Woolf and T.S. Eliot, which took place on Sunday March 20th, 1921 and was recorded in her diary two days later, as follows:

We had Eliot to dinner on Sunday & went to Love for Love . . . Eliot & I had to drive in to Hammersmith in a taxi, having missed our train [from Richmond]. We passed through dark market gardens. "Missing trains is awful" I said. "Yes. But humiliation is the worst thing in life" he replied. "Are you as full of vices as I am?" I demanded. "Full. Riddled with them." "We're not as good as Keats" I said. "Yes we are" he replied. "No: we don't write classics straight off as magnanimous people do." "We're trying something harder" he said. "Anyhow our work is streaked with badness" I said. "Compared with theirs, mine is futile. Negligible. One goes on because of an illusion." He told me that I talked like that without meaning it. Yet I do mean it. I think one could probably become very intimate with Eliot because of our damned self conscious susceptibility: But I plunge more than he does: perhaps I could learn him to be a frog. He has the advantage of me in laughing out. He laughed at Love for Love: but thinking I must write about it I was a little on the stretch.[1]

---

1   Virginia Woolf [VW], *The Diary of Virginia Woolf* [Diary], edited by Anne Olivier Bell, with Andrew McNeillie, Volume II, (Hogarth Press, 1978) / (Penguin, 1981), 103, Tuesday 22 March 1921, writing of Sunday, 20 March. The entry is referred to in Robert Crawford, *Young Eliot: From St Louis to The Waste Land*, (Cape, 2015), 369-370.

At the Lyric in Hammersmith, where they went to see the Phoenix Society's production of Congreve's *Love for Love*, produced by the well-known direction Montague Summers, they encountered friends: these productions were fashionable cultural events. There was Virginia Woolf's husband Leonard. There was the Cambridge philosopher George Moore and his friend Eddie Marsh; Woolf's brother-in-law Clive Bell, dressed, Woolf noted, "as effectively as any beauty"; and Bell's lover Mary Hutchinson who said, flirtatiously to Eliot: "Tom, you must come and see the boat race." (Woolf noted: "Well, these women's emotions, which I don't trouble to write about, are amusing; not very serious in my case.") Also her sister Vanessa Bell with her lover Duncan Grant, "shabby as old moths." Virginia Woolf was reviewing the production for their friend Desmond McCarthy, editor of *The Statesman*. Her review, which put her "a little on the stretch" that night in anticipation, was part of her involvement in a network of 1920s literary journalism in which she and Eliot were both entangled.

She knew Congreve's play well. In the pre-war years, she and her friends had a play-reading society for which they read Jonson, Vanburgh, Milton, Ibsen, Dryden, Shakespeare—and, in 1908, Congreve's *Love for Love*. Virginia was the heroine Angelica, and Clive Bell was her lover Valentine, at a time when they were riskily flirting. Lytton Strachey, the pre-eminent gossip of the group, played Congreve's chattering man-about-town, Tattle.[2]

Her 1921 review of *Love for Love* echoes her conversation in the cab with Eliot. She takes pleasure in Congreve's robust, lively comedy: "so pleasant is it to shake out a good, wholesome laugh now and again." She likes Congreve's frank talk about love and money, and the confidence of the dialogue. His world "is a very small society, acquainted with each other's language so that the pellets of repartee which they are forever discharging fly straight, hit hard, and yet have about them an extraordinary distinction." She finds the play much "simpler" than any play would be nowadays, so it makes us feel as if we "breathe sea air and look for miles and miles into the distance."[3]

She wrote again about Congreve. In 1924, reviewing a biography of him by Bonamy Dobrée, she quoted his saying that Restoration Comedy "expressed . . . a desire to try new ways of living." In "Congreve's

---

2   Hermione Lee, *Virginia Woolf* [HL], (Chatto & Windus, 1996) / (Vintage Books, 1999), 248.

3   VW, "Congreve," 1921, *The Essays of Virginia Woolf*, edited by Andrew McNeillie, (The Hogarth Press, 1998), Vol. 3, 295-297.

Comedies" (1937), she admired again the "genius for phrase-making" and "lightning swiftness" of the dialogue: "It seems as if they have to reign themselves in, bursting with energy as they are, alive and alert to their finger-tips." She praised Congreve's lesson in "the discipline of plain speech . . . The phrase is always finished; nothing is left to dwindle into darkness, to sound after the words are over."[4] That's in shadowy contrast to her conversation with Eliot in the taxi long before, where meanings were left to dwindle into darkness, to sound after the words are over.

Eliot often mentions Congreve, and he too is interested in how Congreve's people speak. In "What is a Classic?" (1944), he calls him the writer of "a mature society"; in "Poetry and Drama" (1951), one of "our greatest prose stylists in the drama": "a speech by a character of Congreve . . . has . . . that unmistakable personal rhythm which is the mark of a prose style, and of which only the most accomplished conversationalists . . . show any trace in their talk."[5]

Love for Love is vitally concerned with saying what you mean. The characters talk about feigning, false and true speech, dissembling and speaking your mind. Finally the lovers give up on counterfeiting and speak true. Valentine says to Angelica, who has played word games with him throughout: "Let us think of leaving acting and be ourselves." At the play's end, he says: "I have done dissembling now."[6]

By contrast, how much could Woolf and Eliot "be themselves"? They lived in a world where they needed to watch their words. The little group of theatre-goers watching *Love for Love* might have recognized themselves on the stage in seventeenth-century costume. There is Bell, dressed like a foppish Restoration beau. There is the clever, sexy woman-about-town Mary Hutchinson, involved with several members of the group, of whom Woolf feels a little jealous, as she notes: "Well, these women's emotions . . .." They could be rivals in a Restoration Comedy, in a society known for its talk and treachery and tattle—what Christopher Ricks, writing of Bloomsbury, has called "tit-for-tattle."[7]

4   VW, "Restoration Comedy," 1924, *The Essays of Virginia Woolf*, edited by Andrew McNeillie, (The Hogarth Press, 1998), Vol 3, 445-447. "Congreve's Comedies: Speed, Stillness and Meaning," 1937, *The Essays of Virginia Woolf*, edited by Stewart N. Clarke, (The Hogarth Press, 2011), 114-121.
5   T.S. Eliot [TSE], "What is a Classic?", 1944, "Poetry and Drama," 1951, in *The Collected Prose of T.S. Eliot*, edited by Archie Burnett, (Faber, 2024), Vol. 4, 172-189, 189-207.
6   William Congreve, *Love for Love*, Act IV, line 615, Act V, line 535.
7   Christopher Ricks, "The Ottoline Empire," review of Miranda Seymour: *Life on the Grand Scale: A life of Ottoline Morrell*, *The New Yorker*, 08/09/1993, 82-85.

Eliot, moving as a stranger from America into these London circles, was aware of the need for caution. He wrote to Eleanor Hinkley in June 1919, describing "a society where everyone is very sensitive, very perceptive and very quick and you will see that a dinner party demands more skill and exercises one's psychological gifts more than the best fencing match or duel. The first thing one tries to notice on entering a room is everyone's frame of mind and attitude towards everyone else, individually, which may have changed in twenty-four hours! It does use one's brains!"[8] When Woolf, long after, created in *The Waves* the expatriate businessman who always stands self-consciously apart from the group, she was partly thinking of Eliot. He shadows the figure of Louis, who as a child says: "My eyes are wild; my lips tight pressed"; and who has an adult nervously asks: "What do I think of you—what do you think of me? Who are you? Who am I? . . . Lord, help us act our parts . . . ."[9]

The relationship between Virginia Woolf and Eliot had something performative about it; it's never relaxed. At the time of their outing, she was 39 and he was 32; neither of them was yet well-established. They had first met in 1918. The Woolfs printed and published his *Poems* in May 1919 for the Hogarth Press. In 1920 Eliot had published his essays *The Sacred Wood*, which included "Tradition and the Individual Talent." He had just published an essay on Marvell and was thinking about a volume of essays on seventeenth-century writers. He was working at the bank. His wife Vivienne was very ill, and Eliot was distraught about her and worn out. In May 1921 he told a friend that a visit to Italy "will just save me from another breakdown."[10]

Yet to Woolf he was an intimidating figure. They were both involved with "trying something harder." Harder than what? "We're not as good as Keats": both of them contrasted their own struggles with Keats, always an inspiration and consolation to Woolf: "If ever there was a lovable human being, one whom one would wish to live with, walk with, go on travels with, it was Keats." Eliot often echoes, alludes to or

---

8   TSE to Eleanor Hinckley, 17 June 1919, *The Letters of T.S. Eliot* [TSE Letters], Revised Edition, edited by Valerie Eliot and Hugh Haughton, Vol. 1, 1898-1922, (Faber, 2009), 364.

9   VW, *The Waves*, 1931, (Penguin, 1992), 43, 178.

10   TSE to Sydney Schiff, 3 April 1921, TSE to John Middleton Murry, 22 April 1921, TSE Letters, Vol. 1, 549, 553. TSE to Ottoline Morrell, 17 May 1921, cited in "Chronology," *The Letters of T.S. Eliot*, edited by Valerie Eliot, (Faber, 1988), Vol. 1, xxv. Peter Ackroyd, *T.S. Eliot*, (Hamish Hamilton, 1984), 110. Lyndall Gordon, *Eliot's Early Years*, (Oxford University Press, 1977), 104-105.

parodies Keats, who (in Ricks's words), in contrast to these effortful and anxious modernists, "never relaxes his intelligence but always has a relaxed intelligence."[11]

Woolf began *Jacob's Room* at the start of 1920. In September 1920, after a visit from Eliot, she wrote in her diary: "I kept myself successfully from being submerged, though feeling the waters rise once or twice. I mean by this that he completely neglected my claims as a writer, & had I been meek, I suppose I should have gone under—felt him and his views dominant & subversive." Eliot told her he thought Joyce's *Ulysses* was "extremely brilliant"—he was reading the early extracts published in *The Little Review*. After the visit, Woolf found that "Jacob has come to a stop."[12] She had to tell herself not to feel outdone by Eliot's intellect and Joyce's rich demotic boldness.

During that visit, Eliot said to her: "If anyone asked him whether he meant what he said, he would have to say no, very often." The phrase echoes "The Love Song of J. Alfred Prufrock" when, settling a pillow by her head, a woman says to the narrator: "That is not what I meant at all. That is not it, at all." Eliot's remark anticipates their conversation in the taxi a few months later. The phrase kept sounding in the air between them.

Woolf was acutely aware of Eliot's pride, his edginess, his mask, his discomfort. She was sensitive to his power and to his mighty will. This is how she describes him in December 1920, thinking—as she would again after *Love for Love*—about how laughter might release him from inhibition:

> A mouth twisted & shut; not a single line free & easy; all caught, pressed, inhibited; but great driving power some where—& my word what concentration of the eye when he argues! … A little human laughter comes very welcome to him, as I guess, & I think he would willingly break up his formal ways.[13]

In June 1922 he read *The Waste Land* aloud to the Woolfs at Hogarth House, just after she had sent her finished copy of *Jacob's Room* to her typist. Woolf's vivid account of his reading is well known:

---

11   VW "Personalities," in *The Essays of Virginia Woolf,* edited by Stuart N. Clarke, (The Hogarth Press, 2011), Vol 6, 437. *ATTP*, 170. For TSE and Keats, see eg *The Poems of T.S. Eliot*, edited by Christopher Ricks and Jim McCue, (Faber, 2015), Vol. 1, 541, 629, 1015, 1072, 1148; Vol. 2, 220-221.

12   VW Diary, II, 68, 20 September 1920.

13   VW Diary, II, 77, 5 December 1920.

He sang it & chanted it and rhythmed it. It has great beauty & force of phrase: symmetry; & tensity. What connects it together, I'm not so sure. But he read it till he had to rush . . . & discussion thus was curtailed. One was left, however, with some strong emotion . . . [And then she adds]: Now what *will* they say about Jacob? Mad, I suppose: a disconnected rhapsody: I don't know.[14]

The idea of connection and disconnection connects her work to his: "What *connects* it together, I'm not so sure." "A *disconnected* rhapsody."

Both *Jacob's Room* and *The Waste Land* came out in October, 1922—famously, the same year as the publication of Joyce's *Ulysses*, on which they had not agreed. It would be satisfying to think that they had both been working on those manuscripts on 20th March 1921, before they went to the theatre together. There are affinities. Both darkly celebrate urban life, crossing between English and European cities. Both are weighed down by the presence of war. In both there are elegies for the dead, sexual anxieties, class caricatures and broken legacies from past literatures and civilizations. Both use cinematic techniques. Both construct a modernist life-story out of fragments. And in both, we hear scraps and splinters of speech, voices cut off or trailing away. Like *The Waste Land*, *Jacob's Room* is trying to find a new form—not perfectly finished, not traditional—for representing history, character and emotion. Jacob notices at the Parthenon that "the Greeks, like sensible men, never bothered to finish the backs of their statues," observing "that the side of the figure which is turned away from view is left in the rough."[15]

Eliot and Woolf were in contact for the rest of their lives. They wrote about each other's work: when Woolf commented (in "Character and Fiction," for Eliot's *Criterion* in 1924) on the writing of Lawrence, Joyce, Eliot and others as being "a season of failures and fragments," he responded, as if continuing their conversation in the taxi: "I feel myself that everything I have done consists simply of tentative sketches and rough experiments. Will the next generation profit by our labours?"[16] They published each other more than once—and difficulties sometimes arose. When the Hogarth Press published *The Waste Land* in 1923, it

---

14   VW Diary, II, 178, 23 June 1922.
15   VW, *Jacob's Room*, Ch 12, (Penguin, 1992), 130.
16   HL, 439. VW, "Character in Fiction," (1924), *The Essays of Virginia Woolf*, edited by Andrew McNeillie, (The Hogarth Press, 1988), Vol 3, 435. TSE to VW, 22 May 1924, *TSE Letters*, Vol. 2, 430.

was an imperfect production. Eliot generously blamed on his own proof-reading the fact that in this edition a crowd flowed under, not over, London Bridge. When Woolf gave him her essay "On Being Ill" for his *New Criterion* in 1926, his unenthusiastic response brought back all her anxieties: "I saw wordiness, feebleness, & all the vices in it."[17] Eliot and the Woolfs were editorial rivals and they came to distrust him for that reason. (She asked herself once: "Then what does he mean by what he says? God knows.")[18] Other circumstances divided them, too. Woolf had a horror of Vivienne Eliot, and she was dismayed and baffled by Eliot's conversion to Anglo-Catholicism.[19] Later, as famous writers in the 1930s, they settled into a teasing friendship. Here, in or around 1938, twenty years after they had first met, Eliot is accepting an invitation to tea with the Woolfs, one of many. He writes in verse and in the character of Possum, as was his occasional jocose habit.

> Be sure that Possums can't refuse
> A tea with Mrs Woolf on Tues.
> And eagerly if still alive,
> I'll come to tea with you at five.
> I'd like to come at half past four,
> But have a business lunch before,
> And feel responsibility
> To do some work before my Tea.
> But please don't let the kettle wait
> And keep for me a cup and plate,
> And keep the water on the bile,
> A chair, and (as I hope) a Smile.

Eliot's editor Christopher Ricks annotates "Be sure that" with a quotation from "Address by T.S. Eliot, '06, to the Class of '33" (1933): "Whatever you think, be sure that it is what you think; whatever you want, be sure that it is what you want; whatever you feel, be sure that it is what you feel."[20] Eliot doesn't add: "Whatever you say, be sure that it is what you mean."

Hermione Lee

---

17   VW Diary, III, 7 December 1925, 49.
18   HL, 438.
19   HL, 506.
20   *The Poems of T.S. Eliot: The Annotated Text*, Vol II, *Practical Cats and Other Verses*, edited by Christopher Ricks and Jim McCue, (Faber, 2015), 186-187.

Humiliation and Humility

Early in *True Friendship*, his account of how three poets formed, together with two of their poetic ancestors, a quincunx,[1] Ricks quotes William Empson on the formative influence T.S. Eliot had on him. Empson begins his tribute refusing what might be seen as his duty on the occasion: "I do not propose here to try to judge or define the achievement of T.S. Eliot; indeed," Empson continues—after a semicolon and not a full stop—"I feel, like most verse writers of my generation, that I do not know for certain how much of my own mind he invented, let alone how much of it is a reaction against him or indeed a consequence of misreading him. He has a very penetrating influence, perhaps not unlike an east wind."[2] In this passage Ricks attends to how Empson's "delectable" word "'invented' banters the self-importance that would suppose that what great writers do for us is a matter of their helping us discover ourselves." Banters, mind; not batters. Bantering, I understand, is one of the few effective approaches for talking someone off a ledge and back into the world; bantering, we accept that life is a durable, pleasurable, exasperating thing; bantering, we do not let gratitude grow malignant, and become piety. While influence need not be a matter of anxiety, to feel that one has been invented by another writer is to admit to something more fraught, lasting and inhibiting than influence. To discover that one's mind is not one's own can be as hair-raising as realizing that one's mind's not right, at least until one realizes that it's not wrong, either. The opposition is misleading: just as it would be to conceive of oneself wholly invented by another or others, it's impossible to remain a monad even on an island. What Ricks exacts from this passage of Empson's

---

1   The word, in this case, is Ricks's: "It would please me if, after all these years and all that is owed to these poets, the five of them were to form for others as well as for me the mysteriously persuasive shaping that Sir Thomas Browne delighted in: the quincunx." *TF*, xi.
2   *TF*, 9 in Empson, "The Style of the Master," *Argufying*, ed. by John Haffenden, (University of Iowa Press, 1987), 361.

is what it means to acknowledge and accept being an invented—not a created—being, seriously, without surrender and with gratitude.

Ricks is penetrating too. It would be disgraceful not to admit that he has refined our senses, and helped us to remember that our work as critics begins in noticing, and need not strive for knowledge, ultimate or otherwise. In a remarkable—and remarkably long—interview with Alan McFarlane, he characterizes his own literary critical work, as "a second-order activity, it's a service industry, it's a service well worth rendering . . . ."[3] The pause following this claim is not a trailing off, diminuendo, but a form of emphasis. In this moment he is not soft-selling or soft-pedaling, but offering an exemplary definition.

Ricks strives, and like the rest of us fails, to be in concord with Eliot, who asserts in "Shakespeare and the Stoicism of Seneca": "Humility is the most difficult of all virtues to achieve; nothing dies harder than the desire to think well of oneself."[1] We critics and reviewers like to think well of ourselves; we have influence in the markets of ideas and of books: we move units. It's enough to make one want to quit the business, and one should quit if it's no more than business. Better not to take oneself so seriously, to banter rather than bang on, to express gratitude instead of praise. Praise has a scent; it can be mephitic. Gratitude begins before and ends long after praise has left the building.

Gratitude is a sense about which we should have no illusions, and so here I will try to answer for a remark T.S. Eliot made about Stendhal in a review, published on May 30, 1919 in the *Athenaeum*. I have chosen this example because of its importance to Ricks, and for its extremity; I imagine that what Eliot experienced while reading Stendhal is a limit case, and so for Ricks to refer to it as often as he does, suggests that it might have the strength of a principle.

Eliot is reviewing the second volume of *A History of the French Novel, to the Close of the Nineteenth Century*, by George Saintsbury. Offering several reasons why Stendhal is a more lasting writer than Balzac, Eliot recalls that "Laurent Tailhade was right when he spoke of the work of Balzac as a fresco crumbling away year by year." Then Eliot turns to what is better, stronger, more terrifying about Stendhal:

---

3   From around the 30th minute of Ricks's interview with Alan Macfarlane from
     2013: https://uk.video.search.yahoo.com/yhs/search?fr=yhs-litmus-caerus&-
     ei=UTF-8&hsimp=yhs-caerus&hspart=litmus&p=christopher•ricks•inter-
     view&type=1476589-vsub-2_22598_nwtb#id=1&vid=978b39a6f460deb-
     c5a5d1c149c970064&action=click. Accessed several times.
4   *AHL*, 86.

"Stendhal's scenes, some of them, and some of his phrases, read like cutting one's own throat; they are a terrible humiliation to read, in the understanding of human feelings and human illusions of feeling they force upon the reader."[5] The last thing one might say of an author one is grateful for and mean it. Who would want to read such books? I mean other than T.S. Eliot. Yet this cutting remark is meaningless as criticism unless he expects others to read works of literature for similar experiences.

Stendhal, then, is penetrating, more penetrating than Empson considers Eliot. The difficulty here is how to conceive of, accept and be grateful for literature or for any art that provokes such violent sensations (and imagine for a moment what it would mean to have one's mind "invented" by Eliot's Stendhal). What has Eliot's Stendhal set down that so provokes the reader's imagination that one undergoes terrible humiliations and *goes on* reading? What Eliot praises in Stendhal is his ability to express emotion, for "to express precise emotion requires as great intellectual power as to express precise thought,"[6] and to express the illusion of precise emotion demands a similar power of discrimination.

The reader of Stendhal understands his characters to be feeling strong feelings they cannot admit to feeling, or admitting to strong feelings they do not feel; and observes Stendhal's characters failing to understand that their feelings can change (that what was once strongly felt is dwindling, what was tepid has grown scorching); and failing to distinguish between what they should feel and what they do feel; and that these several forms of disjuncture, this terrible variety, the countless ways to tread lightly the boards above the abyss, may humiliate the reader who has engaged in one, several or all of these forms of subterfuge. The reader of Stendhal will observe characters failing in one, several or all of these ways of avoiding or exaggerating their feelings. Some of those "scenes" Eliot refers to are of characters making scenes, engaging in histrionic displays, remonstrating with others, of wetting their index fingers to tack into prevailing winds, and working hard to prevent others from learning what they feel; and what we feel reading them is not ordinary ambivalence but excruciating humiliation. I take it that this is what is meant by another remark of

---

5   "Beyle and Balzac," *The Athenaeum*, May 30, 1919, 393. This passage, quoted in full, is important to Ricks. He quotes it in the final chapter of *TSEP*, 240, in "Literary Principles as Against Theory," *EIA*, 314 and in *DVOS*, 230n..

6   T.S. Eliot, "Shakespeare and the Stoicism of Seneca," in *Selected Essays* (Harcourt, Brace & Co., 1950), 115.

Eliot's that Ricks quotes late in *True Friendship*, in the Lowell chapter, in the midst of his long examination of the Ser Brunetto passage in "Little Gidding": "With a chastening sense of our responsibility for what we conceive, [Eliot] had said in 1929 that Dante reminds us 'that man is damned or blessed in the creatures of his imagination as well as in men who have actually lived.'"[7]

In Eliot's conception, the close reader of Stendhal is inevitably a *hypocrite lecteur*, which is less often true of a reader of Dostoyevsky. For in his review in which this remark about Stendhal appeared Eliot singles out two scenes in *The Idiot*, and one each in *Crime and Punishment* and *The Brothers Karamazov*. "No one will deny to Dostoyevsky," Eliot avers, "an imagination at least equal to Balzac's; some of the things he tells us are even more unimaginable. But the Imagination is utterly different, and put to different uses."[8] Eliot on Stendhal echoes Prince Myshkin's remark when he encounters a copy of Holbein the Younger's painting of The Body of the Dead Christ in the Tomb in Rogozhin's house in a famous early scene from *The Idiot*. Hearing that Rogozhin likes looking at the picture: "'At that picture!' cried Myshkin, struck by a sudden thought. 'At that picture! Why, that picture might make some people lose their faith.'"[9] If we accept the articles of faith, it is far worse for a believer to lose his faith than for a non-believer to take his own life, but what can it mean for the reader to suffer such acute humiliation that it is "like cutting one's own throat"? The conversation continues, and after Myshkin reports on a murder he has recently heard an account of in a train, "Rogozhin

---

7   *TF*, 213
8   This is not a typo, unless there is a typo in the original. Eliot has "imagination" lower case in one sentence and capitalized in the next.
9   Fyodor Dostoyevsky, *The Idiot*, translated by Constance Garnett, (Modern Library, 1935), 206. There is a useful account of the painting's fame and Dostoyevsky's initial encounter with it: "In 1857 its fame was sufficiently great to lure a Russian author to Basle, and it was powerful enough to bring him to the brink of collapse. Fyodor Dostoyevsky stood mute before the panel, and his wife had to drag him away to avert the risk of an epileptic fit seizing him." *Hans Holbein*, Oskar Bätschmann and Pascal Briener, (Princeton University Press, 1997), 89. Dostoyevsky's biographer Joseph Frank offers a less dramatic account, culled from his wife "Anna's Diary, much closer to the event than her later *Reminiscences*, Dostoyevsky was so impressed with the painting that he climbed on a chair to obtain a closer look; and Anna was terrified that the law-abiding Swiss would fine him for such a violation of museum decorum. So overcome was he by the canvas that 'he pronounced Holbein the Younger a painter of the first rank.'" See Joseph Frank, *Between Religion and Rationality: Essays in Russian Literature and Culture* (Princeton University Press, 2010), 31.

went off into peals of laughter; he laughed as though he were in a sort of fit."[10] Composing but not collecting himself—he will never collect himself—Rogozhin says: "'I do like that! Yes, that beats everything!' he cried convulsively, gasping for breath. 'One man doesn't believe in God at all, while the other believes in Him so thoroughly that he prays as he murders men! . . . You could never have invented that, brother! Ha-ha-ha! That beats everything."[11] Beats everything except what is to come (and the idiom "that beats everything" batters). For Myshkin will lose his mind when Rogozhin cuts the throat of Nastasya Filippovna, the woman neither of them can marry: Myshkin cannot save her by sanctifying her at the altar; and even though he helps her escape from her marriage to the Prince, Rogozhin cannot buy her and thereby keep her from her desire to be saved, which she feels urgently but intermittently. Having been raped and kept by her guardian, she cannot find herself in a society that cannot afford to grant her a place inside it. She might be the tragic Janus counterpart of Groucho Marx, unable to accept membership in a society that would have her, where marriage is the price of membership.

Ricks glosses Eliot's penetrating observation about Stendhal late in his long interview with Alan Macfarlane:

> For Eliot, the great enemy is illusions of feeling. That is, he writes about Stendhal, and says Stendhal's scenes are a positive humiliation to read in their understanding of human feeling, and human illusions of feeling. The world of the newspapers and everything else is a world that makes people pretend that they feel things that they don't. Maybe it would be good if they did feel those things, but they're never going to feel those things if they think they already feel them. Newspapers are committed to making you pretend for a while that you care about this, and you don't care about it, and so on. It's Beckett, it's Swift, it's Eliot and so on. But that hasn't always been the case. We can imagine . . . It's not about cynicism even, it's just that knowing what you actually feel, Eliot says, intelligence of which is an important function of discernment of exactly what and how much we feel in any given situation.[12]

---

10 It can't be a coincidence that in this moment Rogozhin suffers from fits, the same symptom that plagues the prince.

11 Fyodor Dostoyevsky, *The Idiot*, translated by Constance Garnett, (Modern Library, 1935), 208.

12 The transcription is mine, edited lightly for clarity. Substitute "the internet" or "social media," and his remark remains as acute as it is for "the newspapers," perhaps more so. It is thanks to Hermione Lee's "You Talk Like That Without Meaning It" that I learned that Eliot offered, in 1933, an affirmative version of the statement Ricks summarizes here. In his "Address by T.S. Eliot, '06, to the Class of '33" (1933): "Whatever you think, be sure that it is what you think;

When Ricks acknowledges, after a pause, "It's not about cynicism even," I believe he means that these humiliating phrases and scenes are more appalling than any species of cynicism, than any lie. To borrow another penetrating phrase from Eliot's review, "Because most people are too unconscious of their own suffering to suffer much," we suffer for them, are humiliated for them; and yet this process we undergo is not and cannot be cathartic. Otherwise, we would feel something other than a wish to cut our throats.

To read Stendhal's work as Eliot describes his experience of reading him is to suffer, but it is not to invite suffering. To perceive the impoverishment of feeling among the classes Stendhal writes about gives us more than pause (and in that same interview Ricks reminds us that one of the purposes of art is to give us pause).[13] From time to time one has to put down the book that makes one want to cut one's own throat; and if the tension is unbearable, the book unputdownable, go quickly on, ideally to return later, fortified, for a more searching look.[14]

I take it that Eliot's remark sketches, very briefly, a crash course for the senses consistent with the conception Ricks welcomes in Empson's bantering of Eliot: "that what great writers do for us is a matter of their helping us discover ourselves." To read great writers this way is to flatter ourselves, and Eliot's Stendhal is impossible to read that way. It could be argued that great writers are those who succeed in making the most of humiliation. How else can we welcome the experience of reading that produces a feeling of revulsion or compassion so strong that we might want to take our own lives—and consider taking our own life for the sake of the suffering of *imagined* others? How can we be

---

whatever you want, be sure that it is what you want; whatever you feel, be sure that it is what you feel." *The Poems of T.S. Eliot: The Annotated Text*, Vol II, *Practical Cats and Other Verses*, edited by Christopher Ricks and Jim McCue, (Faber, 2015), 186-187.

13   P.N. Furbank writing in the *London Review of Books* 16:4 (24 February 1994) helps me to situate the load of that loaded word "class" by means Eliot and Ricks would approve: "the proper way to study 'class' is by introspection: by prolonged reflection on what is going on in oneself when one thinks 'class' thoughts—a most devious and complex business, full of ruses and logical paradoxes."

14   I have had this turbulent, start-and-stop experience while reading, among others, George Eliot, Jon McGregor, António Lobo Antunes, J.M. Coetzee, Edward P. Jones, Andrey Platonov.

grateful for any art that makes us, even if ever so briefly, contemplate suicide? Unless humiliation, as well as humility, is endless.[15]

Michael Autrey

---

15 "What can I do for You? *Nothing.* This is the answer granted by humility. If this may not be humiliating as an admission, it is none the worse for that, since without the possibility of humiliation there would be no possibility of humility." *DVOS*, 202. The You is capitalized because Ricks is writing about Dylan considering "The Absolute Being Who is God" in his song "What Can I Do for You?" This, I believe, only reinforces my conviction that both are endless.

The Wrong Way Home

Subic Bay Naval Base,
Philippine Islands
February 23, 1902

Dear Uncle Pratt:

Ten days I've had your letter, and I still . . .

He put the pencil down: *So here it is.*
I knew he'd come to that. Or worse. I knew it.

He blacked the passage out. Then tore it up.

The mail is slow here. I just got your news.
How did you even find out where I am?

I hope you know I'm grateful that you've shown
Such generosity to him, the more
Because he trampled down what claim of kin
Your wife's half-brother might have asked from you.
He never was much of a hired man.

I'm also grateful that for those few weeks
When he and I were working on your farm
You did your best to keep from everyone
Just what his true relation was to me.

"My true relation." How odd to call him that.
I never caught the trick of knowing him.

Now Mrs. Pratt remembered how he'd borne
The seven months my mother took to die,
So she forgave him. And kept forgiving him.
I don't remember. Not one single thing.
But when last fall he turned up at your door
I recognized the man that man became.

I'm sorry. I picked an awful time to leave
I hope you got the harvest in without me.

If I had stayed there, what would I become?

I wonder only how he held his tongue.
What kept him back (draped over some drunk stranger's
Shoulder) from shouting out just who I was?
Was that some flaring up of self-control?
Or maybe it was only shame, although
What shame I ever saw him feel was just
A passing sickness, like a hangover.

I notice, in the clipping, the police
Just call him his first name, don't know his last.

Just how he died's the one surprising thing.
I'd always thought he'd die by violence.
It's very strange he couldn't find his path,
However drunk, that little way from town,
No matter what the weather. What made him turn
And go so many miles the wrong way home?
It makes no difference now: don't think I blame you
That you just couldn't find him in the snow.
At last it's over now. For him at least.

John Burt

Essaying Appreciation

W hat is so different about Christopher Ricks's criticism? Why am I so drawn to the man? There's the surface brilliance. Hardly a phrase without a turn of phrase, an allusion, a pun. But usually this a quality that turns me off. I am not drawn to writers who demand we kneel before their genius. That was always my problem with Joyce, or Eco or Rushdie, an intuition that the energy throwing up the sparks is above all a desire to assert the writer's supremacy. You don't feel this with Ricks. At the same time he is very aware of competition, rivalry, envy: "Since the medium of literature is the same as that of literary studies, there will always be not just the possibility but the likelihood of professional envy and ingratitude."[1]

That is from *Essays in Appreciation*, but the idea bears repeating, in *Dylan's Visions of Sin*.

> "Literary criticism enjoys the advantage of existing in the same medium (language) as the art that it explores ... this may be why literary critics are given to competitive envy."[2]

Is Ricks competing? Certainly he can be peremptory dismissing other critics, even the most celebrated writers. In the essay on Gaskell's *Life of Charlotte Brontë* he quotes Henry James remarking that "full as it is of fine qualities, of affection, of generosity, of sympathy, of imagination, [the book] lacks the prime requisites of a good biography." "Wrong," Ricks chides. "There are in biography no requisites as prime as affection, generosity, sympathy and imagination."[3] A moment later he takes on Professor Carolyn Heilbrunn who had objected that, rather than exploring the female aspect of Brontë's genius, Gaskell had merely sought to restore her reputation among Victorians and hence her biography could no longer be considered "salient." "As if," Ricks shakes his head, "that rare thing, a biography which is a true work of

---

1   *EIA*, 348.
2   *DVOS*, 7.
3   *EIA*, 131.

art . . . would have ceased to be 'salient' because of a political shift within a branch of the academic profession."[4]

"Tennyson's Tennyson" more playfully ticks off Robert Bernard Martin's criticisms of the poet's supposed intellectual limitations by pointing out that the title of Martin's biography, *The Unquiet Heart*, is wrested from a line in *In Memoriam* that actually reads "the unquiet heart and brain." "Is Martin entitled, qualified," Ricks wonders, "to practise lobotomy?"[5]

In the essay on Froude's *Carlyle* he exposes the hubris of John Clubbe's claim that in reducing the great book to less than half its length by eliminating its many long quotations to leave only Froude's words, he had given it a new coherence. Froude's words, Ricks objects, constantly echoed and alluded to what he had quoted, "so that it is mistaken of Clubbe to suppose that [they] are left intact or untouched when others' words in their immediate vicinity are excised."[6]

They are all *defences*. Ricks loves to come out on top when protecting the authors he admires. Protecting and defending them above all from condescension and in particular the condescension of those who confuse their modernity with superiority. What is his well-known aversion to literary theory, if not an intuition that it is a form of condescension, a looking at literature *de haut en bas*? If we read through the long list of his publications, we notice they are for the most part tributes to authors he loves, or reverently annotated editions of their work. *Essays in Appreciation*, might stand as a title for the whole Ricks oeuvre. Friendship, *True Friendship*, is also important. Just as he likes to pay tribute, Ricks is quick to find moments when his authors pay tribute to each other. Lowell and Eliot to Pound. Beckett to Joyce. When they sustain each other, befriend each other. When they show gratitude and are loyal. Here he is on Dylan's tribute to Woody Guthrie:

> *Song to Woody* appreciates a life's worth, and it knows about gratitude: that, for a start, gratitude is the due of Woody Guthrie, and not of him alone. That to give gratitude is to be the richer, not the poorer, for the giving. And that it is gratitude that sees through and sees off envy. Gratitude is the sublime sublimation of envy.[7]

---

4   *EIA*, 132.
5   *EIA* 175.
6   *EIA*, 155.
7   *DVOS*, 52.

Here's the point. If the critic's enterprise (which "is a privilege"[8]) puts him at risk of envy, it also offers the opportunity to overcome this most deadly sin through gratitude. "Gratitude will have no truck with envy,"[9] we're told earlier in the book. Ricks is never afraid of repeating himself. Which doesn't mean that gratitude, has to "run to ingratiation,"[10] or oblige us to relinquish our right to rivalry. "After Guthrie," we learn, "in Dylan's creative life . . . there comes—welcomed—a new arrival who is a newer rival."[11] How Ricks loves words, sounds, rhythms, that call to each other and demand we see connections, make distinctions. "The rivalry has its chivalry,"[12] he goes on, and admiringly shows how the song to Blind Willie MacTell, like the tribute to Woody Guthrie, combines gratitude with a "perfectly pitched"[13] presentation of the singer's own credentials. Competes generously, you could say. Honest homage allows Dylan to write a fine song. He is the richer and shines the brighter in his appreciation of the other.

Chivalry, homage, gratitude. There's an antique ring to these words, values not often celebrated today. Ricks doesn't shun the old-fashioned: "self-sacrifice" he observes, defending Hallam Tennyson's unobtrusive service to his father, "far from being a way of losing one's life, is the only true way to gain it."[14] So Hallam can head his biography with the epigraph, quoted from *Morte d'Arthur*, "I have lived my life," and mean the words as much of himself as of his father, or indeed of Arthur. Self-sacrifice gave Hallam his life, and his 'life' of his father.

Who but Ricks could have shone a light on this quiet gem? It's not overdoing it, I think, to say Ricks has given his life to an appreciation of writers past and present. His attentive gratitude to them opens a space in which he can compete, shine, without envy. Shine, principally, through the extraordinary twining, intertwining of his own words and thoughts with those of the writer on whom he turns his light. This is the structure and dazzle of a Ricks essays, this exhilarating, illuminating back and forth between critic and writer, or writers rather, for "genius is not solitary and can thrive only because of all the others that keep it company, 'all the good people' that travel with it—and with the rest of

---

8   *DVOS*, 1.
9   *DVOS*, 4.
10   *DVOS*, 68.
11   *DVOS*, 69.
12   *DVOS*, 69.
13   *DVOS*, 74.
14   *EIA*, 183.

us."[15] So to read about Chapman is also to think about Othello. Beckett keeps company with Johnson and Swift. Rhymes of Herbert, Marvell and Swinburne are rediscovered in Dylan. Shakespeare, Milton and Eliot are rarely absent. Ricks knows them all, loves them all. The range of reference is ... enviable.

I can't recall when I first saw Ricks, perhaps as a student, at a lecture. But I do remember being—in a state of some awe—introduced to him, in my fifties, after a presentation of *True Friendship*, and being taken at once by the generosity of his attention to all around him, an almost flaunted eagerness to put people at ease and have fun together. This first impression was confirmed at a conference in Boston organized perhaps by the Editorial institute. I think in 2011. An endeavour to gather a community of readers and writers, where, again, inevitable rivalries and envies would be sublimated in the appreciation Ricks encouraged each to show to others. The continuity with the spirit of his criticism was palpable. But if I could claim to have got to know the man a little it was as one of the five judges for the 2013 International Booker Prize. Ricks was Chairman. At our first meeting, after stressing the sense of privilege we should feel—at that time the prize was awarded to any writer worldwide for a lifetime's achievement— he warned us that disagreements would be par for the course, but we must not arrive, when it came to choosing our winner, at a public falling out, such as had befallen the judges the year before us. That would be ugly and a dereliction of our duty to the prize organizers, to the writers we were reading and to ourselves. It was a chastening, but actually rather cheerful recognition of the animosity that can poison literary debate. Something he knew about. Duly cautioned, we proceeded to our deliberations in good spirit.

I was surprised that Ricks had accepted the onerous responsibility of judging a novel prize. I would have imagined he had more rewarding projects in hand. It is largely a thankless task. One reads too much too quickly. If one doesn't skive. Ricks didn't. He took intercontinental flights to be present at our meetings, produced doughtily succinct summaries of all the books we were reading (handwritten on the same cards he shuffles through when he gives a lecture), listened to long and sometimes tedious discussions. How much was this costing him? I wondered. Sometimes I noted a flash of impatience in his eyes. Sometimes the usually kind voice became sharp and peremptory. Then he might close a meeting quite abruptly, as if to go on were to

---

15   *DVOS*, 491.

risk some kind of crisis. Meantime, he was kind to me personally. He had noted my ambition of course and responded with sympathy, as if it were a kind of affliction. To my partner, now wife, at a reception after one of the judge's sessions, he teasingly remarked, "Tim always wants to be the most intelligent, doesn't he?" We laughed. It seemed funny coming from the one I had always thought of as beyond emulation. But I saw he was teaching me something. In a friendly way. If I look back now at the emails we exchanged that year, I remember the temptation I felt to try to match, in my responses, the witty phrasing he always, apparently effortlessly, found, the puns and allusions. Then the decision, not to.

"Gratitude is the sublime sublimation of envy," then, yes. But Ricks goes on: "Meanwhile, all this is of course easier said than done."[16] Of course, of course! Meaning, you would have thought, that envy is no easy beast to slay, that it's a lot to ask of a man to spend his life praising others ("What I'd like to know," we heard earlier, "is why *I* am attending to *Tennyson*, instead of his attending to *me*").[17] But no sooner has he suggested the scope of the task, than Ricks covers his tracks somewhat, as if he'd been talking, not about disposition, but technique. "For there is, from the very start, a challenge about how you are going to end any expression of gratitude. The expression of it has to end without ever suggesting for a final moment that the feeling itself has come to an end."[18]

This problem would never have occurred to me, but now that it has been conjured up, sure enough here comes the temptation to show that I'm equal to it, that I can rise to the challenge of ending in style this brief expression of my gratitude to Christopher. It's disheartening. All I'll say is, every time his name comes up–an email, a conversation, or searching for a quote in a book–I deeply regret not having spent more time in his company, not having learned, as I'm sure I would have learned, even more from him than I have. Still, and however inappropriately, given the subject of the song he's discussing, my eye falls on a line I underlined, one of Ricks's many expressions of gratitude:

"So I hope that I am right in feeling grateful for Dylan's line 'Be grateful for what we've shared together and be glad.'"[19]

Tim Parks

---

16   *DVOS*, 52.
17   *DVOS*, 7.
18   *DVOS*, 52.
19   *DVOS*, 277.

Where Darkness Makes Abode

> Visionary power
> Attends upon the motions of the winds
> Embodied in the mystery of words;
> There darkness makes abode, and all the host
> Of shadowy things do work their changes there
> As in a mansion like their proper home.
> Even forms and substances are circumfused
> By that transparent veil with light divine,
> And through the turnings intricate of verse
> Present themselves as objects recognized
> In flashes, and with a glory scarce their own. (Wordsworth, 1805. V. 619-29)[1]

Recently I recited this passage for Christopher and he brightened, which I took as a sign that he likes it. So here, in his honor, is a close-reading of it, along with some speculation about the defense of poetry it advances. The passage appears in Book V of *The Prelude*, titled "Books." Here Wordsworth describes, not the familiar experience of being haunted *by* words, but the intuition that there is a hauntedness *in* words. The idea that words create a site of the supernatural is surely a Romantic conceit. There are parallel moments in Shelley's poetry and in his "Defence," and hints of similar notions in Coleridge and De Quincey. What is it about poetic language that leads them all to adopt the metaphor of haunting? Can we cash out the metaphor, in Wordsworth at any rate? We *could* identify the "ghosts" of poetry with its sonic aspects (rhyme, rhythm, sound values, assonance and alliteration) or with its more oblique semantic features (nuance, allusion, affect). But Wordsworth's imposing yet rather vague figures of speech, and their obscure pathos, seem to resist translation into a technical vocabulary. What, in particular, is the elaborate system of relays, the density of figures and the many degrees of separation in the passage meant to signify? (Visionary power *attends upon* the

---

1   All the quotations from *The Prelude* in this essay derive from William Wordsworth, *The Prelude: 1799, 1805, 1850*, ed. by M.H. Abrams et. al., (W.W. Norton, 1979).

motions of the *winds embodied* in the *mystery* of words. The "host of shadowy (metaphor) things" work "changes" there (two metaphors and one fuzzy deictic) "as in a mansion like their proper home" (a simile containing two more metaphors). Clearly Wordsworth's purpose cannot be to explain the power of literary language. He seems rather to evoke it in terms that emphasize the mystery, characterizing it as involving complex mediation, with hints of the alien and transcendent. It is thus probably a mistake to try anatomizing the metaphor, but it should be possible to illuminate its rhetorical ground—the origins and affiliations of this way of thinking and talking about poetry. The productive question would be not: what is Wordsworth saying? But: what is making him put it this way?

The original version from 1805 suggests that the question has critical stakes. We can index its urgency by comparing the 1805 with the 1850 version:

> Visionary power
> Attends the motions of the viewless winds,
> Embodied in the mystery of words:
> There, darkness makes abode, and all the host
> Of shadowy things work endless changes,—there,
> As in a mansion like their proper home,
> Even forms and substances are circumfused
> By that transparent veil with light divine,
> And, through the turnings intricate of verse,
> Present themselves as objects recognised,
> In flashes, and with glory not their own. (1850.V. 595–605)

The first version has a spontaneity and a sense of wonder lacking in the later version. Part of the change can be attributed to the fussy commas of 1850. This version literally takes the breathlessness out of 1805: the new punctuation provides *too many* places to stop for breath. Moreover, the uninteresting new adjectives "viewless" and "endless" enfeeble. But the major change substitutes "not their own" for "scarce their own." The sense of exclamation disappears. These changes effect a subtle shift in the narrative voice. Authority displaces a measure of excitement and enthusiasm. With the wonder goes the hint of surprise and vulnerability (as we register it in the idiom "*taken* by surprise"), yet both versions preserve the idea that the visitations are sudden and involuntary, appearing only "in flashes."[2]

---

2   "Flash" is a common word in Wordsworth's vocabulary, employed to depict the ephemeral visitations of desirable, privileged experiences. Cf. among many other examples, "But I have been discouraged: gleams of light/Flash

The imagery of transient intimations links the "Visionary power" passage to the Gothic patterns familiar from Wordsworth's "spots of time" episodes. Gothicism helps to describe—or to create—sublime effects, particularly in the strain of imagery involving ambiguous phenomena that fascinate because they have no clear ontological ground.[3] The spots of time tend to issue in experiences of awe and disorientation that draw upon tantalizing figures of ungraspable, otherworldly power—shadows, ghosts, winds, intimations of opaque being, darkness on the move. There is the boat-stealing scene, in whose aftermath Wordsworth is haunted by the "huge and mighty forms that do not / Live like living men" (1805, I, 424-5), the nest-robbing scene in which "the sky seemed not a sky / Of earth, and with what motion moved the clouds" (1805, I, 349-50) and the "homeless voice of waters" (1805, XIII, 63) representing the Imagination rising up through the bank of clouds atop Mount Snowden. In Wordsworth's instances of the sublime, hitherto unrecognized power outside the self and (sometimes) within the self emerges. In the "Visionary Power" passage, Wordsworth deliberately links the experience of literary power to those dislocating episodes that challenge the sense of self and its relation to its environs.

The power of poetry launches the transient passing of the greater through the lesser world. We see this notion particularly in the second half of the passage (ll. 619-29), where forms and substances

_____

often from the east, then disappear, / And mock me with a sky that ripens not/ Into a steady morning." (1805.I.134-6.)

3   The passage closest in language and imagery to "Visionary power" specifically praises "moods/Of shadowy exultation" for providing the excitement and provocation of liminal experience:

and I would stand
Beneath some rock, listening to sounds that are
The ghostly language of the ancient earth,
Or made their dim abode in distant winds.
Thence did I drink the visionary power.
I deem not profitless those fleeting moods
Of shadowy exultation: not for this,
That they are kindred to our purer mind
And intellectual life; but that the soul—
Remembering how she felt but what she felt
Remembering not—retains an obscure sense
Of possible sublimity, to which,
With growing faculties she doth aspire,
With faculties still growing, feeling still
That whatsoever point they gain, they still
Have something to pursue. (1805.II. 306-322)

are "circumfused" with the "divine light" of visionary power by the "transparent veil" of words. Those forms and substances, seen through the intricate turnings of verse (a dynamic phrase going back to the "motions of the winds" and the changes "worked" by shadowy things)—can now only be recognized evanescently "and with a glory scarce their own." The chief "mystery of words" is evidently how they change what they name or describe by investing it with a new glamour and glory that "scarcely" belongs to it. Their power is specifically figured as alien. It seems not to belong to this world, but to come to us from "the other side." The Gothic vocabulary suggests so, but more particularly the figure "*As in* a mansion like their proper home." The "shadowy things" find only a temporary simulacrum of their true dwelling; an elemental foreignness or alterity clings to them. The pathos of this idea is somehow familiar, and sure enough, the Norton editor points out, at the time Wordsworth was composing Book V, "he ha[d] very probably just completed the *Intimations Ode*."[4] The metaphor of homelessness links the passage to stanzas 5 and 6 of the Ode, especially to the lines recapitulating the Gnostic and Neoplatonic account of the descent of the soul—"Our birth is but a sleep and a forgetting"—as well as those that dramatically re-cast the role of Nature, whose goal is now to make Man "Forget the glories he hath known, / And that imperial palace whence he came" (80-84).

The language of the "Visionary Power" passage implicitly draws on this ancient paradigm of the soul's displacement, its tragic incarnation in a dulling material world, and its fleeting intuition that it belongs elsewhere. In fact, earlier in Book V, Wordsworth had linked youthful literary passion to what he calls elsewhere "the might of souls / And what they do within themselves / while yet the earth is new to them" (1805.III.178-81). As the early power fades, we begin to feel our unbelonging and to rebel, and we find an ally in the freedom of imaginative literature:

---

4   William Wordsworth, *The Prelude:1799,1805,1850*, ed. by Jonathan Wordsworth et al., (W.W. Norton, 1979), 178.

And in that dubious hour,
That twilight when we first begin to see
This dawning earth, to recognize, expect—
And in the long probation that ensues,
That time of trial ere we learn to live
In reconcilement with our stinted powers
To endure this state of meagre vassalage,
Unwilling to forego, confess, submit
Uneasy and unsettled, yoke-fellows
To custom, mettlesome and not yet tamed
And humbled down—oh, then we feel, we feel
We know, when we have friends. (1805.V.536-47)

This language of domestication is clearly related to the images of imprisonment, and the "weight" of "custom," and "the inevitable yoke" in the "Intimations Ode." Conversely, the "Visionary power . . . Embodied in the mystery of words" resembles the "celestial light, / The glory and the freshness of a dream" still beheld by the young unused to Earth. The "shadowy things" that work their changes "As in a mansion like their proper home" share our own predicament; perhaps some kind of covert identification with this alien appearance causes us to feel that books are "friends." Something in them comes to us from our "real home" far away.

Wordsworth keeps up the parallel in this last stretch of Book V. Literary experience fades out in the same way as "the glory and the dream," even as it participates in the same immortal longings. Wordsworth is moved "Even unto tears" when he thinks of books which did "never fail to entrance" him when he was a boy but "are now / Dead in my eyes as is a theatre / Fresh emptied of spectators" (1805.V.568-575). What was expressed in his old enchantment, and therefore what was lost when it went?

. . . nothing less in truth
Than that most noble attribute of man—
Though yet untutored and inordinate—
That wish for something loftier, more adorned
Than is the common aspect, daily garb,
Of human life. (1805.V. 590-602)

The poignancy of these lines turns on the word "wish": we wish for the transcendent, for a reprieve from the banality of everyday life, but we cannot have it, except in teasing "flashes." This evocation of impotent desire takes us deep into the emotional matrix of the "Intimations Ode."

Naturally Wordsworth makes use of the Gothic when he wants to invoke the other world. But there are other consequences—or virtues— of Gothic rhetoric. Wordsworth's Gothicism lends itself easily to the trope of personification: "Visionary power," "darkness," and "the host of shadowy things" all take verbs that make them agents. The personification of poetic power is far from being particular to Wordsworth. Many discussions of "the mystery of words" resort to it. In Longinus, the sublime "bring[s] power and irresistible might to bear."[5] Heidegger speaks of "the invisible" which "imparts itself in order to remain what it is—unknown."[6] Shelley says that poetry "sends . . . forth among mankind" the "vanishing apparitions which haunt the interlunations of life" and that the "diviner nature" which visits us momentarily leaves "its" eroding "footsteps" behind (532).[7] Perhaps they are surrendering to a rhetorical temptation: the idea of power conduces to the personification of an agent of power, *a* power. But we might also consider what intuitions about poetry are answered by the figure of a poetic Power. Here is one: we know the difference between commonplace and poetic language; we intuit that there is in poetic language something else, something *more,* as if there were in it a distinct quality or energy not present in ordinary language. Because of this distinction we want to say that there is a separate power at work in poetic language. It has *its own* power, which is variable, capricious and unpredictable, only revealed when particular lines or poems exert it, for particular readers. In its elusiveness it is "invisible," and with invisibility come autonomy and authority; it is "The awful presence of some unseen power" (Shelley, "Hymn to Intellectual Beauty," l.1). Neil Hertz once talked in class about the charm of the force that passes through falling dominoes: because it cannot be perceived except through its action on objects, it is imagined as a "viewless," spectral force. The idea of poetic "power"—"Visionary power"—is a similar catachresis.

The apprehension of dark agency lends itself easily to the language of guilt and reprimand. In the "Intimations Ode," the obstinate

---

5   Hazard Adams, *Critical Theory Since Plato*, Revised Edition, (Harcourt Brace Jovanovich, 1977), 71.
6   Martin Heidegger, "Poetically Man Dwells" in *Poetry, Language and Thought* (Harper, 2013), 225.
7   Percy Bysshe Shelley, Shelley's Poetry and Prose, 2nd Edition, ed. by Donald H. Reiman and Neil Fraistat, (W.W. Norton, 2002), 532.

questionings or glances at "the abyss of idealism"[8] in childhood lead
to "Blank misgivings" and the recollection of "High instincts, before
which our mortal Nature/Did tremble like a guilty Thing surpriz'd"
(149-150). With these words (and their allusions to *Hamlet* and *Paradise
Lost*), Wordsworth introduces a moral note, in the felt rebuke to "our
mortal Nature," caught out in forgetfulness and neglect of the "High
instincts" which are its birthright. Often, in similar scenarios of
being brought up short, Wordsworth is explicit about the sense of
correction. He uses the word "admonishment," as when he concludes
that the leech-gatherer of *Resolution and Independence* has offered him
"human strength and apt admonishment," or when he is transfixed
by the spectacle of the Blind Beggar in Book 6 of *The Prelude*, and
he finds himself "as if admonished from another world." Though the
"Visionary Power" passage does not specifically adduce the idea of
admonishment, it does share the sense of surprise with the "spots
of time" passages, and some hint of their typical climax in startled
self-consciousness.

Poetry interpolates the reader–the sole self–subject to warning
and reprimand. Burke and Longinus on the literary sublime, Shelley
on intellectual beauty, Heidegger on Hölderlin's force, Wordsworth
on the "visionary power" of words all share a focus on aesthetic
experience that arrests and confounds. The effect of the experience
is to introduce a new value, and even prompt a re-evaluation of
values.[9] That a work of art may cause existential shock in this way
is an idea familiar to us from other contexts. "You must change your
life." Dramatic accounts of aesthetic impact similar to Rilke's portray
art as the agent of an apprehensive awakening, an awakening to
what has been forgotten or neglected–to self-betrayal and the need
to act against it. Among claims made for poetry in particular, we
have Heidegger's assertion that poetry is extra-ordinary language
that arouses us from the benumbed inertia of "chatter." Certainly
Heidegger, as a late Romantic, an heir of Kierkegaard and a student

---

8   The phrase Wordsworth used in 1843 in his letter to Isabella Fenwick about the
     genesis of the Intimations Ode (quoted in *Wordsworth's Poetry and Prose*, 433).

9   Cf. Shelley's "Defense": "And whether it spreads its own figured curtain, or
     withdraws life's dark veil from before the scene of things, it equally creates
     for us a being within our being. It makes us the inhabitants of a world to which
     the familiar world is a chaos. It reproduces the common universe of which we
     are portions and percipients, and it purges from our inward sight the film of
     familiarity which obscures from us the wonder of our being." (533) Reproduce"
     is used here in the sense of OED, 2a: "To bring again into material existence; to
     create or form (a person or thing) again"–in other words, "recreate."

of Gnosticism, can be seen as channeling Romantic ideas about the banality of everyday life and of poetry's salutary power to disquiet. In these ideas lies an echo of Greek dualism, Orphic and Platonic, which contrasts a distant immaterial reality with a factitious surround. In fact, many modern and even contemporary defenses of poetry that wistfully evoke its power to transport us may unknowingly reprise the ancient dualism, exalting literature because it offers us an "intenser day" than the day we are living through (Shelley, "Ode to the West Wind").

Laura Quinney

Who's to Say?

The professor's past chariness about a Festschrift gave some of us pause. Will he welcome the infliction of these compliments? There's only one thing worse than being given short shrift, he might think, and that's being given a long one when there are Beckett and *Alice in Wonderland* to be re-read. As a matter of tact, is this something that friends and colleagues can pull off for the author of *Keats and Embarrassment*? Have we the art to avoid the possibility of "an embarrassment that clogs, paralyses, or coarsens"? Should we not dread "the shadow of the impure motive" that Mr. Eliot saw hanging about Donne, lending its aid "to a facile success"?

Every tribute of this kind has a potentially unwelcome element of summing up. Eliot was subjected to not exactly a Festschrift but *A Selected Critique* at 60, in 1948, five years after declaring in his last great poem that "next year's words await another voice." But fortunately, he wouldn't lie down, so there was the *Symposium* at 70, and then the reminiscences of *The Man and His Work* in 1966, the year after his death, and then . . ..

In 1963, Christopher adeptly did and didn't write for the double number of *the Review* devoted to Empson, by interviewing him. In 1974 he doubled down, and his sixty pages on "Empson's Poetry" hogged a quarter of Roma Gill's Festschrift. It was then almost two decades since Empson's *Collected Poems*, and more than one since *Milton's God* (1961) had been promptly followed by Ricks's *Milton's Grand Style* (1963). Even so, Empson had ten years left to live, and for Gill's book to describe itself as a "volume of commemorative and celebratory essays" felt too much like a foreclosing. Empson called it "that absurd book."

In Larkin's case, the "Special Number" of *Phoenix* in 1973 was content to reprint Christopher's already eight-year-old review of *The Whitsun Weddings*: "Yes, we ought to be impatient with his having written so little . . .." The Festschrift followed *at Sixty*, but despite this youthfulness, it was already eight years after the last book of poems Larkin ever managed to publish, *High Windows* (1974), and if he was rueful, that was in keeping with the feeling he'd long been trading on that the game was up. His letter of thanks praised Christopher for the way "time after time you show the reader how the perceptive intelligence can provide additional facets to what at first had seemed two-dimensional." After a publication party at Faber, though, he apologized to Kingsley Amis for not having "more of a chance for a chinwag," having "had my bellyful of C. Rix" (among other indigestibles).

Although Christopher had written about Beckett in *Isis* in 1955 as unjustly neglected (before *Godot a changé tout çela*), and wrote about him again in 1964, he is not among the 24 contributors to *Beckett at Sixty* or the 23 (+ Samuel Beckett) who contributed to *As No Other Dare Fail: For Samuel Beckett on his 80th Birthday*. This unjust neglect is probably explained by both books being published, 19 years apart, by John Calder, for whom Christopher had considerably less time than Beckett had himself. Nor, perhaps, was Christopher top of Calder's invitation list for the second volume after his review of several Beckett books including the first hurrah:

> John Calder achieves the bizarre and demeaning feat of selling Beckett as a good read: "Beckett's plots are good, understandable, interesting plots, his situations are believable, his characters quickly become old friends."

With friends like these, one might well decline to be of the party, and when the John Calder brandwagon came round again to Beckett, Christopher's was the tribute of not being aboard. With one or two exceptions, the living writers he has most loved have not clamoured for applause, nor been in the puff'n'blurb business, and it was a sheer surprise in 1982 when a centenary book about James Joyce included a single-sentence tribute from Beckett: "I welcome this occasion to bow once again, before I go, deep down, before his heroic work, heroic being." Although Beckett lived until 1989, this heroic line was written two years before the Joyce centenary, and therefore with the possibility of posthumescence. Christopher duly celebrated it in *Beckett's Dying Words* as "the tragic counterpart to Beckett's declining to be celebrated." Then, placing his essay "Heroic Work by Samuel Johnson and Samuel Beckett" last in *Along Heroic Lines*, which he has said will be his final collection, he took a long look back and bowed out, quoting Beckett's sentence once again as his book's dying words

In truth, Christopher has loved Festschrifts for other people, whether it be Austin Clarke, Irvin Ehrenpreis or William H. Pritchard, just as he has frequently written for centenaries, companions, commemorations, congratulations, celebrations—every kind of appreciation and gratitude. He's brimming with unexpected loves. I was stunned, not so long after graduating, to receive a letter from the King Edward VIIth Professor of English Literature signed "Love, Christopher"—not having realised how promiscuously he chucks it about. (Who else says not just "I love puns" but "I love coincidences" or "I love brackets" (lunulae)?)

However, despite a sheaf of *Ricks's Dicta* being set down twenty-odd years ago by friends (David Ferry, Anthony Hecht, Charles Tomlinson among the poets; Seamus Heaney sent regrets), Christopher has escaped sprightly. Now that he's 91, though, we're catching up with him, and with no actual anniversary he's bound to wonder whether we are late to the *Fest*, or getting in early, lest. (His 90th birthday was comically marked for selected friends by gifts from him: copies of his (expensive) volume (newly published) of the eleven that will constitute the *Selected Writings of James Fitzjames Stephen* (of which he is the instigating co-editor).) As we are reminded on the first page of *Beckett's Dying Words*, I. *Death*, THE WISH TO DIE: "Most people most of the time want to live for ever." But there are other considerations, as always, because Christopher's principles are closer to proverbs than to theories: "after all, most people, some of the time, and some people most of the time, do not want to live for ever."

This buttressing of different-but-not-cancelling truths enables Christopher not to be in two minds but in many minds. *Forever Young*, for instance, is a quite different proposition, and Beckett and Dylan's two minds are "radically different kinds of genius"—both of which Christopher nudged the Nobel committee to recognize—and they are among many in his firmament of genius who have praised, commissioned or reviewed him, asked his advice, corresponded or broken bread with him, tangled with him, loved him. Artists don't always respect their critics like this, let alone artists of genius who cover such a range. How pleasant not only to meet Mr Beckett and Mr Dylan, but to number among your innumerable friends William Empson, Robert Lowell, Anthony Hecht and Frederick Wiseman.

The designation "genius" and its nature matter a lot to Christopher, partly because, as he pointed out, "in America at the moment it is exceptionally difficult to get genius recognised, except in the realm of sport. There is built-in resistance to the idea of genius in an egalitarian society, or one that takes itself to be so, partly dishonestly" (this was a while ago). Important to recognise it, though, because "geniuses are people who notice things and connections between things which others haven't noticed. Genius must be a surprise." If Beckett had gone electric, one feels, Christopher is the critic who would have welcomed it (though had there been a fundamentalist period, I suppose he might have invoked Judas).

"Genius is free to do as it chooses," and it is up to the critic to discriminate precisely what it is up to and what not. What *not* sometimes being what tells. On Johnson: "Genius is better than we are because of its generosity. But because of his old Tory convictions, that the world is as it is, there is almost no sense of *mission* in Dr. Johnson for the improvement of things in general. *Rasselas* and the essays in *The Rambler* are about learning to endure, and to enjoy when we can." Or on Dickens: "see it as a condition of Dickens's genius: say rather that Dickens is at his best in not exploring the most inward of his characters' feelings. Because not to explore can be reticently piercing."

Lawrence has "a genius with words," whereas Dorothy M. Richardson "was a true talent, and the more so in not misconceiving of herself as a genius." Geoffrey Hill, with whom Christopher's relationship was often one of give and take, "may not *be* a genius, but he *has* genius"; and some there are who are "touched with genius" or merely produce "a stroke of genius." As with angels, we shouldn't forget the hierarchy.

The big critical studies are all about individual geniuses and new ways to unlock them: Milton, Keats, Eliot, Beckett... and then the tricky one. There's the coy hint: "Geniuses are at work in the rock music field, and great popularity is no proof you aren't good." Then advocacy, then just thrilled admiration: "a genius with rhyming"; "rhetorical genius"; "a genius in performance"; "I think of his genius as one that has an extraordinary range (as well as depth) of apprehension"; "To this artist, whose genius is given also to gratitude, our gratitude is due." And once you've written *Dylan's Visions of Sin* and edited his lyrics, it's not clear whose are the royalties and whose the gratuities.

The older senses of "genius" predominate in Johnson's Dictionary, with "The protecting power of men, places, or things," backed by quotations from Shakespeare (2), Milton (1) and Dryden (2), leading to "Disposition by nature by which any one is qualified for some peculiar employment" (Dryden, Burnet, Pope, Arbuthnot). Whereas "A man endowed with superior faculties" (to put it mildly) is supported only by Addison, despite Swift having raised the bar considerably forty years before the Dictionary, in his *Proposal for Correcting ... the English Tongue* (1712):

> I do not mean by a true Genius, any bold Writer, who breaks through the Rules of Decency to distinguish himself by the Singularity of Opinions; but one, who upon a deserving Subject, is able to open new Scenes, and discover a Vein of true and noble Thinking, which never entered into any Imagination before: Every Stroke of whose Pen is worth all the Paper blotted by Hundreds of others in the Compass of their Lives.

Even geniuses make mistakes, though. All the players were wrong, Ben Jonson commented, to have praised Shakespeare for never blotting a line. "Would he had blotted a thousand" was his retort—as if we didn't have enough variants. But rather than just editing for a "best text," correcting Keats's misspellings, deploring Empson's misquotations, or despairing of Dylan's vagaries in performance, how much richer to mine and compare the variants, thinking all the time about intentions, conscious and unconscious. "All revisions by geniuses have something to be said about them," says our man—who has often proved to be the man to say it.

Christopher, though, resists accusations of being a genius himself, not knowing what he would do with the thought if he believed it were true. It might lead him to thoughts of Robert Lowell, "who wasn't vain, although he knew he was a genius and was tormented by it," or of Dylan disliking, if not quite disowning, this label among many others: "Genius is a terrible word, a word they think will make me like them."

Well, like it or not, Christopher finds himself disavowing it suspiciously often. When compared once with Empson, he wrote, "I know that I am without genius, even a streak of it, and Empson had scarcely a streak of anything else." And again, with Johnson, "I'm not in that class. I'm without genius" (but the coincidence of sharing a birthday with him—what's not to love?).

Christopher and Geoffrey were in violent agreement in thinking that critics often think too much of themselves, and shouldn't have pretensions to parity with the artists they write about. Criticism can be creative, and there are critics of genius, for sure, but it helps if they've done a bit of geniusing elsewhere as, say, poets or translators of Norwegian drama. For the centenary of Tennyson's death, Christopher tried to keep the "service art" of the editor-critic-biographer in perspective:

> Someone in *Punch*, cleverly clowning, once went so farcical as to describe me as "the domed genius who brought Tennyson out of the doghouse." Well, domed I can understand (it is encoded baldism), and genius I know myself to be entirely without, but who ever believed that Tennyson had

been in the doghouse? His poems have become dog-eared, so repeatedly have they been read and loved by millions . . ..

Yet even Oxford's former Professor of Poetry might agree that here and there *The Idylls of the King* "leaves us in doubt," in Edward Young's words, "whether genius is more evident in the sublime flights and beauteous flowers of poetry, or in the profound penetrations, and marvellously keen and minute distinctions, called the thorns of the schools." There are times when one would rather read the critic.

Coleridge was fascinated by Genius yet lapsed so egregiously into humility as to claim "My inner mind does not justify the Thought that I possess a Genius." When it comes to this critical distinction, as with most other things, then, self-identification must give way to scientific tests. If it quacks like a duck, and has flights of fancy, and ornithologists such as Mary Douglas classify it as a duck . . .. That is to say, pieces of evidence must be produced, perhaps each slight in itself, but having a cumulative plausibility.

Coleridge's own tests are many, so let us try some. "The sum total of all intellectual excellence is good sense and method. When these have passed into the instinctive readiness of habit, when the wheel revolves so rapidly that we cannot see it revolve at all, then we call the combination Genius." Yes: Christopher is extremely many things, among them extremely moderate, balanced and ready with copious good sense and method. Like Groucho Marx, he has principles, and if you don't like them, he has others. "But there are ways in which we should be simply grateful for his not always standing by his convictions," as he writes of Eliot. "There is a generosity in all such acts of overriding oneself."

"It is one contradistinction of genius from talent," writes Coleridge, "that its predominant end is always comprised in the means; and this is one of the many points which establish an analogy between genius and virtue." Again, Christopher distinguishes himself with high marks. He's sometimes partial to an argument, but he's not partial in argument: truth's the thing, and never compromised for wit or victory's sake. Well, hardly ever. (In his Table Talk, Coleridge added a further contradistinction, that "Talent, lying in the understanding, is often inherited; genius, being the action of reason and imagination, rarely or never." Perhaps sadly he cannot pass it on, but when a man has had seven children, he has certainly done his polyphiloprogenitive best.)

So how about Coleridge's discernment in genius of "an originality in intellectual construction: the moral accompaniment, and actuating principle of which consists, perhaps, in the carrying on of the freshness and feelings of childhood into the powers of manhood"? Yes, and children sense his love of them (see above) and will toddle impressive distances to be with him.

To Coleridge, genius meant "the faculty which *adds* to the existing stock of power, and knowledge by new views, new combinations &c." and in Christopher's case the *et caetera* includes ingenious readings, new aphorisms and other observations. In Coleridge's terms again, "Man of genius places things *in a new light.*"

Christopher might be happier to agree with Madame de Staël that "Next to genius what is most like it is the power to know it and admire it," but to judge his lifelong exercise of gratitude and generosity, critical and personal, as less than the genius of generosity would be sucking the blood out of it. Isn't genius often a unique brew that you otherwise can't put a name to? If he had been anybody else, he'd have been the first to recognize it in himself.

Humility is useless. Christopher, you've often shown judgment as precise as a musician with perfect pitch, but on this exacting question—it's not for you to say.

Jim McCue

"People Like Us"

P
eople like us," said Christopher, pulling a book from the shelf of a here-no-longer bookshop in New York, referring to the kind of place "people like us" like to explore. I can still hear him saying that; and with that "us" he welcomed me into his orbit. (Thank you again, Christopher; and knowing praise makes you uneasy, I place these words between parentheses.)

One of the great good fortunes of my life is to have studied with Christopher Ricks and for him to encourage me, read my poems closely, befriend me and be a true friend. To study with Christopher means to listen to how he listens, engaging with language with absolute intensity and clarity. To read Christopher is to enter a realm where clarity intensifies thought that does not lose its power. I recall turning to someone next to me in a lecture hall where Christopher had just given a talk in which he considered vicissitudes of syntax and punctuation: my audience-mate and I concurred that hearing Professor Ricks attend to commas and semicolons—in a sentence or a line—was a mouthwatering experience. As for readers and writers for whom the physicality of a poem is a living force impelling us to run *to* rather than away from poetry: devoted to comprehending and appreciating this force, Christopher has produced many gifts, including his essays in *The Force of Poetry*, where he quotes Dr. Johnson's words defining this force "which calls new power into being, which embodies sentiment, and animates matter."

When I first met Christopher, he was a Professor of English Literature at Cambridge University and a visiting professor at The CUNY Graduate Center in New York. I was twenty-five; it was the fall of 1979 or spring of 1980, and I had moved to a tiny apartment in the West Village the year before, after completing a graduate degree in poetry at The Johns Hopkins Writing Seminars and spending an extra year in Baltimore as a special student at the Humanities Center. As a doctoral student at The Graduate Center, I signed up for the first course Christopher taught there: Allusion from Dryden to Eliot. The experience was transformative for everyone in our class; I felt a sense

of euphoria, especially as a young poet already disenchanted by
theoretical discourse and ambivalent about literary criticism. This may
have been the same academic year when I signed up for Christopher's
short course entitled Beckett and Death. Though I had fallen in love
with Beckett's plays in high school and his prose works in college,
death did not intrigue me as a subject (I still felt immortal); but I had no
doubt that Professor Ricks would enthrall us with his comments and
that it would be foolish to miss a chance to study with him again. The
joy of being in one of his seminars was shared by anyone who, from
prior experience, could anticipate the effect of his insights but could
never predict what those insights might be. The third course, also a
shorter one, consisted of several class meetings in which we discussed
Bob Dylan's lyrics—not only by closely attending to the words but by
listening to different versions of songs that Dylan recorded, versions
that Christopher played for us. Around that time, a Shakespeare
scholar on the faculty took me aside and in a conspiratorial tone told
me that studying Dylan was beyond the bounds of what should be
taught in an English Department's curriculum; I had to brush off this
attempt to dissuade me from taking the course seriously (or at all).
This was my first encounter with something apparent in retrospect,
the envy one professor might harbor for another. What a conundrum
Christopher must have presented: for the person who wrote *Milton's
Grand Style*, arguably the finest book on Milton, to apply his nuanced
understanding to a popular singer-songwriter.

Some of the most-treasured memories return as a fragment or a
flash. Being invited to lunch at the apartment on Leroy Street where
Christopher and his wife, the photographer Judith Aronson, were
staying: cucumber sandwiches, delicious conversation. On my first
visit, Judith was still pregnant with their second child. At some point
during this lunchtime visit or another, I walked with Christopher to an
Italian bakery on MacDougal Street, Christopher pushing Alice in a
stroller: we had coffee and then selected pastries to bring back to the
apartment, probably for dessert. Another vivid memory is of walking
with Christopher to the Phoenix Book Shop: upon opening the door we
saw Geoffrey Hill stepping out of a shadow, moving toward us, a book
in one hand. A few years earlier I had started reading Hill's poems; he
was words on a page, I never imagined a chance to meet him face to
face would arise. Christopher introduced us: he must have arranged
this brief encounter, knowing how much it would mean to meet a poet
whose work I keenly admired. That's how things happen when one is
young (and lucky). Soon after that, Christopher sent me a pamphlet,

"Geoffrey Hill and 'The tongue's atrocities'" (the first published version of a talk he delivered on 15 February 1978 at the University College of Swansea). I assume many of us have received from Christopher one of his published works and discovered on some pages the corrections he penciled in. I had not yet read a critical essay on Hill's poems and was struck by Christopher's calibrated observations, how beautifully he articulated subtle aspects of tone, syntax, sound, allusion. That pamphlet remains my touchstone for how to read and hear a poem, " and how to evoke the experience.

One of the things that always impressed me is how much Christopher loves babies; I saw this in his relationship with Alice and James, but also in his reaction to other people's children. Infants and toddlers provoke in him a sense of glee. I cherish the photos Christopher sent of his grandchildren, including one of Sylvia smiling in her baby carriage, wearing a big pair of sunglasses: "Swinging Sylvia" is the email's subject line. The ease with which Christopher moves between unselfconscious feeling and deliberated thought reminds me of the quality Eliot valued so highly in Donne's poetry: an association of feeling and thought, not the "dissociation of sensibility" he rued. I wonder if a child's unfiltered authentic response, a pre-linguistic relation to the world, is related paradoxically to Christopher's linguistic sensitivity, to "new power" called into being at least in part through nonverbal elements, rhythms and formal patterns that generate and shape a literary work.

W.H. Auden said that Christopher Ricks is "the kind of critic every poet dreams of finding." How true that is. Auden was alive but I was too young to have a chance to meet him when I memorized some of his poems in childhood, not aware why I was drawn to them, drawn to them nevertheless. "Another time has other lives to live" was a line that haunted me, its music and truth inextricable—though the weight of its meaning and the sorrow I savored when reciting it were a weight and sorrow beyond my years. The chance to meet Christopher occurred at just the right moment in my life and his influence never ebbed, beginning the first day of his course on allusion, where so much I needed to learn was illuminated and so much that mattered to me as a writer was affirmed—beyond anything I could have hoped for. A few weeks into the seminar, Christopher met with me in conference: he had read a sheaf of my poems and began by saying aloud the title of one poem, "Winter Sculpture," remarking on the soundscape those two words created. The off-rhyme clearly pleased him; so did a particular line, "Between the crystal and its melt," which arose spontaneously in the composition process but I wasn't sure would make sense to anyone else. Although "melt" felt right to my ear I knew it was an odd use of the word, could only hope this verb behaving as a noun would sound true and convey meaning (it is an actual noun, if one looks back far enough). Homing in on sonic effects, Christopher let me know how much sound mattered to him; and instead of criticizing "melt" as diction too archaic, he appreciated that monosyllable.

From what he gleaned by reading this recent group of poems, all in free verse, Christopher could not have known that since the age of nine I had been writing in longhand almost every day, mostly poems composed in rhyme and meter or blank verse, some longer ones sprawling across the page (experiments influenced by Cummings and Ferlinghetti), and a few plays and stories. When I arrived at college with a binder containing a transcription of my writing, three-hundred typed pages, I soon discovered that my peers would find my poems old-fashioned. Why are you trying to sound like Shakespeare? asked another freshman in my dorm. I wanted my work to be more idiomatic but didn't want to sacrifice my love of sonic play. I began writing free verse, found ways to create echoes with internal rhymes instead of the end rhymes my earlier poems deployed. The week before classes started at Sarah Lawrence College, students were required to "interview" any teacher whose course they were interested in taking. I lugged my heavy binder to Galway Kinnell's office: he had just finished playing tennis and towered over his desk in his tennis whites. When Galway asked me to show him some poems, I doubt he was pleased when I handed him that binder: he started flipping through the pages, stopping at one poem then another until he asked me to find something in the first person. I did; he read it, then asked me to find a poem in the first person that wasn't in rhyme and meter. I could not find anything that fit this requirement except one poem loosely composed in blank verse, lines of which he read aloud. Until that moment it hadn't crossed my mind that I was unable to compose a poem in the first person, one that felt "personal," without entering the zone of meter or the enclosure of rhyme; my shyness, not yet overcome, could be transcended only if I lost myself in a pattern that possessed me, the rhythms themselves generating the lines. I didn't register for Kinnell's poetry workshop or any workshop that semester but continued writing poems.

At the age of twenty-five, feeling old because the manuscript of my first book was still in limbo, the struggle against my aesthetic predilections ended. In letters Par Avion on tissue-thin blue paper and later in emails, Christopher corresponded and responded, sharing news and meticulously describing what did or did not work (for him) in the poems I shared. Christopher opened the door. It may embarrass him that I say this, but even the notion of embarrassment reminds me of how, during one of his talks, Christopher placed a curved hand on either side of his face to demonstrate the relation between shyness and words in parentheses. When I simulate this visual analogy, my students grasp the connection—words quietly living (or hiding) between brackets.

Opening one of my favorite books by Christopher Ricks, *True Friendship: Geoffrey Hill, Anthony Hecht, and Robert Lowell Under the Sign of Eliot and Pound,* I see his inscription from March 2010 in the script that grew so familiar. By chance I turn to page 156 and read: "Allusion is always a return, and the word *return* within an allusion will align the use of poetry with the use of memory." That is the first sentence of a paragraph preceding a passage Christopher quotes from *Little Gidding,* a passage that begins: "This is the use of memory: / For liberation—." True friendship and the memory of its liberating force realign us.

Phillis Levin

A Thank-You Note for Christopher

Dear Christopher, it's been some years
 Since last I saw you—maybe Boston—
 Yes it was there—before the fears
Of plague descended. I had tossed on
An ugly hat: rain came in spears,
 Or dribs and drabs. But it was lost on
The cab-ride back—so go the years!—
 That conference that honored—very
Rightly—gentle David Ferry.

The hat I mention, well because
 It is a memory that sticks.
Not just a useful hat, it was
 A hat remarked on by a Ricks—
"What a hat!" perhaps—the laws
 Of memory can play some tricks,
It might have been something like that—
 But it was a remarked-on hat,

And now it's gone, which makes me sorry,
 Because remarkable, no less.
(It also kept me dry.) But worry
 Not, I shall cease to digress,
And focus on another story
 Back in the past's vague wilderness.
Another time, when I met you
At ALSCW—

(Muse, help me remember better—
 At that time just ALSC,
Without that final cretic letter?
 I think so.) Anyway, for me
Notable, for my being wetter

Behind the ears—figuratively—
And on a panel presentation
On didactic and translation—

Lucretius, in this case, who met
A metaphor, as he would sing,
In letters of the alphabet,
(And weaving too, with so much string):
Just like the atoms, there's a set
Can spell out this and everything.
And you, as I recall to mind,
Asked questions that were keen and kind.

Even before, though, when I came
Through Boston, I think, for a reading,
Bob Clawson came up with a scheme
For entertainment, one exceeding
Curious—because he'd claim
That as the gathering was needing
A venue, that we might repair
To your house. But were you aware?

Ay, there's the rub, we realized.
Were you aware? Perhaps a hitch in
Such a plan: you seemed surprised
To find some poets in your kitchen,
But not unpleasantly, and sized
The party up, and who would pitch in.
(Then did I blush, cheeks red as beets,
With an embarrassment, like Keats?)

I don't remember—but I think
You were amused, and we were jolly,
Some with verse, and some with drink
(which sometimes leads to melancholy,
The verse, I mean—"it hurts to think.")
I blame and praise Bob for the folly.
You showed us, as if on a bet,
A note from T.S. Eliot.

But that's enough for a preamble.
This is a celebration—send
For fine champagne, cavort and gambol!
Thus all would celebrate a friend,
Friend to the singers. (I might ramble,
But wandering's a way to wend
From stanza to its near successor,
From poet to poetry professor.)

And so I wear another hat,
And tip it to you. As one chooses,
A life is spent in this and that,
One labors, and another boozes.
But some ascend the ziggurat
(That's mount Parnassus) of the Muses,
By solving cruxes that arise
(And shepherding a Nobel prize),

And reading deeply, who have heard
The tuneless ditties of the Urn.
They are the lovers of the word.
For love's precision, to discern
The song in songster, trilling bird,
Or sea-girls in the ocean's churn.
So Christopher, I wish you, dearly,
Felicitations. Yours, sincerely.

A.E. Stallings

Moi, Marcellus eris:
Proust and Vergil[1]

Just what role classical literature played in Marcel Proust's writing has been debated for years, especially in the context of *A la recherche du temps perdu*. While Proust's treatment of the classics surfaces often negatively in the novel, most often to portray a character such as Cottard or Brichot unsympathetically, Proust's correspondence offers additional insight. As Miguet-Ollagnier notes,

> Critical in the novel concerning those who display their knowledge of antiquity indiscreetly through quotation, Proust is no less so in his correspondence, when he spots a gaffe, a misidentified Latin line. The critic Paul Souday, reviewing *Swann's Way* in *Le Temps* had made cutting remarks about Proust's French mistakes, citing a line from Ovid's *Metamorphoses*, "materiam superabat opus" ('the work transcended its material'), but attributing it to Horace. Proust countered in scathing fashion, advising him to check his Latin quotations: "It's not Horace who spoke of a text whose *materiam superabat opus* but Ovid," adding, "This latter poet did not say that critically but for purposes of praise." Note the two reproaches from Proust: author error and perversion of sense.[2]

---

1   This paper was inspired by a talk by William Flesch at the ALSCW conference in New Haven in 2022 on Proust's adaptation of the Orpheus story from Vergil's fourth *Georgic*. It is dedicated to Christopher Ricks in the hopes that it will add to our longish list of shared delights.

2   "Sévère dans le roman vis-à-vis de ceux qui étalent indiscrètement par des citations leur connaissance de l'antiquité, Proust l'est pourtant aussi dans sa correspondance, lorsqu'il peut relever une bévue, un vers latin mal identifié. Le critique Paul Souday rendant compte dans *Le Temps* de *Du côté de chez Swann* avait fait des remarques acerbes sur des fautes de français de Proust et avait cité un vers des *Métamorphoses* d'Ovide: "materiam superabat opus" ("le travail surpassait la matière", II, 5) mais l'attribuant à Horace. Proust lui répond de façon cinglante en lui conseillant de vérifier ses citations latines: "ce n'est pas Horace qui a parlé d'un ouvrage où 'materiam superabat opus' mais Ovide" et il ajoute : "ce dernier poète avait dit cela non pas sévèrement, mais en manière d'éloge" (III, 1592). Retenons les deux griefs de Proust: erreur sur l'auteur et détournement de sens." Marie Miguet-Ollagnier, "Citations d'auteurs anciens dans l'oeuvre de Proust," *Bulletin d'informations proustiennes*, 23, (1992), 13-28, esp. 14.

Paul Souday was a writer who frequently reviewed literary works, including those of Proust, and with whom Proust often argued about the classics. But there is a second letter from Proust to Souday, dated April 7, 1922, that offers even greater insight into Proust's classicism. Dated April 7, 1922, Proust writes: *Cher monsieur et ami*, "I have many excuses to offer you concerning the stag dinner the other night." He continues by explaining that there were no women present at this event because he scheduled it too late to invite them. He then laments the misfortune the two men have had over the years, since whenever the possibility for a rendezvous arises, the timing is off: one date is too close to publication of a review by Souday, another occurs at a time when Proust has delayed too long in getting a manuscript ready for publication. Proust concludes the letter by explaining that

> to the extent that it is not only *libelli* [little books] that have *sua fata* [their destiny] but me, who will be that Marcellus (that I have not been) who failed to break bitter destiny, since one way or another, my invitations seem to create the appearance of thanking you for your review, if not manipulating it. I am not such a man of letters as that would suggest, although I'm proud of being one at all. And I would love it if our relationship might be (as it is in reality, except for annoying "dates," as Jacques Blanche says, that take away the appearance of being so) the relationship of man to man—with amenable women *sub rosa*—who pass the evenings conversing about literature when I am not, as I was the other day, half-aware.[3]
>
> Please accept, my sir and friend, my grateful and devoted respect,

Marcel Proust

References to classics, especially Latin, abound. Starting with the insertion of Latin *libelli . . . sua fata*, the letter moves from lamenting a failed social event to a complicated statement about memory and experience, the very topics the seven volumes of *A la Recherche* return to again and again. And, even more to the point, it makes

---

3   "De sorte que ce n'est pas seulement les livres (*libelli*) qui ont *sua fata*, mais moi, *Marcellus eris*, que je n'ai pas été, n'ayant pas rompu l'âpre destin et sûr d'une façon ou de la contraire, mes invitations ont l'air tantôt de remercier mon critique, tantôt de le ménager. Je ne suis pas si homme de lettres que cela, quoique très fier de l'être. Et j'aimerais que nos rapports soient (ce qu'ils sont en réalité, mais que de fâcheuses "dates", comme dit Jacques Blanche, leur ôtent l'apparence de l'être) des rapports d'homme à homme avec d'aimables dames *sub rosa* et en devisant de belles-lettres les soirs où je ne suis pas, comme avant hier, demi-apathique. Veuillez agréer, cher Monsieur et ami, mes hommages reconnaissants et dévoués, Marcel Proust. *Correspondance de Marcel Proust*, ed. by P. Kolb (Plon, 1993), 21: 112-14.

these arguments precisely through classical references, especially to Vergil.

Libelli . . . sua fata, it must be said, is not Vergil but Terence. By Proust's time this phrase had become an oft-quoted sound bite, used precisely to demonstrate pseudo-erudition. Proust's pedantic character, Bichot, uses it in the final volume of *A la recherche*, and it appears in the popular culture of the day and after, indicating that books have lives of their own.[4] It is, I would suggest, just the kind of Latin that Proust would expect Souday to use without knowing its source or meaning; in the context of the letter, it's almost an inside joke. Less wry and more significant are the references that follow. The *fata* from Terence here triggers references to *Aeneid* 6 where fate also plays a significant role. Having tuned us to Latin through the Terence quote, Proust dives deeper into classical allusions; the highly evocative *Marcellus eris* is followed immediately by *n'ayant pas rompu l'âpre destin*, (failed to break bitter destiny) both of which echo the end of *Aeneid* 6 and evoke the figure of young Marcellus, Augustus' nephew who died at nineteen, a death editorialized by the observation that despite what we wish, our fate is unchangeable:

heu, miserande puer, si qua fata aspera rumpas,
tu Marcellus eris . . .[5]

(Pitiful boy, if you could but break your fate! Alas, you will be Marcellus.)

To dwell on Marcellus for a moment: in 1910 Proust bought an 1832 etching by James Pradier of an 1812 Jean-Auguste-Dominique Ingres' painting of Vergil reading the Marcellus passage to Octavian, Vergil's patron and future emperor, his sister Octavia, and his wife Livia; the painting shows Octavia fainting. As Antoine Compagnon has commented: "But even more, this Vergilian Marcellus, would he not be identifiable as Proust, given Proust's [classical] predilections and maybe also because of the blows of fate he has experienced?"[6]

---

4   *Habent libelli sua fata* is a phrase from Terence, *De litteris, de syllabis, de metris*, verse 1286. It is often quoted, including by Walter Benjamin, *Illuminations*, and Umberto Eco, *The Name of the Rose*. Proust, *A la recherche du temps perdu*, (Pléiade, 1987), 4:371.
5   Vergil, *Aeneid* VI, ed. by R.A.B. Mynors, (Oxford University Press, 1972), 881-2. Translation is mine.
6   "Mais plus encore, ce Marcellus virgilien ne serait-il pas identifiable à Proust, penchant qu'avait ce dernier lui-meme, peut-être aussi pour les coups subits du destin (*fata aspera* . . .)." Antoine Compagnon, Canalblog, leçon 4, Tuesday 29 January 2019: compaproust.canalblog.com; pub. Jan 31, 2019.

In the 1922 letter to Souday Marcel Proust indeed identifies explicitly with the ancient Marcellus, an identification that, despite his assertion to the contrary, he may have assumed for quite a while, given the date he purchased the etching. In the context of the letter, he too muses over whether he can change his fate and alter the nature of his relationship to Souday. He appears to lament the fact that their social events up to now have been marred by coincidence and things beyond his control. He opines that if circumstances would change, they could become just two regular guys who like to talk about literature, preferably in the presence of women.

And yet: while that is the surface message, the letter offers further indication of what Proust actually believes, and, in the process, also guides us in the depth of his classical learning. His mention of Jacques Blanche and his collection of essays known as *Dates*, together with the superfluous mention of *sub rosa*, would presumably have meant nothing to Souday beyond the literal reference. Blanche's book argues that dates create accidental associations: in the same way, Proust and Souday are cursed by the accidental fact that publication—of a review, of a book—happened too close to invitations to dinner and so there appears to be an ulterior plan, one that, at the end, Proust suggests maybe they can revise.

In the context of *Aeneid* 6, however, and the story of Marcellus, the mention of *Dates*, together with the author's name, *Blanche*, and the enigmatic reference to *sub rosa* take on further classical resonance. In Vergil, the very half-line that identifies Marcellus, quoted above, is followed by:

> ...manibus date lilia plenis
> purpureos spargam flores...[7]

(Allow me to scatter handfuls of lilies with crimson blossoms...)

Fate has weighed in: Marcellus will not survive, and his funeral is here indicated by the strewn flowers. Even as Proust is suggesting to Souday that it would be nice if things could change, I would argue that he alludes to these very lines in Vergil to indicate they cannot: the

---

7   *Aen.* 6. 883-4. Although it is unknown which version of the *Aeneid* Proust used, a popular translation of the time clearly distinguishes two types of flowers: "& les lis & les roses" (M. de Segrais, (Paris, 1712), 265). There is much debate about the exact translation of these lines. See especially F.E. Brenk, "*Purpureos Spargam Flores*," *Classical Quarterly* 40 (1990), 218-23 for discussion of the colors and substantial bibliography.

title of Blanche's book, *Dates*, echoes the key verb, *date*. The author's surname means white, like the lilies, and the superfluous *sub rosa* adds red to the mix. Together they evoke the putative funeral for Marcellus, the passage that declares that fate is beyond our control. But the point is more barbed than that, because Proust would have assumed that Souday would not catch those references, would not see the larger picture that requires solid learning in Latin. Not only will they not get over their social misfortunes, they will never become men of letters discussing literature. It's just not possible, since such discussions could only happen between men of equal erudition, which these two, it appears, are not.

In the broader context of his writing, it does seem that when Proust wants to talk about the past he often turns to Vergil–other ancient authors as well, but primarily Vergil (and especially *Aen.* 6, like others before and after him, from Dante to David Ferry). Memory, he comes to argue, is enhanced by time and change: the new brings the old back to life even as the old grants depth to the new. The last pages of *A la recherche* speak of "This notion of embodied time, of past years not being separated from us," which has "no break in continuity," enables him to "still find it, still go back to it." Human bodies contain "every hour of the past" and are "perched atop living stilts which never stop growing."[8] Proust directs his final words at the reader, as he urges us to look back on our lives even as we think back on the seven volumes we have just read; both journeys, according to him, are continuous and retrievable. The blurring of text and experience is here asserted, and the counterexample offered by the letter to Paul Souday continues to play in the background as an instance of failed responsibility, but also lost opportunity. Marcel Proust may share the fate of the ancient Marcellus and be unable to rewrite his relationship with Souday, but at the same time he revives that Marcellus, as he brings him back into the conversation. The image he provides is telling: he does not see our relationship with the past as that of dwarves on the shoulders of giants. Rather, we are perched on living stilts, "juchés sur de vivantes échasses," where the emphasis is not on vision but on life and growth: the past in whatever form is revived by the present which, in turn, enables that present to draw on what came before.

Sarah Spence

---

8   Proust, *A la recherche*, 4:623-25; Ian Patterson, tr. *Finding Time Again* (Penguin Classics, 2002), 390-2.

You Might Have Rhymed

When is a poem a rhyming poem? T.S. Eliot saw that the *vers libre* pursued by his most innovative contemporaries involved as a founding principle "[t]he rejection of rhyme," and he was certainly not sorry himself to see the back of the "comforting echo" created by "the recurrence of identical sounds."[1] Of course it seems obvious that verse wishing to be free should spurn rhyme: opponents have always objected to it as a form of constraint, the "troublesome and modern bondage" described by Milton which hampered a more "ancient liberty."[2] Looking back on his own revolutionary times, Hazlitt made out a similar sort of connection: "rhyme was looked upon as a relic of the feudal system," he claimed to remember, something naturally to be discarded by a generation in which "[e]very one did that which was good in his own eyes."[3] But the left-libertarian politics in such statements are hardly Eliot's ("it is a battle-cry of freedom, and there is no freedom in art") and his response to the rejection of rhyme is finely ambivalent: "The question is of course just *what* is free and *what* is bound," as he had asked in a philosophical paper at Harvard.[4] For, he says, it is not so much that poetry is liberated from the bondage of rhyme as that rhyme is freed to be called upon for different kinds of local work: "There are often passages in an unrhymed poem where rhyme is wanted for some special effect, for a sudden tightening-up, for a cumulative insistence, or for an abrupt change of mood."[5] Had Eliot been asked for an exemplification of his claim he could not have done better than suggest the Milton of *Paradise Lost*, whose polemic

---

1   "Reflections on Vers Libre," in *The Complete Prose of T.S. Eliot*, ed. by Ronald Schuchard et al, (8 vols.; Johns Hopkins University Press, 2021), Vol. 1, 516.

2   "The Verse," in *The Poems of John Milton*, ed. by John Carey and Alastair Fowler, (Longman, 1968), 457.

3   "On the Living Poets," from *Lectures on the English Poets*, in *The Complete Works of William Hazlitt*, ed. by P.P. Howe, (21 vols.; Dent, 1930-34), Vol. 5, 162.

4   "[The Relationship between Politics and Metaphysics]," in *Complete Prose*, Vol. 1, 98.

5   "Reflections on *Vers Libre*," in *Complete Prose*, Vol. 1, 516.

against rhyme cannot disguise an auditory imagination that was, as Christopher Ricks once put it in a finely Miltonic double negative, "not indifferent to rhyme" at all.[6] When, then, Eliot warmly praises "[t]he peculiar feeling, almost a physical sensation of a breathless leap, communicated by Milton's long periods, and by his alone," and judges such effects "impossible to procure from rhymed verse," he really means to celebrate verse that very often deploys rhyme to exquisite effect, just not in ways that organise themselves into a pattern of line-endings as, say, heroic couplets or quatrains do:[7]

> in his face
> Divine compassion visibly appeerd,
> Love without end, and without measure Grace,
> Which uttering thus he to his Father spake.

Ricks: "grace, with miraculous simplicity, is as sweetly obvious, as effortless, as the rhyme of 'grace' and 'face.'" The lines could only be by Milton, needless to say, but similar resources might be utilised to quite different ends, for example (the connection is offered by Ricks) by Eliot himself, in "Marina," writing about the way that all those who mean Death

> Are become unsubstantial, reduced by a wind,
> A breath of pine, and the woodsong fog
> By this grace dissolved in place
>
> What is this face, less clear and clearer ... [8]

Here is a recurrence of sounds alright, but hardly a comforting echo, nor yet a sense of being bound, unless it is being spellbound: the feeling is one of suspended animation, "a cumulative insistence," the verse paused wonderingly in a particular sound space before gathering itself and moving on to the next phase of its journey.

---

6   "John Milton: Sound and Sense in *Paradise Lost*," in *TFOP*, 71. George Saintsbury points out the oddity that "the man who thirty years earlier had issued, and eight years later than that had reissued, work by far the larger part of which had been in rhyme, and who—for the moment let us put it in no stronger fashion—had certainly shown himself not unapt therein, now affected contempt and disgust at the very idea of rhyming. Nobody, so far as we know, made any observations on this anomaly [...] And the thing still remains odd." George Saintsbury, *A History of English Prosody from the Twelfth Century to the Present Day* (3 vols.; Macmillan, 1906-10), Vol. 2, 236.
7   "Milton II"; in *Complete Prose*, Vol. 7, 32.
8   *TFOP*, 69.

Such effects are about encountering rhymes where you had not been led to think you would find them, what Stephanie Burt calls "foreground rhyme"; but the interplay between the rhymed and the unrhymed can work in the opposite way too, not finding a rhyme when you *were* expecting one—a phenomenon that, of course, only becomes possible within a regime of "background" rhyme;[9] and that is my main interest here.[10] Among the many possibilities enabled by "expressing sentiments in short lines having similar sounds at their ends," Larkin's somewhat dour account of his lyric vocation—"the jingling sound of like endings" in Milton's words—is *declining* to produce a similar sound;[11] and the effects can be various and striking. Flushed with success after the performance of *The Mouse-Trap*, Hamlet recites a poem to Horatio: "For thou dost know, O Damon dear, / This realm dismantled was / Of Jove himself; and now reigns here / A very, very – pajock." This is clearly disrespectful though the nature of the disrespect is complicated. Hamlet is not saying the word "ass," but to call Claudius a peacock, or perhaps a patchcock, is just being rude about him in another way:[12] it is as though it is the refusal to rhyme, to discharge that obligation, that is in itself somehow the gesture of contempt. "You might have rhymed," says Horatio, sounding rather taken aback by his friend's scurrility: you had the opportunity to rhyme; but also, more judgmentally, you could have done the correct thing and rhymed. Good rhymes have good manners, like decent servants, said Robert Graves, "whose presence at the dinner-table gives the guests a sense of opulent security; never awkward or over-clever, they handle the dishes silently and professionally."[13]

In a late essay, Eliot singled out for praise an aspect of Herbert's genius which had a kinship with awkwardness: "Herbert knows the

---

9   "Cornucopia, or Contemporary American Rhyme," in *The Monkey and the Wrench. Essays into Contemporary Poetics*, ed. by Mary Biddinger and John Gallaher, (University of Akron Press, 2011), 61.

10   Burt traces a decline in "background rhyme" in modern American poetry (though not British or Irish). J. Paul Hunter summons the reasons why the practice once appealed: "Seven Reasons for Rhyme," in *Ritual, Routine and Regime: Repetition in Early Modern British and European Cultures*, ed. by Lorna Clymer, (University of Toronto Press, 2006), 172-98. Writing in 1980, Donald Wesling identified a kind of "sporadic sound linkage that, in time, will perhaps become the norm rather than the deviation." *The Chances of Rhyme. Device and Modernity* (University of California Press, 1980), 120.

11   To Barbara Pym, 22 January 1975: *Selected Letters of Philip Larkin* (Faber, 1992), 521. Milton, 457.

12   *Hamlet*, ed. by Harold Jenkins, (Methuen, 1982), 305, n..

13   *Collected Writings on Poetry*, ed. by Paul O'Prey, (Carcanet, 1995), 6-7.

effect of denying a rhyme where it is expected," said Eliot, and he gave
as an example

> When my devotions could not pierce
>   Thy silent eares;
>   Then was my heart broken, as was my verse:
> My breast was full of fears
>   And disorder.[14]

Herbert's poem, "Denial," does come out of denial in the end,
discovering the union of a closing couplet where it had so far
found only disjunction, what Helen Vendler calls "extraordinary
derangements":[15] "That so thy favors granting my request, / They and
my mind may chime, / And mend my rhyme." Rhyme there is being
used very emphatically to dramatize a return to a wholly salutary
form of bondage. Milton offers a different and more subtle case of the
unexpectedly unrhymed in what Ricks calls "the masterly rhyming
of 'Lycidas,'" a performance which famously encompasses some
masterly *un*rhyming along the way.[16] F.T. Prince described the poem
as "irregularly but closely rhymed, so that the few unrhymed lines
pass unnoticed";[17] but of course many readers have indeed noticed to
puzzle at them: Johnson, for instance, found "the rhymes uncertain."[18]
He did not mean to praise, and several scholars have attempted to
exonerate Milton's practice by reference to Italian models that he had
in mind, some even denying that, properly understood, there are any
unrhymed lines in the poem at all;[19] but Johnson's perception is acute,
and Saintsbury must be right to say that the poem's extraordinary
"symphonic effect is very mainly produced by the uncertainty of the
rhymes themselves." The effect is established from the off:

> Yet once more, O ye laurels, and once more
> Ye myrtles brown, with ivy never sere,
> I come to pluck your berries harsh and crude,
> And with forc'd fingers rude
> Shatter your leaves before the mellowing year.

---

14   "George Herbert," in *Complete Prose*, Vol. 7, 522.
15   *The Poetry of George Herbert* (Harvard University Press, 1975), 260.
16   *TFOP*, 71.
17   "'Lycidas' and the Tradition of the Italian Eclogue," *English Miscellany 2*, ed. by
     Mario Praz, (British Council, 1951), 96.
18   Samuel Johnson, *The Lives of the Most Eminent English Poets*, ed. by Roger
     Lonsdale, (4 vols.; Oxford University Press, 2006), Vol. 1, 278.
19   Alberta Turner, "The Sound of Grief: A Reconsideration of the Nature and
     Function of the Unrhymed Lines in *Lycidas*," *Milton Quarterly* 10 (1976), 67-73.

Saintsbury writes about the cultivation of uncertainty most beautifully: "Here the attention, aroused at first by the failure of the rhyme [. . .] is reassured by the prompt appearance of it, and yet warned by the irregularity of that appearance that it must not go to sleep."[20] The effect is sonic rather than semantic: as John Crowe Ransom pointed out, the ten unrhyming lines "do not seem more important than ten others" and are not lines by which Milton might have "set special store."[21] But they create a soundscape in which we can detect the poem taking soundings from some part of language or experience that lies outside its otherwise determining codes and conventions: it is an aspect of what Michael Longley once described as "the tug-of-war between sincerity and artifice in 'Lycidas'";[22] or, in Ransom's handsome phrase, "the gesture of his rebellion against the formalism of his art," a sequence of aural "defiances," which show "the man unwilling to give way to the poet." And it is this, says Ransom, that makes Milton a modern poet.[23] No doubt he has in mind practice such as:

> Let us go then, you and I,
> When the evening is spread out against the sky
> Like a patient etherized upon a table;
> Let us go, through certain half-deserted streets,
> The muttering retreats
> Of restless nights in one-night cheap hotels
> And sawdust restaurants with oyster-shells:
> Streets that follow like a tedious argument
> Of insidious intent
> To lead you to an overwhelming question . . .

Whether to call something a missed rhyme or a skewed rhyme is often a nicety: here, "table" might be found belatedly to find a partner in "hotels," but Hamlet's word "question" remains quite unaccommodated, a real outlier in a world of rough couplets, keeping the attention from going to sleep.

The whole matter of unexpectedly unrhyming lines inevitably brings into view questions about intentionality which literary theorists once considered effectively banished from the scene; and naturally the questions are not always straightforward to decide. Take, for example, the stanza from Arnold's "Stanzas from the Grand

---

20   Saintsbury, Vol. 2, 221.
21   John Crowe Ransom, *The World's Body* (1938; Kennikat Press, 1964), 10.
22   Michael Longley, *Sidelines. Selected Prose 1962-2015* (Enitharmon, 2017), 118.
23   Ransom, 11; 12.

Chartreuse" which, throughout a long publishing history, never fulfilled the rhyme scheme that otherwise the poem accomplished impeccably:

> For the world cries your faith is now
> But a dead time's exploded dream;
> My melancholy, sciolists say,
> Is a past mode, an outworn theme—
> As if the world had ever had
> A faith, or sciolists been sad!

The Allotts, Arnold's editors, say of this verse that "[t]he defective rhyme-word 'say' is found in all editions," perhaps with the implication that his eyes saw what his hand did:[24] the alternative explanation is sheer inadvertence on Arnold's part, but it is intriguing at the least that a solution involving "avow" should have been so near to hand and not pursued.

A poet, said Wordsworth, enters into "a formal engagement" with the reader, and he was acutely conscious that his own practice was likely to be charged with having "not fulfilled the terms of an engagement thus voluntarily contracted."[25] But he offers a solemn example of the rich expressiveness that such non-fulfilment might make possible in the "Intimations" Ode:

> We will grieve not, rather find
> Strength in what remains behind;
> In the primal sympathy
> Which having been must ever be;
> In the soothing thoughts that spring
> Out of human suffering;
> In the faith that looks through death,
> In years that bring the philosophic mind.

For, of all words, "death" to go unrhymed is to add a special kind of emphasis, but Peter McDonald observes keenly the additional poignancy of a particular rhyme that is left undone: "Wordsworth achieves a startling effect, speaking the word which has made its power felt often in the "Ode," but now isolating it as a word which will *not* be permitted, by the choosing voice, to dictate a rhyme—not least,

---

24 *The Poems of Matthew Arnold*, ed. by Kenneth Allott, second edition ed. by Miriam Allott, (Longman, 1979), 306n.
25 "Preface" to *Lyrical Ballads*, in *William Wordsworth*, ed. by Stephen Gill, (Oxford University Press, 2010), 58.

with that most Wordsworthian word for the poetic activity, 'breath.'"[26] (Wordsworth had used that missing rhyme buoyantly to oppose the vigour of the one with the sterility of the other in "We are Seven": "A simple Child, / That lightly draws its breath, /And feels its life in every limb, / What should it know of death?")

Byron liked a phrase he came across in William Gifford: "the wicked necessity of rhyming."[27] Gifford used the phrase while maladroitly defending his verses against the hostilities of the *Edinburgh Review*: it was the exigencies of his rhyme scheme, he said, which had unfortunately led him to say something which he otherwise wouldn't have chosen to.[28] Robert Graves would not have been impressed: for him it was a key principle that the rhyme "must on no account appear to guide the sense."[29] Byron enjoyed, too, the thought that an alternative, and more virtuous, necessity might always come into play: the compulsion to tell things as they are. He wrote a footnote to the dedicatory stanzas of *Don Juan*, acknowledging a rackety rhyme ("Laureate"/ "Iscariot"), in which he re-told an apocryphal story of Ben Jonson, who, challenged by a fellow poet to rhyme with "I, John Sylvester, / Lay with your sister," answered, "I, Ben Jonson, lay with your wife." "Sylvester answered, 'that is not *rhyme.'*–'No,' said Ben Jonson; 'but it is *true.'*"[30] In its jocular way, the anecdote makes an important point about a poetry that admits sorts of truth or self-awareness so compelling that they override the requirements of mere art. Donald Davie once described a quality to some poems which he especially admired: "words are thrusting at the poem and being fended off from it [. . .] certain words would never be allowed into the poems, except as a disastrous oversight."[31] The unrhymed lines I am considering might be considered as calculated minor disasters, as

---

26 Peter McDonald, *Sound Intentions. The Workings of Rhyme in Nineteenth-Century Poetry* (Oxford University Press, 2012), 113.

27 He quotes the phrase twice in the manuscript of *Don Juan: Byron's Don Juan*, ed. by T.G. Steffan and Willis W. Pratt, (4 vols.; University of Texas Press, 1957), Vol. 3, 348; 392; and also in a letter to Moore, 22 January 1821: *Byron's Letters and Journals*, ed. by Leslie A. Marchand, (13 vols.; John Murray, 1973-1994), Vol. 8, 68.

28 "I regret, indeed, that the wicked necessity of rhyming obliged me to sophisticate the title, which is, the 'Boke of gode maners,'" where he had put "Boke of good advice" so as to rhyme with "price": "Advertisement to the Second Edition", *The Plays of Philip Massinger,* ed. by W. Gifford, (4 vols.; Nicol etc., 1813), Vol. 1, v.

29 Graves, 7.

30 Lord Byron, *The Complete Poetical Works*, ed. by Jerome J. McGann and Barry Weller, (7 vols.; Clarendon Press, 1980-1993), Vol. 5, 672.

31 *Purity of Diction in English Verse* (Chatto and Windus, 1952), 5.

though words forced their way past the artist, "the man unwilling to give way to the poet" in Ransom's phrase, and thus making a creative virtue out of "the consciousness of the inadequateness of our own powers" that, according to Wordsworth, almost always accompanies our attempts to communicate impassioned feelings.[32]

Hardy's genius for unrhyming created the natural idiom for his poetry of disconnection, set in a world in which, as Jude discovers, "[e]vents did not rhyme quite as he had thought."[33]

> I thought her behind my back,
> Yea, her I long had learned to lack,
> And I said: 'I am sure you are standing behind me,
>   Though how do you get into this old track?'
> And there was no sound but the fall of a leaf
> As a sad response; and to keep down grief
> I would not turn my head to discover
>   That there was nothing in my belief.

If, as Charles Tomlinson has it, "[t]he chances of rhyme are like the chances of meeting" ("The Chances of Rhyme"), this is a great verse of failing to meet:[34] for no meeting is possible, a thought which the poem struggles to keep at bay but which is only enhanced by the subdued mordancy that it should be upon a note of "discovery" that prosodically things fall apart. Hardy's greatest follower, Philip Larkin, often occupied similar territory, sometimes with similar devices.[35] In "Counting," for instance:

> Thinking in terms of one
> Is easily done—
> One room, one bed, one chair,
> One person there,
> Makes perfect sense; one set
> Of wishes can be met,
> One coffin filled.
>
> But counting up to two
> Is harder to do;
> For one must be denied
> Before it's tried.

---

32 Note to "The Thorn"; in Gill, 728.
33 *Jude the Obscure*, chapter I.2.
34 Wesling, 131, notes that the phrase is from Baudelaire: "Je vais m'exercer seul à ma fantasque escrime, / Flairant dans tous les coins les hasards de la rime" ("La Soleil").
35 The use of an unrhymed line in the stanza of "Church Going" is remarked by B.J. Pendlebury, *The Art of the Rhyme* (Faber, 1971), 80-81.

Vendler observes how much of the odd potency of this playful little
lyric lies in "the sinisterly unpartnered and unrhymed line 'One coffin
filled'":[36] formally, the poem is committed to the idea of two-ness in its
couplets, an act of wishful thinking which reaches its sadly comical
apogee in the stutter of "to two." But the heart's not in it: the unrhymed
line gives the game away, as it does in a bigger poem, "Talking in Bed."

> Talking in bed ought to be easiest,
> Lying together there goes back so far,
> An emblem of two people being honest.
> Yet more and more time passes silently.
> Outside, the wind's incomplete unrest
> Builds and disperses clouds in the sky,
> And dark towns heap up on the horizon.
> None of this cares for us. Nothing shows why
> At this unique distance from isolation
> It becomes still more difficult to find
> Words at once true and kind,
> Or not untrue and not unkind.

The repetitive non-rhymes of the last non-couplet are a masterclass
in not being able to find the words; but it is the curiously unhoused
word "far," in the second line, that speaks most powerfully of human
distance and remoteness.

But quite other effects may be worked with the unrhyming, even
the celebratory, as in Ruth Stone's "In an Iridescent Time," with which
I shall end:

> My mother, when young, scrubbed laundry in a tub,
> She and her sisters on an old brick walk
> Under the apple trees, sweet rub-a-dub.
> The bees came round their heads, the wrens made talk.
> Four young ladies each with a rainbow board
> Honed their knuckles, wrung their wrists to red,
> Tossed back their braids and wiped their aprons wet.
> The Jersey calf beyond the back fence roared;
> And all the soft day, swarms about their pet
> Buzzed at his big brown eyes and bullish head.
> Four times they rinsed, they said. Some things they starched,
> Then shook them from the baskets two by two,
> And pinned the fluttering intimacies of life
> Between the lilac bushes and the yew:
> Brown gingham, pink, and skirts of Alice blue.

---

36 "Why aren't they screaming?," *London Review of Books* 36.21 (6 November
    2014).

This lovely work of recollected companionship evokes domestic harmony in the "two by two" work of its rhymes: "starched," which might look like an only child, can in fact find sisters in "red" and "head" and "roared." The only end-word that really stands alone in this poem is "life": here, its singularity communicates nothing of loneliness, but rather of a repleteness or self-sufficiency that clearly needs no further confirmation. The poem is wonderfully conscious of the good luck it memorialises, and in its casually discovered rhymes, too, it seems mindful of the way that, as Peter McDonald says, "in rhymed poetry, intentions need to have luck, and to know about luck":[37] a poem of good luck with "life" itself as its take-home message.

Seamus Perry

---

37   McDonald, 30.

The Letter Thorn

For C.R.

To thank, Old English *Þancian, þoncian,* "to reward,
to recompense," from Proto-Germanic *thankōjanan,*
Old Saxon *thancon* and Old Norse *þakka,* Danish
takke, Old Frisian *thankia,* Old High German
danchon, German, Middle Dutch, Dutch *danken*
from *thankoz,* "thought, gratitude"; *tong,* the root
Proto-Indo-European, "to think, to feel."

(To thank in irony, from 1550's onward.
"To thank for nothing" recorded from 1703.)
Compare Old English noun *þanc, þonc,*
originally "thought," also "good thoughts, gratitude."
Related phonetically to "think" as "song" to "sing."
For sense evolution, compare Old High German
minna "loving memory," originally "memory."

Alissa Valles

Aby Warburg and the Aspect of the Interval

"Our realm is that of the intervals." (*Zwischenreich*].
Sigmund Freud to Wilhelm Fleiss. April 16, 1896[1]

Interval has been defined as the space between one point and another, one object to another. In music, an interval is the space between two notes, in both the harmonic distance between two simultaneously sounding tones (physical space) and the melodic distance between two subsequent tones (temporal space).[2] Likewise, the term "Interval" in painting refers to both space and time: a time betwixt, a space between two figures. It is not an empty space devoid of meaning, rather it is charged and multivalent.

For German art historian and cultural theorist Aby Warburg (1866-1929) the Interval had particular significance. He was interested in the spatial organization of images and their chronological context, suggesting the dialectical nature of the Renaissance appropriation of antiquity.

There are two aspects of the interval I'll address: the explicit reference to the "Iconology of the interval" concerning his Memory Atlas and the exploration of relationships, archetypes, lineages and suggested meanings in the figure of the Nympha.[3]

Warburg studied "the body striding in motion," the expressive movements revealing a figure's ecstatic nature. In Botticelli, *Birth of Venus*, (1484-86), the beautiful nude figure of Venus, positioned on a half shell, is blown toward the shore by the wind god Zephyrus. She is contrasted with the figure of Flora, goddess of Spring, dressed in a billowing garment, who holds out a windswept robe to cover Venus.[4]

1   Philippe-Alain Michaud, *Aby Warburg and the Image in Motion* (Zone Books, 2004), 251.

2   Thanks to Christoph Wolff, Ricardo Bloch and Janet Gezari for their helpful comments and suggestions and Maria Wuerker for her assistance.

3   For a succinct summary of Warburg's use of the term see Matthew Rampley, "Iconology of the interval: Aby Warburg's legacy." *Word & Image*, Vol. 17, No.4, (October-December 2001): 303-324.

4   Aby Warburg, *Sandro Botticelli's "Birth of Venus and Spring, An Examination of Concepts of Antiquity in the Italian Early Renaissance (1893)* in *The Renewal of Pagan Antiquity*, (Getty Research Institute for the History of Art and the Humanities, 1999), 116. Warburg writes of "female figures with garments in

Warburg identified a universal figure in motion, "in the guise of the nymph with flowing hair and windblown veil . . . the reworking of Antiquity . . . ceased to appear in its Apollonian aspect and reveled instead its ecstatic, Dionysian nature."[5] The Nymph signals Warburg's interest in Nietzsche and the polarities of the Apollonian and the Dionysian. Gombrich notes that "there was sufficient evidence for Warburg to regard the 'Nympha' as the very embodiment of Renaissance 'paganism.'"[6]

Warburg believed that the conflict of the rational vs the irrational is a fundamental tendency in culture and reverses the idea of the Italian Renaissance as a refuge of timeless order and beauty. He sought the reappearance of the living gesture of antiquity and the spatial organization of images, in their *Vorleben*, previous life, and *Nachleben,* afterlife. Most notable is the ecstatic Nymph or Nympha, a multivalent figure with antique origins, who appears in early Renaissance paintings of religious themes. The motif of the Nymph might be seen under the aspect of the interval between Antiquity and the Renaissance.[7]

In Domenico Ghirlandaio's fresco *Birth of John the Baptist* (1486-1490) (Santa Maria Novella) formally posed women, including Lucretia Tornabuoni of the donor family, visit Elizabeth, sister of Mary, mother of John, lying-in majestically on her bed. Through the door on the right, the nymph bursts forcefully onto the scene. The platter of fruit she bears on her head hovers precariously at an angle, barely grasped by two fingers. Larger than the other figures, she goes unseen, or at least, unnoticed. The space immediately around her is unoccupied. Warburg refers to this figure as Nympha or Ninfa, as he came to call the idealized female figure in motion.[8] What is she doing there? What

---

motion and of nymphs in filmy billowing garments."

5   Michaud, 68.

6   E.H. Gombrich, *Aby Warburg, An Intellectual Biography* (Oxford University Press, 1986), 122.

7   I asked Christopher if he is interested in the concept of the Interval. He replied that though he hadn't published or written about the interval, it is significant in his reading and teaching of Milton's *Paradise Lost.* He explained that the Interval is a kind of time out, a non-temporal pause, a pause but not a temporal intimation. Milton's epic is divided into two books with an interval between them. "All of these moments may gain from being attended to (with awareness of) what it is to see or hear, anyway imagine, something under the aspect of an interval. Nor is this an interval but what do we gain by seeing it under the aspect of an interval?" Email January 4, 2025.

8   Gombrich, 65.

is her role? Does the platter prefigure that on which the decapitated head of John the Baptist will lie? Is she a quasi 'double interval,' the figure of Salomé (anticipating the threatening death) and the angel of the Annunciation (anticipating the birth)? The wind sweeps in such a way that the nymph appears to be moving figuratively from the past into the future. Is she predictive, bridging the gap between early Christian motifs and the Renaissance?[9] The Nympha is an enigmatic interval in the dramatic flow of the story, moving across space, not only as a messenger from antiquity but also across time, recalling or foreshadowing, a marginal figure of considerable power in the range of periods and meanings she evokes and embodies. Gombrich notes "She is a 'pagan spirit' because in and through her form elemental passions could find an outlet."[10]

Certain figures have visual traits of the Nympha but are sinister and menacing. They fall into a category Warburg called 'the hunters of heads' such as Salomé, Judith, the maenads. As Roberto Calasso notes: "The Nymph could be both salvation and devastation or both at the same time."[11] And Georges Didi-Huberman observes, "For Warburg ... *Ninfa* remains a floating signifier traipsing from one incarnation to another without anything trying to draw her limits."[12]

Fra Filippo Lippi in his *Feast of Herod* (1460-1464) (Choir Chapel at the Church of San Stefano, Prato) painted another incarnation of the Nympha. Salomé, step-daughter of King Herod, demands the head of John the Baptist at her mother's request. Three moments are represented: in the center, Salomé dances; on the left, she receives the head of John the Baptist on a platter; to the right, she presents the head to her mother, while other figures recoil. "The speed of . . . [Salomé's] movements and imbalance of her posture signal impropriety . . . ."[13] as

---

9   "Warburg examined with particular insistence the multifarious and mul-
     tivalent relationship between pagan antiquity on one hand and Christian
     worship and imagery on the other: the way in which pictorial formulas
     conveying uninhibited motion introduced an invigorating-but also an equi-
     vocal-element that was equally likely to reinforce the image or to shatter it."
     Kurt W. Foster and David Britt, "Warburg: His Study of Ritual and Art on Two
     Continents," *October*, (Summer 1996), 5-24, 17.
10   Gombrich, 124.
11   Roberto Calasso, "La folie qui vient des Nymphs," *RES: Anthropology and Aes-
     thetics*, No.26, (1994), 125-133, 127.
12   Georges Didi-Huberman, "*Dialektik des monstrums; Aby Warburg and the symp-
     tom paradigm,*" *Art History*, Vol. 24. No.5, (November 2001), 621-645, 631.
13   Jane Long 'Dangerous women: observations on the Feast of Herod in Floren-
     tine Art of the Early Renaissance," *Renaissance Quarterly*, Vol. 66 no.4, (winter
     2013), 1153-1205, 1194.

does her looking out directly at the viewer. Frenzied and tempestuous, for Warburg she represents a phase of paganism in antiquity.

The sequence of paintings in the Choir Chapel on the life of John the Baptist concludes with Domenico Ghirlandaio's *Herod's Banquet* (1486-1490) (Cappella Tornabuoni, Santa Maria Novella) influenced by Lippi's painting, Salomé dances before the Tetrarch while the head of the Baptist is presented. She lurches forward, her robes agitated. This is a seductive and destructive Nympha. As Michaud points out, "Their works bear the stamp of a force that is not harmonious but contradictory, a force destabilizing the figure ... the divine serenity that served as a model of ideal beauty was transformed into bacchantes with convulsive gestures and violent outbursts."[14] The figure in motion which Warburg wrote about in 1905 "became associated with the subject's entrance into the image, with rites of passage, and with the dramatizations affecting his or her appearance ... Warburg was trying to elucidate the devices—independently of their significations—by which the artist, by inserting a figure into the picture plane, indicated a change of place."[15]

Botticelli, *The Temptations of Christ,* (1480-1482) (Sistine Chapel, Panel 46) presents a nymph striding forth, her dress and hair swept backward. She balances a bundle of cedar wood on her head, perhaps a prefiguration of the crucifixion and resurrection. The space surrounding her is dark, forming a somber nimbus. She seems unnoticed or unseen by the men in front of and behind her.

Might we regard the Nympha here as a kind of interval, in a space from a different time? She is not integrated into the scene but rather appears, literally from the margins, emblematic of a more complex view of the tradition, incorporating the demonic and the beatific, the Dionysian and the Apollonian. Gombrich writes, "the 'Nympha' could become the very symbol of liberation and emancipation."[16]

Joseph Koerner observed:

> Warburg's genius as an art historian rests in his capacity to localize the essential rupture and to uncover the hidden origins. Warburg reverses the concept of the High Renaissance as a timeless refuge of order and beauty. Sometimes he discovers an essential fracture/break in the midst of a masterpiece, in the ruptures of style or the expression of temporality. Decisive importance is given to the fractures and contradictions.[17]

---

14   Michaud, 28.
15   Michaud, 32.
16   E.H. Gombrich, 127.
17   Interview with Koerner for *Aby Warburg, Metamorphosis and Memory,* (2016), a

There is a more literal manifestation of the Interval in Warburg's work in the incomplete magnum opus, a picture atlas entitled *Bilderatlas, Mnemosyne*, Atlas of Images: Mnemosyne or *Memory Atlas*. It was begun in 1927 a few years after his return from Kreuzlingen psychiatric hospital and worked on until 1929 with his untimely death of a heart attack. The last version of the Atlas, consisting of 971 images on 63 panels, each one meter-fifty by two meters. Warburg pinned photographs of various art works and artifacts in constant rearrangements suggesting different associations and meanings. The subtitle of the Atlas: "Image Sequence for the Cultural Study of Expressive Material Reminiscent of Antiquity in the Representation of Cosmic and Human Movements during the European Renaissance."

Warburg used the term "Interval" in his introduction to the Mnemosyne Atlas: *Zwischenreich* (in space) and *Zwischenzeit* (in time).[18] The underlying concept was the "afterlife of antiquity," the *nachleben*, and how ancient ideas carry on. The use of the interval is apparent in the constantly shifting positions of the reproductions on the panels of the Mnemosyne Atlas, whose juxtapositions render different meanings beyond texts and include references from various media and genres. Warburg wanted the viewer of the Memory Atlas panels to be aware of the spaces between images, their variations and their repetitions. He established "an iconology of intervals," *eine Ikonologie des Zwischenraumes* "based not on the meaning of the figures . . . but on the interrelationships between the figures in their complex, autonomous arrangement, which cannot be reduced to discourse."[19]

The Atlas imagery was constantly shifting, a vast array of classical antiquity, Renaissance art, maps, calendars, contemporary postage stamps and more. The nympha is a frequent motif. It was designed to follow the migration of figures through the history of representation across areas of knowledge from the from antiquity to the present. Underlying the Atlas was the idea that the Renaissance was a time of transition and uncertainty. Warburg used the Interval to suggest the complexities and underlying tensions.

Two aspects of the Interval are brought together in Warburg's concept of the transmission of culture—as the space between figures

---

film by Judith Wechsler.

18 Claudia Wedepohl, Archivist of the Warburg Institute wrote in emails to me that the terms also appear in Warburg's many late notes and in the unpublished manuscript on the Nympha. She also notes that *"Zwischenraum"* is very closely related to *"Denkraum"* (thought space).

19 Michaud, 252.

in a painting or the space between images on his Atlas, and the figure of the Nympha, who might be seen as an interval in space-time. The motif of the Nymph played an essential role in Warburg's concept of the transmission of culture. Seeing her under the aspect of the interval, between antiquity and the Renaissance, is key to understanding her position and significance for Warburg.

Judith Wechsler

The Women

I met Marion in a convenience store.
She was staying there, in the liquor section,
and she showed me out on to the roof
of the house in which the convenience store
was located which had more privacy.
Back in the convenience store
I found I was talking to a group of women,
not saying much, but I found out that they knew
Varteni and visited Goxwa in Paris.
Soon I was to learn I was at a Hollywood party.
People were thrown out because they put
racing sheets in their identification envelopes,
signaling that they were gay. Everyone was
Carriage Trade or the remnants of Carriage Trade,
beautiful English silks transported to Hollywood.
I was with a group of five women, three quite attractive.
But there was one who I instantly knew meant something
deeply to me. I, the trained lover, ignored them all,
and took care not to make eye contact with the one
to whom my deepest affections were betrothed.
When I was for a moment alone with her behind the
threshold of another room, I said something
abrupt and intimate, ending with the phrase "near me."
Back with the others we talked with each other. She said
she admired the grace of a Thirties starlet
who wore French blouse-arms. I looked.
Her own sleeves and shoulders were wrinkled on one side,
and faintly stained or faded. I remembered the picture,
and myself years ago telling her this as we came out of it,
and wondered whether she were making an allusion to that
or simply had absorbed my influence over the years.
I couldn't make out if she remembered me.
I passed Marion on our way to a different area of the party

but failed to recognize her because she was dressed
in a man's suit. At the party directors laughed at me, "How's Delmore!"
I went with the women to a great lounge sofa on which dozens
of aging, worn-looking women spread their wings, preening
and commiserating. They were all served special desserts.
The men weren't. I lay my head against the breasts of my true love,
and one of them said, "Now she has tits! Those are tits!"
When I woke I was doubly disappointed.
My love was gone and my life was the same.

Ben Mazer

A Real Thing:
Henry James in Norman Mailer's
The Executioner's Song

C hristopher Ricks, in correspondence: "They said, a while back (it may even be that Richard Poirier said), that Mailer was Carlyle redivivus, which I thought and think true if it accommodates their both being, when at their best, great *comic* writers."[1] But Mailer as James redivivus? Strange to say, but it catches at something distinctly impersonal and delicate in the brutality of *The Executioner's Song*. Consider the critical aperçu that is Thom Gunn's epigram, "Jamesian":

> Their relationship consisted
> In discussing if it existed.[2]

Now, Mailer's account of Schiller's final farewell to Gary Gilmore:

> They shook hands, Gilmore's grip kind of weak, and Schiller walked away not knowing whether he had handled the moment the way he should. Didn't even know if it was a moment to be handled. He felt like he had no real relationship to Gilmore. (1015)[3]

The touch of the "hands" becomes "handled," as what Schiller cannot firmly grasp is what to make of the moment owing to his unshakeable uncertainty as to whether he had a "real relationship to" Gilmore (Schiller's "grip kind of weak" in the moment). "Relationship to" and not "relationship with," the preposition refusing to assert what Schiller cannot know, "to" drawing a line, and not shared bond between objects—where even that line may not exist.

The real thing that is a real relationship depends on a shared imaginative act. Gilmore presents all who seek a relationship with him the quandary of his being too much of a fiction, a collaboration of his own posing and their own minds. But this is also at the root of Schiller's desire to turn Gilmore's life into art—or at least into something that has the chance at becoming a work of art. James's "The Real Thing"

---

1   August 4, 2022.
2   Thom Gunn, *Collected Poems* (The Noonday Press, FSG, 1994), 450.
3   All quotations from Norman Mailer, *The Executioner's Song* (Grand Central Publishing, 2012).

apprehends how Gilmore's lack of realness resists relationships and invites representation:

> She was always a lady certainly, and into the bargain was always the same lady. She was the real thing, but always the same thing. There were moments when I was oppressed by the serenity of her confidence that she was the real thing. (242)[4]

The artist of "The Real Thing" much prefers those who yield to the Jamesian task of correctly "placing": "You may say that this was my business, was only a question of placing her" (241). It is Mailer's business, receiving the thousands of documents and recordings from Schiller, to place, arrange, and distil them so as to give shape to Gary Gilmore's story.

Among the most excruciatingly poignant moments of the book takes place between Gilmore's uncle Vern Damico and Gary, where the magnanimous decency of the former is set against the dignity of the latter in his final moments. The moment turns a self-revelation that, as often in James, depends on gesture, pose, and attitude, rather than action or words:

> Vern walked over into the light that was on Gary, and his nephew looked up at him with those baby-blue eyes of his, and Vern felt he'd like to pull him out if that chair, just pull him out of that chair and make him free again. Vern was feeling a great deal of emotion. He didn't want him in that chair really.
>
> They shook hands and Gary started to squeeze his hand, right there in the chair as if he could crush Vern's knuckles. He said to Vern, "Come on, I'll give you a go," and Vern said, "Gary, I could pull you right out of that chair if I wanted to."
>
> Gary said, "Would you?"
>
> Vern went back to his place behind the line and thought of the conversation he'd had weeks before when Gary asked him and Ida to be witnesses, and Vern had said, "I don't want Ida to see it," and Gary had said, "but I want you there, Vern."
>
> "I don't know whether I can take it or not," Vern had said, "I don't think I can." Gary had said, "Well, I want you there."
>
> "Why?" Vern asked, "Why do you want me?"
>
> "Well, Vern," Gary said, "I want to show you. I've already shown you how I live"—he gave his most mocking smile—"and I'd like to show you how I can die." Vern thought all this now must be part of what he had said then because, back behind the line, feeling Gary's hand still on his, Vern wanted to tell him, "That was so good, Gary, what you just did." (1014)

---

4   Henry James, "The Real Thing," *Major Stories and Essays* (Library of America, 1999), 229-254.

"Must be part of what he had said then": Vern sees into things, as James might say, and his response to Gary is Jamesian too: "That was so good, Gary, what you just did." "What you just did" is precise in its phrasing but imprecise in its object: the handshake? Something else, something that we cannot see or share? Vern, at this moment, relates to Gary as no other in the book does. There is, of course, a risk of moral muddle. But "so good" does not pretend Gary Gilmore is a hero and "what you just did" specifies to exclude all that he did not "just" do; for much of what he did at other times was cruel and morally debased. "He didn't want him in that chair really." That "really" catches Vern's nerve: without it, would it be less real? With it, the force of what Vern really wants is made somehow more uncertain, a matter of a story being unfolded in the experience of Vern's discovering what it is he wants; this is it, the arrival of what he really didn't want, and yet for taking so long to dawn, the dawning is an event and achievement both, something that happens to Vern's sense of what is real in himself.

The uncertain moral status of any gesture owes to the possibility that it is a mere put-on. James repeatedly shows us not that all conduct can be valued as an artistic creation, but that we need to be stringent in our judgment of both morality and art, realizing the continuity of our standards for judging both—and realizing also how both art and action-that-is-not-art must be "placed" within an occasion, not mistake their "relationship to" what is beyond their limits. The writer Barry Farrell is not suspicious that Gary is turning his self-presentation into art, but that his self-presentation is too neatly split between dramatic modes, that it does not establish the proper relations between its various parts, and even refuses to recognize how they do bear on one another:

> Farrell got formidably suspicious of those letters. The mood, he noticed, often changed at the beginning of a new page. In effect, each sheet was being worked on as a separate composition. Gilmore—good old Renaissance man—wasn't about to sully the calligraphy of a pretty page with obscenities, not if he was planning to finish the pretty page with a drawing of an elf. (865-6)

The artistry is too conscious of the poses it wants to strike; this is the wrong sort of fiction being presented, or so Farrell thinks. But then at another extreme, is Schiller, trying to accomplish reportage so perfect that the eye is transmitted through the hand, to the page, without the conduit of the mind:

> He realized that if he was going to take accurate notes at the execution, he
> might not have a second to remove his glance from the scene, and so he had
> to learn to separate his hand from is eye, and do it without even referring
> to the pad, and to himself he said, "For the first time, Schiller, you can't
> fictionalize, you can't make it up, you can't embroider." (889)

This scene, Schiller thinks, needs to be the real thing. But then Schiller
is foiled. He gets the colors wrong: of the chair, of the room, of the
canvas behind which the shooters—whom he catches himself calling
"assassins," in the secrecy of his own thoughts. The impossibility of
what he intends is foiled already in the expression of how he intends
it: "he had to learn to separate his hand from his eye." But what he
wants might also be expressed by saying that he had to unite his hand
and eye perfectly. He means he cannot afford to look down, to see
the calligraphy of his pen on the page (recall Farrell's "calligraphy
of a pretty pen with obscenities," where the calligraphy is too self-
conscious, too much an object of the authorial eye's attention); but
what it might also mean to separate the hand from the eye is that the
hand writes what the eye does not see, that the fiction happens without
the eye's realizing it, which is just what does happen with the mistaken
colors. Schiller is compelling because of his desire not to be seen as
imposter, a hack whose fiction is parasitic of the real, but whose work
is instead a revelation of the real, which depends on his standing in
proper relation to his subject:

> He said to himself, "I don't know any longer whether what I'm doing is
> morally right," and that made him cry even more. He had been saying to
> himself for weeks that he was not part of the circus, that he had instincts
> which raised him above, a desire to record history, a true history, not
> journalistic crap, but now he felt as if he was finally part of the circus
> and might even be the biggest part of it, and in the middle of crying, he
> went into the bathroom and took the longest fucking shit of his life. It was
> all diarrhea. His system, after days of running nonstop and nights with
> crummy sleep, was by now totally screwed up. The horrors were loose. The
> diarrhea went through him as if to squeeze every last rotten thing out, and
> still it came. When he thought he might be done, he looked out the window
> at the snow and made the decision that in no way was he ever going to sell
> Gary Gilmore's execution. (888)

This is, on the surface, in its awareness of excremental functions, so
unlike James as to make the comparison perverse, except that, at a
deeper level, James invites us to find in the symptoms and experience
of sickness the proof of life's moral strength: "Let him [the poet] deal
with the sickest of the sick, it is still by the act of living that they appeal

to him, and appeal the more as the conditions plot against them and prescribe the battle."[5] The specificity and crassness of "the longest fucking shit of his life . . . all diarrhea" is twin to the suggestively unspecified ailments of James' invalids. "The horrors were loose" is, transposed into Mailer's visceral scatology, a Jamesian metaphor, the moral imagination made somatic. It culminates in pristine white snowfall and a crucial decision. Schiller is starkly unlike Gilmore in that he succumbs to self-dramatization in his very effort to resist it. This is not a matter of his blending too readily with the roles he must perform if he is to establish the necessary intimacy with his interview subjects. Instead, it is a consequence of his uncertainty about his relation to himself, to who he is in his own eyes. And he is curiously passive in the face of becoming a character, an actor on stage with one's agency compromised:

> "Actually," said Schiller to himself, "I have become part of it. All around me, I'm becoming part of the story." (739)

And this is his problem: a distinctly Jamesian bind of distance and nearness: the nearness that affords him the capacity to see well enough to make a worthy fiction of what is real, but also a nearness that implicates him in the suspicion that such a fiction is worth too much to him, personally, financially—vulgarly, as James might say— and that undermines the fiction he would offer:

> Yet if he, Larry Schiller, were to offer examples of interesting human qualities in Gilmore, no one would accept them. They would say he was painting that nice picture for his own financial benefit. Therefore, he had to have the portrait painted by somebody else. Right now, that was going to be Bill Moyers. (844)

Ultimately, that somebody else would be Mailer, and the portrait would not be of Gilmore alone, but of how others pictured and portrayed, to themselves and one another, their relationship to Gilmore. Gilmore consistently represents himself as existing in relation to nobody except Nicole: the sense he presents to others of his own reality, his real self and the world that is real to him, is inseparable from what he says about her and to her and through her. She is the target of his most persistent violence, and Mailer registers this in an extraordinary moment when Gilmore is on the way to the firing squad:

---

5   Henry James, "Preface," *The Wings of the Dove* in *Henry James: Novels 1901-1902* (The Library of America, 2006), 198.

> As soon as they started, Gary reached in with both manacled hands to a pocket of his pants and took out a folded piece of paper and put it on his knee so that he could look at it. It was a picture of Nicole clipped from a magazine, and he stared at it. (1007)

Their relationship consists in so great a certainty that we doubt it exists as they believe it to—but there we fall back because cannot know what they did believe, and Mailer respects this limit. "He stared at it" is as blank in its outward expression as Gilmore's inner life is blank to Mailer. But this much, Mailer will intimate, and without biting wit, but with a sense of latent significance: that there is, in Gilmore's gaze at Nicole, violence. "Clipped" and "magazine" comport uneasily with the hands that held the gun and killed with it, twice.

Owen Boynton

Friend of Mind

It all started sixty-two years ago. After graduating from the University of California at Berkeley, spending eight months as an assistant editor at McGraw-Hill in New York City and six months on active duty in the U.S. Coast Guard Reserve, I was at loose ends, direction unknown. I bumped into Professor John Searle, from whom I had taken three undergraduate philosophy courses. He had been a Rhodes Scholar at Christ Church, Oxford, earning a B.A. and D. Phil. He had spoken to me about Oxford and revived his idea of my going there, urging me to apply to do a B.A. in English Language and Literature.

For Searle, Oxford was Mecca. For me, it seemed the moon. He said the most important thing was your tutor. He had heard from John Carey, later Merton Professor of English, about their Oxford contemporary Christopher Ricks. He received the highest first in thirty years and was the coming man as the English don at Worcester College. Searle said make him your number one choice, adding, characteristically, 'I don't know him, but use my name."

Among the blue aerograms I received in the Sixties and Seventies from Christopher is his first letter to me:

Dear Mr. Isenberg,

Thank you for your letter about the possibility of coming here. I'm afraid I haven't any specific advice as to how you need apply; I am sure that it will be best simply to do so, and I assure you that your application will receive scrupulous and fair-minded consideration (not, in the first place, from me ...). So I'm passing your letter on to the Tutor for Admissions, and you will be hearing from him. Don't trouble, please, to write to me acknowledging this. With all good wishes,

Yours sincerely,
Christopher Ricks

Here was my introduction to an application process entirely unfamiliar to an American and to the relationship within an Oxford college of a tutor to the system of admissions, "not, in the first place, from me ...."

And to the mind and way of expressing itself, gracious, complex and pointedly holding himself and the college to standards, "scrupulous and fair-minded," while ready to examine my record.

The letter is dated November 22, 1963. That day in Dallas, President John F. Kennedy was assassinated. Never such innocence again for my country, yet the beginning of the happiest adventure of my young life that helped shape my mind and my reading.

My application comprised the academic transcript of my courses and grades, recommendation letters from Berkeley faculty—Searle, Mark Schorer, Howard Hugo and Thomas Barnes—and a letter from me presenting my case. Some months later, I cried when an acceptance letter arrived. Late that September, I took a Greyhound bus from my home in Los Angeles to New York, and then sailed on the S.S. France to Southampton, carrying my first passport and steamer trunk.

My first tutorial was in October, 1964 in my tutor's room in the wing of once medieval monks' cottages that overlook the perfect grass quad, across from the 1776 building where I lived. I arrived in coat, tie and short commoner's gown, seeing Ricks for the first time, waiting with poised intensity for me to read aloud my unremarkably earnest essay on, gulp, reality and illusion in *King Lear*.

Ricks raised the discussion with his questions and illuminating quotations from the play and elsewhere in Shakespeare (all from memory). Then in a pointed framing he reported that in an earlier tutorial John Lahr, later the drama critic for *The New Yorker*, offered "the play ended as it had begun with Lear trying to coax words from Cordelia." I had never heard a teacher so generously use another student's observation to awaken my noticing and I was caught by "coax," a word I suspected was his in the retelling. He asked: "Does this mean we remain the same over our lives, becoming more and more who we are? Or can we change?"

Immediately, the wholeness of the play, Lear's character and dilemma, the parental poignancy, the powerlessness of a king and father in the face of death and the very nature of how we live as who we are were newly defined, even if made more complex.

This was to happen over and over again. Ricks led an examination of the architecture, craft, sensibilities and diction of a literary work, always connecting art to the human experience. The tutorial would end with some things settled, more often stirred.

John Masterman, a former Provost of Worcester and the architect of the British double-agent spy system in World War II, held that the "weekly talk and discussion between pupil and tutor . . . is the essence of Oxford life." So true. But what made for a great tutor and tutorial? I found it was the rigorous questioning, the spur to avoid lazy thinking, the critical thrust against unexamined assumptions, the suggested readings, and a commanding knowledge that brought other ideas, works and appraisals to the moment.

The tutorial setting is immediate and intimate, focused. Tutor and pupil sit several feet apart, no one else is present. Christopher's presence was theatrical; animated by his energy and pace, the snap of his wit and sarcasm (his schoolboy nickname was "Sarky"), the sweep of his allusions and gatherings, the span of his knowledge and the force of mustering argument and analysis. I hovered between being struck by wonder, laughing and coming to attention to answer a question, trying to cement his best remarks in my memory before putting forward my own take on the matter. It all moved so quickly, from particulars to principles, weighing words, their beauty and felicity, their telling power and grip. He made clear, and urged the same, that evidence should bolster a line of thought. (As an undergraduate, he spent an hour a day memorizing, both for exams and more importantly to have the best proving words readily at hand.) He disliked and avoided "bullying words" like "surely" and "obviously." He listened with seismographic attentiveness. The circumference of what he had read, recalled and made germane was intimidating, yet it was given over generously, so we seized the day because of what he drew from us.

At eighty-four, I am now his oldest student, hoping to convey what has been deeply felt and cherished by Christopher's students. We all have memorable anecdotes. He left a mark on our sensibilities as readers and writers, enlivened our language, sharpened our noticing and thinking. He taught us when and how to dwell on a word. He encouraged us to be alert appreciators, to talk about novels and poetry, above all, the vitality of language, in spacious and exacting ways, free of jargon, with enthusiasm. His javelin toss will always outspan ours and almost all others, yet we have some of his technique.

At the heart of his wisdom is the necessity of "bracing" and "holding fast" to antitheticals: " ... you use your mind in the full consciousness that reason cannot guarantee that you will be right but it is better, much better than relying on feeling alone (just as your feelings forbid you to rely on reason alone.)" *Poems and Critics*, Introduction.

His cornerstone came from Samuel Johnson: "the task of criticism [is to] ... establish principles; to improve opinion into knowledge and to distinguish those means of pleasing which depend upon known causes and rational deductions . . .."

He led us to the critical works he admired such as William Empson's *Seven Types of Ambiguity* and Donald Davie's *Purity of Diction in English Verse,* and the rich wonders of the Oxford English Dictionary. We learned to attend to the history of a word and its shades of meaning, the shaping force of syntax and the signals of punctuation. He noted the essential difference between poetry and prose is the poet determines line endings so they merit special regard. He insisted both forms had the capabilities of beauty, concision, sound and sense. In his initial lecture as Oxford Professor of Poetry he suggested there ought to be an Oxford Professor of Prose. The novel was my long suit and our tutorials on Dickens and George Eliot, as well as George Orwell's essays, were high points.

The fuse for me from those days has been long, and deepened by our friendship. When I went down from Oxford, returning to America, I dropped the academic baton, and followed other impulses that brought me to New York City Mayor John V. Lindsay, the law, newspapers, university governance and later on teaching and PEN, the literary human rights organization. Christopher gave his blessing and encouragement to all my careers, and loved to talk about the worlds of politics and journalism. I had the happiness of his meeting my bosses and colleagues, charming them with his intelligence and humor, and showing discerning interest in our circumstances, challenges and characters.

Christopher never stopped being my tutor, especially when I became the Chairman of the Board and interim president of Adelphi University and then a visiting professor of humanities at Berkeley and the University of Texas at Austin. We shared each other's counsel on academic governance and administration, aspirations and fault lines. He gave me the inspiration to teach a class on Fathers and Sons which should include Edmund Gosse and J.R. Ackerley. He offered ideas on reading for my courses on war literature, literary journalism and the novel. As you would expect, I brought Ricks into those classes through his essays such as on Norman Mailer's *The Executioner's Song* and recently at a summer seminar at St. John's College in Santa Fe, I used his introduction to an edition of *Paradise Lost*. His promptings show how to get to the quick of a work and its complexity. When he visited me in Austin, his energetic willingness to put his oar in our waters with observations and questions delighted the students.

Last, Christopher as my editor. He had me review books about British war poetry and Philip Larkin for *Essays in Criticism*, helping make my essays more cogent and in trim. Recently, we both greatly admired M.W. Rowe's biography of J.L. Austin. While I could size up and synthesize Austin's World War II years in military intelligence and the dynamic of his Oxford lecturing and tutorials, I weakened at the prospect of assessing his philosophical dominance and original thinking in the way it deserved. I disappointed myself because while starkly unique in his manner, many things about Austin's love of words, his magnetism and relationships with American students, reminded me of Ricks. I wrote Christopher saying I couldn't review it. He was so kind about my note saying he wouldn't even joke about it. To fail Christopher was to know, again, his generous understanding heart.

Later this year his correspondence with Empson will be published, its coda an essay of mine recollecting my luncheons with E.M. Forster and Philip Larkin, Christopher figures in each, and the memorable lunch we had with Empson. I couldn't be happier than to be the caboose on Empson-Ricks train.

Because of the time we now live in, I am often reminded of Christopher's sure-handed way of finding the right words for a large moment by the telegram he sent me when President Richard Nixon resigned over Watergate. It was a perfect slice of Bob Dylan: "The ladder of the law has no top. Congratulations." Ah, but that was then.

Over seven decades, Christopher has been part of my work, my family and friends. He has connected to them by loving attention, powered by his vivacious chemistry and joyful humanity. The pleasure of his company is a wealth meant to be shared. And now, in retrospect, all of it seems to have begun with a hunch by my tutor to accept my application. Lucky me.

Steven Isenberg

In Memoriam:
Saskia Hamilton (1967-2023)

With sorrow, we report the death of the poet, scholar, editor, and professor Saskia Hamilton. Saskia was a long-time member of ALSCW, and worked with extraordinary energy and imagination to support the Association. In 2012-14, she co-edited *Literary Imagination* with Archie Burnett. She joined the faculty at Barnard College in 2002, and in 2018 was appointed Vice Provost for Academic Programs and Curriculum while continuing to teach her passionately attended courses in poetry and poetics. As Vice Provost, she often hosted local meetings of ALSCW for poetry readings and discussions, giving the Association a dignified home in New York City.

In her lifetime, Saskia published four volumes of delicate, intensely suggestive poetry, three with Graywolf Press, and *Canal: New and Selected Poems* with Arc in the United Kingdom. Her final collection, *All Souls*, came out from Graywolf in October 2023. She edited *The Letters of Robert Lowell* for Farrar, Straus, and Giroux (2005); *The Dolphin Letters, 1970-1979: Elizabeth Hardwick, Robert Lowell and Their Circle* (Farrar, Straus, and Giroux, 2019); and a new edition of Lowell's *The Dolphin: Two Versions, 1972, 1973* (Farrar, Straus, and Giroux, 2019). With Thomas Travisano she edited *Words in Air: The Complete Correspondence Between Elizabeth Bishop and Robert Lowell* (Farrar, Straus, and Giroux, 2008). These editions drew renewed attention to Lowell's poetry and were rewarded with significant prizes: the Pegasus Award for *The Dolphin* and *The Dolphin Letters*, and the Morton N. Cohen Award for a Distinguished Edition of Letters from the MLA. Her poetry earned her fellowships from the Guggenheim Foundation, the Ruth Lily Foundation, the NEA, and an Arts & Letters Award from the American Academy of Arts & Letters.

Saskia's very being was a reward for all who knew her and cared about her. We have lost a singular intelligence, and a model of magnanimity and attentive friendship.

Rosanna Warren

From "All Souls"

How strange—but then '*strange* should be dried out
for a millennium,' Ricks says. *Journey*,
too. Poor old words. Even so, how *out
of the way* – *?* to be the subject.
To whom would it be otherwise?
Who becomes familiar with mortal
illness for very long. I was a stranger, &c.
Not everyone appreciates it, no
one finds being the third person
becoming, it's never accurate,
and then one is headed for the past tense.
Futurity that was once a lark, a gamble,
a chance messenger, traffic and trade, under sail.
The boy touches your arm in his sleep
for ballast. It's warm in the hold. Between
ship and sky, the bounds of sight
alone, sphere so bounded.

Saskia Hamilton

"Duly and happily noted"

A selection of lines from recent emails from Christopher:

Two suggestions for the talk (but not limited to these):

"Adaptations of the sound to the sense"
Johnson > Empson; John Wallis (1653) > J.L. Austin (the 1950s)

Preludes, particularly those of T.S. Eliot

Change of subject for 27 March, please (given the present world):

Crisis
"But these were mere crises, and what are crises compared to all that never stops, knows neither ebb nor flow" (Samuel Beckett)

*

Alright?

The snow. Herrick always the heartener, as you'll remember.

The comming of good luck

So Good-luck came, and on my roofe did light,
Like noyse-lesse Snow; or as the dew of night:
Not all at once, but gently, as the trees
Are, by the Sun-beams, tickel'd by degrees.

And Ambrose Philips (attached).*   * "A Winter Piece" (poem)

Over the past few decades, Christopher has taught me, and many others, about this kind of love for *les mots justes*. He impresses upon his listeners and readers the necessity and the rewards of using language well. When I speak with him, I feel a strong urge to take notes to capture his deft use of syntax, the sense of anticipation as each syntactical unit unfurls. I want to return to what has been said to see what I have missed and what I can newly absorb.

Christopher makes us become aware of, as Francis Beaumont put it, words "so nimble, and so full of subtil flame." His genius works in tandem with his sense of play. I think of some of the words that have peppered his emails over the years: *corrigendum, cunctator, bantling, dunderhead, tergiversation.* I never stop learning from him of the value of this playfulness when it comes to language (and to teaching). In "Geoffrey Hill's Grievous Heroes," an essay from *Along Heroic Lines,* Ricks quotes Hill who quotes Eliot (from *The Three Voices of Poetry* 1953):

> When the words are finally arranged in the right way—or in what he comes to accept as the best arrangement he can find—the poet may experience a moment of exhaustion, of appeasement, of absolution, and of something very near annihilation . . . .[1]

Listening to or reading Christopher—who, as a friend says, speaks in complete sentences—gives us a version of this kind of release: not absolution, because he would insist that we are sinners when it comes to using language, even him—not quite annihilation, although I have in some moments felt self-conscious about speaking in his company—but blessed, because when he gives, he gives largely and lastingly, "the words . . . arranged in the right way."

My friend Saskia Hamilton, who died in 2023, and I were ever in awe of Christopher when we were students. He had been our teacher in graduate school. Some time back, she had been reading *The Force of Poetry,* and she wrote to him an email of her gratitude: "Your prose is improving." Afterwards, she panicked, thinking it might be read the wrong way. The height of delight for the two us was to go out to dinner after poetry readings at BU with Christopher and whatever visitors to campus there were. The laughter that lit up the dim corners of those restaurants. For a while, we frequented "Petit Robert," a little bistro near campus that has since closed its doors. He ensures a lively occasion. Not many people can inspire me to choke with laughter, but he does. I recall a story about his walking down a street in Cambridge (England) with Eric Griffiths. They passed a chap whom they knew, and Eric uttered, "Asshole." Later, after some worrying, Christopher suggested to his friend that that wasn't a kind thing to

---

1   *AHL,* 232.

say. Eric responded: "I was talking about you." I recall a note he had once written (I think) to Carmen Bugan, the Romanian poet: "from c to shining c."

Beyond the wit, there is something quietly shepherd-like about him. I smile as I type this, knowing he would resist the notion (and advise me to choose another descriptor). Few professors care as much about the material taught and the students' development of skills as he does. I remember being drawn to the way in which Heaney, no matter to whom he spoke, children or Harvard faculty members, sounded like himself and treated those he spoke to with respect. Christopher is like this too. He is the furthest thing from aloof you can find. He is always gracious. When you visit him in his office, he offers tea and biscuits, or lunch. And asks you to choose a book or two from the shelf to take away. He has never failed to treat me as a fully-fledged colleague, although internally I still register myself as his student. I sometimes receive cross-campus mail from him, with copies of articles or poems or books he thinks I might find interesting. I would say that his attention to the details of human relationships is uncanny, but this is his way in almost everything he does. He is the great appreciator of the power of subtlety. He is also steadfast. When Saskia was dying, Christopher and Judith would zoom every week with her. Sometimes Saskia would doze off as Christopher read aloud to her; the cancer treatment was brutal, and she had lost much of her strength. But she found nourishment in listening to him read poems and I know she cherished his friendship. As Christopher said, "So painful and sad, the losses and all the diminished things, the deep unignorability of it all."

And he is full to the brim with love. In the last few years of the poet David Ferry's life, I would feel a mingling of grief and delight whenever I was in his company—that feeling of the majesty of both the man and the moment and how it would soon be a memory. In the summer of 2023, Christopher, Judith and I had lunch with David in Lexington, MA. I have photos from the occasion and to see the way the two gentlemen interact with and adore each other, well, my words cannot do justice to their tenderness. That to me is what love should be like, generous and generative. When I moved to France briefly in my thirties, what I missed most was the warmth of this poetry circle. Not only was the poetry, the language used around it, exquisite, but the company made me feel as if I might belong somewhere.

A former undergraduate student of mine, now a senior who recently became a student of Christopher's, visited me in my office recently, a gob-smacked expression on her face, because not only had Christopher purchased for her a membership to the Association of Literary Scholars, Critics and Writers, but he had also spent over two hours with her going over her essay. He had color-coded his comments. As I said, the attention he pays to nuance is extraordinary. At some poetry event or another (was it a Core Curriculum Poetry reading?), I read John Clare's "The Badger." I mispronounced "blackguard." He corrected me immediately afterward, but never in a way that felt scornful. I think he was trying to save me from future embarrassment.

I had the great luck to be invited to take part in several dissertation committees at the Editorial Institute. The dissertations were always brilliant. Both he and Archie Burnett would insist at the outset that the committee tell the candidate straight away whether or not they had passed, even before the discussion began. Those two would hold back their comments until after the candidate and other members of the committee had spoken. More often than not, Christopher spoke last.

Over the years, he and Archie hosted a number of literary events at the Institute, a remarkable place where literary labor was undertaken. My mind swings back to the familiar faces around the long wooden conference table, the bottles of wine being passed around. How we would smile at each other when Christopher spoke. I heard that students used to play Bingo in his classes. A point for every time he said T.S. Eliot, double-bind, Dylan, Tennyson, Beckett, etc. Their choices were more nuanced than my memory can produce, but you get the idea.

And how we have cherished his litany of dislikes: the BU administration (where the *cunctator* held sway), a certain poet, a particular literary critic. In many a far-ranging conversation, these topics would arise. BU's inability to appreciate the gift that the Editorial Institute was and is a thorn in his side, in our side. I recall a time at Harvard, a day-long event on William Empson hosted by the English Department. When Helen Vendler (another recently lost star!) began to speak, Christopher rose in indignation, his face as red as a valentine, and critiqued her misguidedness about Empson. I am not even sure why it pleased us so much that he became so irate. Because he is both perspicacious and feels things strongly? He is certainly willing to express his dissent. Whatever the case, he is and was our hero. (When I say "our," I am referring to Saskia Hamilton, although there are others who feel similarly). Colm Tóibín came to speak at BU about his book, *The Testament of Mary*, and I had asked Christopher to be the respondent. What an experience to hear Tóibín speak movingly about the Catholic church, the signal place of beauty and order where he grew up in Ireland. And then to hear Christopher, like a teakettle beginning to sing, say something about the preposterousness of Christian belief.

Even watching him as he listens to someone speak at a podium is a treat. Sometimes he presses his face into his hands, which I at first took for concentration, his shining pate pinkening, but I now see as his attempt to suppress a groan. When the speakers simulate having a pulse (say something honest and refreshing), Christopher will laugh and then clap his hand over his mouth, sometimes looking to the side and uttering under his breath, "Now that is good." Ever alert to "erroneous aptness"[2] and the value of rereading books and people ("We had better not wince from the fact that we good people are often imperceptive, or from the fact that bad people often are not"[3]), his engagement with others is real and constant. While the rest of us do what we can to block out the noise and turn from the too muchness of this world, Christopher faces, examines, and offers us a form of apprehension flooded by his light.

Meg Tyler

---

2   *TF*, 218.
3   *AHL*, 90.

I offer this poem to Christopher with gratitude for his graciousness and kindness back in the day when I was an attendant lord and seeking to please and impress him, face to face or in writing, by reacting laterally to a brilliant argument he had made. His reaction to this attention-seeking was to honour me (and perhaps other attendant lords up to the same tricks) by reacting in kind and raising the stakes. "If you want to play that game, I'm up for it", was his grownup reaction. Finally, Christopher has pointed out that there is no noun for those who are grateful. The opposite, however, exists: ingrates. A pox on them. If you go online and look for antonyms for "ingrate" you won't find any nouns.

From Leopardi's Prose Dialogue between Plotinus and Porphyry

For Christopher Ricks with affection and gratitude

Let us live, my dear Porphyry,
and take comfort from each other;
let us not refuse to bear
those human ills
destiny has assigned to us.
Let us protect each other
and encourage each other,
help and support each other
so that we may bear
as best we can
the burdens of life,
which doubtless will be brief.
And when death comes,
we will have no regrets,
and in those last hours
our friends and companions
will comfort us, and we shall rejoice
because when we are no more,
they will remember us often,
and love us still.

Anthony Rudolf

CONTRIBUTOR BIOGRAPHIES

Michael Autrey (editor and contributor): is a poet and an essayist. His first collection *Our Fear* (The Cultural Society) was published in 2013. Recently, he won the 2025 River Styx Poetry Prize. His essays have appeared in, among others, *Asymptote, Bright Wall/Dark Room, Chicago Review, Essays in Criticism, The Hopkins Review, Literary Matters, Raritan, The American Scholar* and *The Threepenny Review*.

John Barnard is Emeritus Professor of English Literature, University of Leeds. He has published widely on Keats, the second-generation Romantics, seventeenth century drama and literature, and book history.

Owen Boynton works at Collegiate School in New York City. His most recent critical pieces have been for University of Pennsylvania's Andrea Mitchell Center for the Study of Democracy, in their online "Poetry and Politics" series.

John C. Briggs (PhD Chicago, 1987) is a Professor of English, Emeritus at the University of California, Riverside, where he has taught for forty-five years. He is the author of *Francis Bacon and the Rhetoric of Nature* (Harvard University Press, 1989) and *Lincoln's Speeches Reconsidered* (Johns Hopkins, 2005) as well as numerous writings on Shakespeare, Lincoln, Homer, C.S. Lewis, literary catharsis, and the history of rhetoric. He was twice president of the Association of Literary Scholars, Critics, and Writers. He is the founding director of the UCR University Writing Program and the first director of the campus-based Inland Area Writing Project. In 1995 he was the winner of the Senate faculty's Outstanding Teaching Award.

Archie Burnett was born in Scotland. He is a graduate of the Universities of Edinburgh and Oxford and is currently Professor of English at Boston University. In 1981 he produced *Milton's Style: The Shorter Poems, Paradise Regained and Samson Agonistes,* and this was supplemented by scholarly editions of *The Poems of A.E. Housman* (1997), *The Letters of A.E. Housman* (2007), *The Complete Poems of Philip Larkin* (2012), and *The Collected Prose of T.S. Eliot* (2024). He was for many years Co-Director with Christopher Ricks of The Editorial Institute at Boston University. He started writing poetry when he was 60. A collection of his poems, together with a selection of essays on Milton, Housman, and Larkin, is to be published by the Un-Gyve Press, Boston.

John Burt is Paul Prosswimmer Professor of American Literature at Brandeis University. He is the author of *Lincoln's Tragic Pragmatism* (Harvard U.P. 2013), and *Robert Penn Warren and American Idealism* (Yale U.P. 1988). He is the editor of *The Collected Poems of Robert Penn Warren* (Louisiana State University Press, 1998). He is also the author of three books of poetry, *The Way Down* (Princeton University Press, 1988), *Work without Hope* (Johns Hopkins University Press, 1995), and *Victory* (Turning Point Press, 2007). His novel *A Moment's Surrender* won the 2023 Prize Americana and is forthcoming from Hollywood Books International.

Clare Cavanagh is Frances Hooper Professor of Arts and Humanities and Professor of Slavic Literatures and Comparative Literary Studies at Northwestern University. Her book *Lyric Poetry and Modern Politics: Russia, Poland, and the West* received the National Book Critics Circle Award in Criticism for 2010. She received a 2018 American Academy of Arts and Letters Award in Literature for her many volumes of Polish poetry in translation. Other honors include the Harold Langdon Translation Award from the Academy of American Poets; the PEN Translation Award; the MLA William Riley Parker Award; and fellowships from the NEH and Guggenheim Foundation. She is editing Adam Zagajewski's *Collected Poems* and working on an authorized biography of Czesław Miłosz, both for Farrar, Straus, and Giroux.

Bill Coyle's poems and translations have appeared in journals such as *Poetry*, *The Hudson Review*, and *Modern Poetry in Translation*. His collection of poetry *The God of This World to His Prophet* won the New Criterion Poetry Prize. In 2010, he received a translation grant from the National Endowment for the Arts, and the resulting collection of his translations of the Swedish poet Håkan Sandell, *Dog Star Notations: Selected Poems 1999-2016*, was published by Carcanet. He received his PhD in Editorial Studies from Boston University in 2023.

Greg Delanty's latest collection is *The Professor of Forgetting*. His next book, *Sweeney Now* is due in Fall, 2026. He is the author and editor of more than twenty poetry books. He teaches at Saint Michael's Collage, Vermont. He has received many awards, including a Guggenheim for poetry. In 2021 he was awarded The David Ferry & Ellen LaForge Poetry Prize. He is considered both a US/Vermont poet as well as an Irish poet. His work is frequently anthologized and broadcast. Recently one of his poems, "The Alien," appeared in Wes Anderson's movie, *Asteroid City* (2023). He has poems forthcoming in numerous venues including *The Irish Times* and *The Best American Poetry 2025*. He is also a past president of the ALSCW.

William Flesch is Professor of English at Brandeis University. He is the author of several books, including *Comeuppance: Altruistic Punishment, Costly Signaling, and Other Biological Components of Fiction*. He served as Secretary-Treasurer for the Association of Literary Scholars, Critics, and Writers when Christopher Ricks was President in 2008.

Jeffrey Gutierrez is a lecturer at Boston University. He is co-editor, with Christopher Ricks, of *As to Empson* (2025).

Judith Hawley is Professor of Eighteenth-Century Literature in the Department of English, Royal Holloway, University of London and frequently appears on BBC radio. She works on a range of subjects from gin to Grub Street and has a particular interest in the history of amateur performance. As well as publishing essays on private theatricals, she has edited various eighteenth-century texts, including Jane Collier, *The Art of Ingeniously Tormenting*; Henry Fielding, *Joseph Andrews and Shamela*; Laurence Sterne, *Tristram Shandy*, and works by the Bluestocking, Elizabeth Carter. Currently, she is writing a group biography of Pope, Swift and the Scriblerus Club.

Mark Halliday teaches at Ohio University. His seventh book of poems *Losers Dream On* was published in 2018 by the University of Chicago Press.

Saskia Hamilton (1967-2023) authored 3 previous poetry collections, *As for Dream, Divide These* and *Corridor*, all published by Graywolf. A fourth, *Canal: New and Selected Poems*, by Arc in the UK. She was the editor of several volumes of correspondence, including *The Dolphin Letters, 1970-1979: Elizabeth Hardwick, Robert Lowell, and Their Circle*.

Kenneth Haynes, Professor of Comparative Literature and Classics at Brown University, edited Geoffrey Hill's collected poetry and collected criticism.

Geoffrey Hill (1932–2016), poet, taught English literature at the University of Leeds from 1954 to 1980 before moving to Cambridge, where he taught from 1981 to 1988. He then became Professor of Literature and Religion at Boston University, later working there with graduate students in the Editorial Institute, which he cofounded with Christopher Ricks in 1998. He retired from Boston University in 2006 and returned to England. In 2010 he was elected the Oxford Professor of Poetry. In 2012 he was knighted for services to literature. His poetry was collected in the volumes *Broken Hierarchies* (2013) and *The Book of Baruch by the Gnostic Justin* (2019) and his criticism in *Collected Critical Writings* (2008).

Philip Horne is Professor of English at University College London. He is the author of *Henry James and Revision: The New York Edition* (Oxford University Press, 1990); and editor of *Henry James: A Life in Letters* (Penguin, 1999). He is co-editor of *Thorold Dickinson: a world of film* (Manchester University Press, 2008). He has also edited Henry James's *A London Life & The Reverberator*, *The Tragic Muse*, *The Portrait of a Lady* and *Autobiographies;* and Dickens's *Oliver Twist*. He is the founding General Editor of *The Complete Fiction of Henry James* (Cambridge University Press). He has written on subjects including telephones and literature, zombies and consumer culture, the films of Powell and Pressburger and Martin Scorsese, the texts of Emily Dickinson, the criticism of F.R. Leavis, and poetic allusion in Victorian fiction.

Steven L. Isenberg was chief of staff to New York City Mayor John V. Lindsay, publisher of New York Newsday and Executive Vice President of The Los Angeles Times, visiting professor of humanities at the University of California at Berkeley and the University of Texas at Austin and Executive Director of PEN, and is the chair of the board, emeritus, at Adelphi University. He has written for *The American Scholar, Essays in Criticism* and *The Los Angeles Review of Books*. He holds degrees from Berkeley, Yale Law School and Worcester College, Oxford, where he is an Honorary Fellow. He is a senior advisor to The Committee to Protect Journalists.

George Kalogeris's most recent book of poems is *Winthropos*, (Louisiana State University Press, 2021). He is also the author of *Guide to Greece* (Louisiana State University Press, 2018), a book of paired poems in translation, *Dialogos*, and poems based on the notebooks of Albert Camus, *Camus: Carnets*. His poems and translations have been anthologized in *Joining Music with Reason*, chosen by Christopher Ricks (Waywiser, 2010).

Daniel Karlin's PhD thesis on "Composition and Creation in the Poetry of Browning" was supervised by Christopher Ricks at Cambridge, 1975-1978. He retired in 2020 as Winterstoke Professor of English Literature from the University of Bristol, where he is now Emeritus Professor. His previous posts were at University College London, Boston University, and the University of Sheffield. He is the author of *The Courtship of Robert Browning and Elizabeth Barrett* (1985), *Browning's Hatreds* (1993), *Proust's English* (2005), *The Figure of the Singer* (2013), and *Street Songs* (2018). He is co-editor of the Longman Annotated English Poets edition of Robert Browning (most recently *The Ring and the Book*, 2022), and he has also edited works by Edward FitzGerald, Rider Haggard, Rudyard Kipling, and Henry James. He is a Fellow of the British Academy.

Hermione Lee is a literary biographer and Professor Emeritus of English Literature at the University of Oxford. She held the Goldsmiths' Chair at New College from 1998 to 2008 and from 2008-2017 was President of Wolfson College, where she founded the Oxford Centre for Life-Writing in 2011. Her publications include biographies of Willa Cather, Virginia Woolf, Edith Wharton, Penelope Fitzgerald and Tom Stoppard; critical books on Woolf, Elizabeth Bowen and Philip Roth; and books on life-writing such as *Biography: A Very Short Introduction* and *Body Parts: Essays on Life-Writing*. She was awarded the 2020 Bio Award for her contribution to the art of biography. She is currently writing a life of Anita Brookner.

Angela Leighton is Senior Research Fellow at Trinity College, Cambridge. In addition to many works of 19th-21st-century literary criticism, including *Victorian Women Poets: Writing Against the Heart* (Harvester, 1992, 2019), *On Form* (Oxford University Press, 2007) and *Hearing Things: The Work of Sound in Literature* (Harvard University Press, 2018), she has published six volumes of poetry, most recently *One, Two* (Carcanet, 2021) and *Something, I Forget* (Carcanet, 2023).

Phillis Levin is the author of six books of poetry, most recently *An Anthology of Rain* (Barrow Street Press, 2025). Her previous collection, *Mr. Memory & Other Poems* (Penguin, 2016), was a finalist for the Los Angeles Times Book Prize. She is the editor of *The Penguin Book of the Sonnet* (2001). Levin's honors include the Poetry Society of America's Norma Farber First Book Award, a Fulbright Scholar Award to Slovenia, and fellowships from the Guggenheim Foundation, the National Endowment for the Arts, and the Trust of Amy Lowell. Her poems have appeared in *AGNI, The Atlantic, Michigan Quarterly Review, The New Republic, The New Yorker, Paris Review, PN Review, Poetry London, The Poetry Review, Raritan,* and *The Yale Review.* She lives in New York.

Ben Mazer was educated at Harvard and the Editorial Institute at Boston University. He is the author of several poetry collections, including most recently *Selected Poems* (Madhat Press, 2017). He is the editor of *The Collected Poems of John Crowe Ransom* (Un-Gyve Press, 2015), Landis Everson's *Everything Preserved: Poems 1955-2005* (Graywolf Press, 2019), which won the first Emily Dickinson Award from the Poetry Foundation and *The Collected Poems of Delmore Schwartz* (FSG, 2024).

Jim McCue was baffled in his first term at Cambridge by Christopher's lectures on T.S. Eliot, but was lucky enough to hear them again in his third year, by which time he could follow the argument as well as marvel at the presentation of what became *T.S. Eliot and Prejudice.* He could not have imagined that decades later he would jointly edit *The Poems of T.S. Eliot* with Christopher. In the interim, he worked as an editor and writer at *The Times,* wrote a study of *Edmund Burke and Our Present Discontents,* and ran the Foundling Press, which produced limited editions of neglected writings by Eliot, Empson, Pope, Housman, Henry James and others (as well as *Ricks's Dicta,* for Christopher's 70th birthday).

Peter McDonald is a poet and critic, born in Belfast in 1962. His first collection of poetry was published in 1989, and his most recent, *One Little Room,* in 2024; a *Collected Poems* appeared in 2012. He is the author of four books of criticism, including *Sound Intentions: Form and Authority from Yeats to Hill* (2012), and many essays on poets and poetry. He is editor of *Louis MacNeice: Collected Poems* (2007), and three volumes so far of *The Poems of W.B. Yeats* for the Longman Annotated

Poets series. He taught at the Universities of Cambridge, Bristol, and Oxford, and is now Emeritus Professor of British and Irish Poetry at Christ Church, Oxford.

Cassandra Nelson is a visiting fellow in literature at the Lumen Center in Madison, Wisconsin, and an associate fellow at the University of Virginia's Institute for Advanced Studies in Culture. Her scholarship centers on faith and technology in American literature and contemporary culture. She received a BA in English and MA in Editorial Studies from Boston University, followed by a PhD in English from Harvard University. She is the author of *A Theology of Fiction* (Wiseblood Books, 2025) and editor of Samuel Beckett's *More Pricks than Kicks* (Faber, 2010). Her master's thesis—an edition of *Selected Stories of Betty Wahl*, which was completed at the Editorial Institute in 2007 under the direction of Christopher Ricks—is forthcoming from Catholic University of America Press.

Julie Nemrow is co-founder of the Un-Gyve Limited Group and publisher of Un-Gyve Press. Co-editor, with Christopher Ricks and Lisa Nemrow, of *The Lyrics. Since 1962.* by the Nobel Laureate Bob Dylan, she is a multi-instrumentalist, composer and cartoonist.

Lisa Nemrow, who is published also as L.A. Nemrow, is co-founder of the Un-Gyve Limited Group and publisher of Un-Gyve Press. She is co-editor, with Christopher Ricks and Julie Nemrow, of *The Lyrics. Since 1962.* by the Nobel Laureate, Bob Dylan.

Lee Oser's most recent books are *Christian Humanism in Shakespeare: A Study in Religion and Literature* and *Old Enemies: A Satire.* A former president of the Association of Literary Scholars, Critics, and Writers (ALSCW), he teaches at College of the Holy Cross. His record album, *Windmills on the Moon*, is due out with Regional Records in 2025.

Tim Parks is a British novelist, essayist, travel writer and translator based in Italy, where he has lived for forty years. Author of twenty novels, he has translated works by Moravia, Pavese, Calvino, Calasso, Tabucchi, Pasolini, Machiavelli and Leopardi and was for many years director of a postgraduate degree in translation in Milan. He writes regularly for the NYRB, the LRB and the TLS. His non-fiction works include various accounts of Italian life, a history of the Medici Bank, a memoir of chronic pain and mediation, an analysis of Italian translations of the British modernists, and four collections of critical essays. His latest novel is *Mr. Geography*.

Tim Peltason taught in the English Department at Wellesley College from 1977 to 2021. He is a life member of the ALSCW, which he served as Treasurer and Council member from 2009-2015. He has published *Reading In Memoriam* (1985) and several other essays about Tennyson; edited *Matthew Arnold: Selected Poems* for Penguin (1994); and also published essays about J.S. Mill, George Eliot, Charles Dickens, John Ruskin, Matthew Arnold, Oscar Wilde, and other Victorians; online commentaries about five plays by Shakespeare, including *Othello*; essays about literary education and the practice of critical judgment; and most recently essays about Mark Twain, Jane Austen, and American crime fiction. He is currently writing about Anthony Trollope.

Seamus Perry is a Fellow of Balliol College, Oxford, where he teaches English Literature. He has published books and essays on many aspects of modern poetry, and is editor, with Christopher Ricks and Freya Johnston, of the journal *Essays in Criticism*.

Laura Quinney teaches English and Comparative Literature at Brandeis University. Her field of specialization is Romanticism, but she has also taught courses on epic, poetry and myth, poetry and philosophy, British devotional poetry and the poetry of Hell. Her publications include three works of literary criticism: *Literary Power and the Criteria of Truth* (Florida, 1995), *The Poetics of Disappointment: Wordsworth to Ashbery* (Virginia, 1999) and *William Blake on Self and Soul* (Harvard, 2010). She has also written three volumes of poetry. *Stumbling, and Other Poems* (Borderland Books) is the most recent.

Anna Razumnaya earned a doctorate from the Editorial Institute at Boston University in 2013. She is the author of *Under the Sign of Contradiction: Mandelstam and the Politics of Memory* (2021); her essays and book reviews in English and Russian have appeared in *Essays in Criticism, Literary Imagination, Translation and Literature, Los Angeles Review of Books, BERLIN.Berega*, and elsewhere.

Anthony Rudolf lives in London, where he was born in 1942. He is a poet, a poetry translator from French and other languages, and a literary essayist (on George Oppen, Primo Levi, Byron, Balzac and others). He taught Life Studies at London Metropolitan University for a few years. For the last 26 years of Paula Rego's life, he was her principal male model and partner. He also, unsurprisingly, publishes about art in various journals.

Sarah Spence, distinguished research professor emerita of classics and comparative literature at the University of Georgia, has published widely on classical reception, where she is especially interested in the adaptation of Vergil by later authors. Her publications include *Rhetorics of Reason and Desire* (Cornell, 1988), *Texts of the Self in the Twelfth Century* (Cambridge, 1996), and, most recently, *The Return of Proserpina* (Princeton, 2023). She also edited the volume *Poets and Critics Read Vergil*, featuring essays by poets Mark Strand and Rosanna Warren and literary critics Michael Putnam, Bruce Redford, and Craig Kallendorf. She was the first editor of *Literary Imagination*, the journal of the Association of Literary Scholars, Critics, and Writers, and has since edited several academic journals, including *Vergilius* and *Speculum*.

A.E. Stallings is an American poet, translator and essayist who lives in Athens. She is the 47th Oxford Professor of Poetry.

Garrett Stewart is the author of twenty monographs, and elected to the American Academy of Arts and Sciences in 2010, Garrett Stewart is James O. Freedman Professor of Letters at the University of Iowa. He has written before on Hopkins in *Reading Voices: Literature and the Phonotext* (1990), has more than once reviewed Ricks, most extensively in "Metallusion" for *MLQ* (2004), and has a chapter on Hopkins' phonetics in the forthcoming *Closer Reading: Garrett Stewart's Essays in Refraction*, ed. David La Rocca.

Harry Thomas is the author of *Some Complicity: Poems and Translations*, *The Truth of Two: Selected Translations*, and *Haiku* (also in a limited edition with a number of the poems translated into Japanese), all three of these books published by Un-Gyve. He is the editor of *Selected Poems of Thomas Hardy* (Penguin UK), *Montale in English* (Penguin UK), and *Poems about Trees* (Knopf). His poems, translations, essays, and reviews have appeared in dozens of magazines. From 2001 to 2010 he was editor-in-chief of Handsel Books, an imprint of Other Press. He brought out thirty-five books from Handsel, including, he is honored to say, two by Christopher Ricks, R*eviewery* and *Selected Poems of James Henry* (editor).

Tomas Tranströmer (1931-2015) won the 2011 Nobel Prize in Literature.

Meg Tyler is Associate Professor of Humanities at Boston University. A book of poems, *More Feathers in the Lake Than Swans*, is forthcoming from Finishing Line Press.

Alissa Valles is the author of the poetry books *Orphan Fire* (2008) and *Hospitium* (2019), as well as *Anastylosis* (2014), a limited thermal paper edition published for the Whitechapel Art Gallery in London; she has been the recipient of fellowships from the NEA and the Ruth Lilly Poetry Foundation and awards from Poetry magazine, the Modern Language Association, AATSEEL and the Polish Book Institute. She has published translations of Polish poets Zbigniew Herbert, Zuzanna Ginczanka, and Ryszard Krynicki, among others, and worked at the BBC Russian Service, the Dutch Institute for War Documentation in Amsterdam and the Jewish Historical Institute in Warsaw. She has taught writing, translation, literature and film at Boston University since 2019, and received a doctorate from the BU Editorial Institute in 2021. Her translation of Aleksander Wat's *Diary Without Vowels* is forthcoming from New York Review Books in 2025.

Rosanna Warren retired in 2023 from the Committee on Social Thought at the University of Chicago. Her most recent books are *Max Jacob: A Life in Art and Letters*, and *So Forth*, a collection of poems, both from W.W. Norton in 2020. A new book of poems, *Hindsight,* was published by Norton in September 2025.

Judith Wechsler has written books on Cézanne, Daumier, *A Human Comedy, Physiognomy and Caricature in 19th century Paris,* and edited *On Aesthetics in Science.* She wrote and directed 30 documentary films, for the Louvre on drawing, the Metropolitan Museum on Manet, on 19th century actress Rachel for the Comédie Francaise as well as films on Walter Benjamin, Isaiah Berlin, Svetlana Boym, Nahum Glatzer, and Aby Warburg. The French government awarded Wechsler Chevalier de l'Ordre des Arts et des Lettres. Wechsler was the National Endowment for the Humanities Professor in the Department of Art history at Tufts University, taught at MIT, Rhode Island School of Design, and was visiting professor at Harvard, Ecole Normale Supérieur in Paris and the Hebrew University.

Michael Wood studied French and German at Cambridge University and was a fellow of St John's College. He taught at Columbia, Exeter and Princeton, where he is now Professor Emeritus of English and Comparative Literature. He has written books on Stendhal, Nabokov, Yeats, and Hitchcock, and is the author, most recently, of *On Empson* (2017), *The Habits of Distraction* (2018), and *Marcel Proust* (2023). He writes regularly for the *London Review of Books*, and for several other journals.

Susan J. Wolfson is Professor English at Princeton University since 1991. Receiving her PhD from University of California, Berkeley in 1978, she joined Rutgers University in New Brunswick the same year. Her core interests, in teaching and publication, are the British Romantics and their contemporaries, with forays into Shakespeare, Milton, Tennyson, Yeats, and Frost. Recent publications include *A Greeting of the Spirit: Selected Poetry of John Keats, with Commentaries* (2022), a hybrid of anthology, biography, and critical essays; and *On Mary Wollstonecraft's* A Vindication of the Rights of Woman: *"the first of a new genus"* (2023). She has coedited volumes for Christopher Ricks's Penguin Poets series: *Lord Byron: Selected Poems*, and *Selected Poetry of Thomas Hood, Winthrop Mackworth Praed, Thomas Lovell Beddoes.*

www.ingramcontent.com/pod-product-compliance
Lightning Source LLC
Chambersburg PA
CBHW021224130626
46554CB00004B/1358